The Seven Mountains' message redefines the map for how we d a paradigm shift, as any who hear it properly proclaimed can attest. By redefining the map with a fresh template the church can redeploy its massive underutilized capacity in a manner that not only makes sense, it alters the trajectory of nations. The church can never prevail against the gates of hell if it refuses to move into proximity to where the gates are located - at the summit of the seven mind molders of culture.

The crumbling structures of our society are a direct reflection of the absence of salt and light in the very centers of influence where we are needed most right now, specifically: government, economics, and media where the people desperately need to understand and discuss the real facts and issues. By yielding these high places to the enemy we have surrendered the power of truth and left decision making and influence shaping to the hands of people under the influence of darkness.

The only hope for nations and the church is a move of God that raises up children of light to turn the battle at the gates. This is what is promised in Isaiah 60:1–3 where God's people are told they will arise and shine in the midst of darkness that seeks to cover the earth.

Tommi Femrite understands this and has given us a major missing piece within the pages of this book. If the Lord is going to arise upon you, there will be a concerted effort made by Hell to stop you. Therefore you will need the extra power of organized, intelligent intercession to guide, guard and protect you, your family and your flanks. I trust nobody more than Tommi Femrite in this matter. She understands the 7M world and knows how to come along side you to ensure your success. This book is a must read for those who refuse to be spectators in the conflict of the ages—it is written for the wise ones who know they are called to do exploits, and also know they can't do it without prayer.

—LANCE WALLNAU
FOUNDER, LANCE LEARNING GROUP AND 7M UNIVERSITY

Tommi Femrite is a mighty woman of God who literally practices what she preaches. It is without hesitation that I recommend her newest book, *Invading the Seven Mountains With Intercession*. This is a powerful compilation of truths, facts, stories, and testimonies that apprehends your spirit to take action and to no longer sit by idle. Tommi does an excellent job at explaining the Seven Mountains, bringing revelatory insight into the various types of intercessors, and providing divine strategic prayer tactics along with the pivotal key for global societal transformation to be established. God's kingdom must reign throughout the earth, just as it is in heaven.

—CHÉ AHN
SENIOR PASTOR, HROCK CHURCH, PASADENA, CALIFORNIA
PRESIDENT, HARVEST INTERNATIONAL MINISTRY
INTERNATIONAL CHANCELLOR, WAGNER LEADERSHIP INSTITUTE

In this critical hour of human history, God has trained and prepared Tommi Femrite to bring forth a "textbook" to empower the body of Christ for true transformation. Many talk about invading the Seven Mountains of society but few have really grasped the role and necessity of intercessory prayer in this process, yet prayer is the one thing that is foundational to all the Seven Mountains.

Intercessory prayer is the foundational building block needed to open the heavens for God's will and purposes to be realized. Tommi's prophetic insight and background in this area has prepared her for such a time as this.

I encourage everyone who is serious about transformation to study this book in prayer. Then realign your strategies to God's timing and team anointing needed to shift things in the heavens.

—NAOMI DOWDY
NAOMI DOWDY MINISTRIES
NAOMI DOWDY MENTORING AND CONSULTING
FORMER SENIOR PASTOR, TRINITY CHRISTIAN CENTER, SINGAPORE

Tommi has a timely message for the body of Christ. Knowledgeable and effective intercessors are the key to fulfilling God's purpose for reformation. The kingdom of God is to be demonstrated in all the seven cultures of mankind and in every nation of the world. Every Christian needs to read this book. It is a very effective manual for every intercessor to follow. The truths in this book are desperately needed for the body of Christ to fulfill its end time destiny. Thanks Tommi for your years of experience and revelation knowledge that has made this book possible.

—Dr. Bill Hamon
Bishop of CIAN
Author, *Day of the Saints*,
Prophetic Scriptures Yet to Be Fulfilled,
and *The 3rd Reformation*

Tommi has provided a much needed tool to help "mountain climbers" understand and apply strategic prayer that is required to influence the seven cultural mountains of society. If you're going to be an effective influencer, you'll need the truths in this book to succeed.

—Os Hillman
President, Marketplace Leaders
Author, *Change Agent*

"God does nothing...but in answer to prayer," a familiar John Wesley quote. In Tommi's new book, she applies the power of that statement to the timely issue of taking the Seven Mountains for the kingdom of God. With wisdom, practicality, and spiritual acuity, Tommi addresses the role of intercession in advancing His kingdom in every facet of society. It is the only prayer-centric book designed to equip intercessors with effective tools to stand in the gap for believers on the Seven Mountains. Who should read this book? Everyone passionate about impacting their world!

—Jane Hansen Hoyt
President/CEO, Aglow International

Tommi Femrite has given a clear road map on how to pray and achieve both reformation and the transformation of nations! This is not just a book but a teaching manual to be used in prayer movements around the world.

—Cindy Jacobs
Generals International

Tommi Femrite is an apostolic leader and strategist. She skillfully invades the Seven Mountains with anointed intercession mixed with practical knowledge and understanding. Tommi presents a master strategy that will help you win the mountaintop!

—DR. JOHN P. KELLY
VISIONARY FOUNDER, LEAD (LEADERSHIP EDUCATION
FOR ADVANCEMENT AND DEVELOPMENT)
CONVENING APOSTLE, ICA (INTERNATIONAL COALITION OF APOSTLES)

Tommi Femrite is an incredibly spiritual, but very practical, leader in the body of Christ. Through the many years that I have known Tommi, I have always seen within her an intense passion to help God's people enter His plan for today. *Invading the Seven Mountains With Intercession* is a book to encourage each individual in God's kingdom to intercede for where they are positioned in society. Many have written how transformation works. But this book is more practical on how to seek God in the midst of the place that you are called to transform. Jesus exhorted us to be in the world, but not of the world (John 17:14–16). This is the perfect book to help you accomplish that mandate.

—CHUCK D. PIERCE
PRESIDENT, GLOBAL SPHERES, INC.
PRESIDENT, GLORY OF ZION INTERNATIONAL MINISTRIES, INC.

Intercession has shifted to a new level! Tommi Femrite's newest book is destined to be used for transforming culture in many nations. *Invading the Seven Mountains With Intercession* awakens intercessors to a fresh sense of destiny. She provides them with practical prayer points for each of the Seven Mountains of culture. Tommi also reveals the necessity for the alignment of intercession and leaders in each mountain. Her practical approach ignites an intercessory fire in the reader that will result in God's kingdom advancing throughout the earth. I highly recommend this book for intercessors, leaders, pastors and anyone longing to see transformation come to their mountain of influence!

—BARBARA WENTROBLE
PRESIDENT, INTERNATIONAL BREAKTHROUGH MINISTRIES
PRESIDENT, BREAKTHROUGH BUSINESS NETWORK
PRESIDENT, BUSINESS OWNERS FOR CHRIST INTERNATIONAL
AUTHOR, *FIGHTING FOR YOUR PROPHETIC PROMISES*,
REMOVING THE VEIL OF DECEPTION, AND *PRAYING WITH AUTHORITY*

This book is a wealth of insight on how you can more effectively pray for all areas of society. Read it, and then Pray! Tommi shows you how you can make a difference today!

—Dr. Rev. Diane Wigstone
Director, Ywam Hollywood
Author, *Discovering Your Destiny*
and *Hope For Hollywood: Reclaiming the Soul of Film & Tv*
Actress and Producer

When I consider endorsing a book, I also consider the author. Does the author demonstrate, live out the content they are writing about? This book comes right out of Tommi's life, out of the core of her belief system as well as her accomplishments. She has a fundamental belief in the power of prayer to change things. Prayer creates a dynamic power that will transform the Seven Mountains through changing people and creating strategic intervention and advancement. I highly recommend both the author and the book.

—Barbara J. Yoder
Senior Pastor and Lead Apostle
Shekinah Regional Equipping and Revival Center
Breakthrough Apostolic Ministries Network
Shekinah Leadership Institute

INVADING
THE SEVEN
MOUNTAINS
WITH
INTERCESSION

TOMMI FEMRITE

CREATION
HOUSE

INVADING THE SEVEN MOUNTAINS WITH INTERCESSION:
HOW TO RECLAIM SOCIETY THROUGH PRAYER
By Tommi Femrite
Published by Creation House
A Charisma Media Company
600 Rinehart Road
Lake Mary, Florida 32746
www.charismamedia.com

Design Director: Bill Johnson
Cover design by Terry Clifton
Cover illustration by James Nesbit

Visit the author's websites: www.AIN-GKI.org and www.GateKeepersIntl.org

Library of Congress Cataloging-in-Publication Data: 2011936191
International Standard Book Number: 978-1-61638-666-5

E-book ISBN: 978-1-61638-726-6

While the author has made every effort to provide accurate telephone numbers and Internet addresses at the time of publication, neither the publisher nor the author assumes any responsibility for errors or for changes that occur after publication.

First edition

11 12 13 14 15 — 987654321
Printed in Canada

DEDICATION

This book is dedicated to my precious family: my husband Ralph, daughter Carri and her husband Bart, son Eric and his wife Jaclyn, granddaughter Ashley and her husband David, granddaughter Alexia and grandsons Andrew and Zach. I am so very blessed to have such a wonderful family. Thank you for your love, encouragement and support. I could not do what I do without you and I am so very proud of each of you.

ACKNOWLEDGMENTS

My heartfelt thanks to:

❖ My daughter Carri Bell for all of your hard work and many hours of transcribing my teachings and proofing my manuscript. Your attention to details helped keep me moving forward.

❖ Peter Wagner, my apostle, for your continual encouragement and support.

❖ Dianne Emmons, my Administrator for Apostolic Intercessors Network (AIN), who carried my load and relieved my burden.

❖ Kelli Drury, my Executive Administrator, for seeing to fine details, tying up loose ends and keeping me focused.

❖ My friend Lance Wallnau for igniting a passion in me for the Seven Mountains.

❖ My Korean friend Mr. H. Hwang for spending countless hours doing research on the demonic root structures of each of the Seven Mountains.

❖ All who shared their personal stories recorded in this book.

❖ My friend Marcus, for affirming my passion to invade the Seven Mountains of society with intercession.

❖ My Wagner Leadership Institute (WLI) and Kingdom Leadership Institute (KLI) students who asked many questions that helped bring clarity to my Seven Mountain teachings in Colorado, New York, California and Aruba.

❖ My many faithful intercessors who pushed back the darkness and opened the heavens so I could complete this assignment with great grace.

❖ Al Hauck for leading my AIN prayer shield and Joyce Shaver for leading my GateKeepers International prayer shield. You paved the way for me to walk in peace.

❖ James Nesbit, a gifted prophetic artist with an amazing ability for capturing the theme of this book and putting it in art form. You did a wonderful job.

❖ The Creation House team for all of your hard work to make this book a reality.

TABLE OF CONTENTS

FOREWORD

THIS IS THE best book I have ever seen on the Seven Mountains! Yes, I must admit that I have said that before. I first said it when Johnny Enlow's *The Seven Mountain Prophecy: Unveiling the Coming Elijah Revolution* was published in 2008. Then I said it again when Robert Henderson's *A Voice of Reformation: An Apostolic and Prophetic View of Each of the Seven Mountains in a Reformed State* came out in 2010. But for me, the newest one always seems to be the most exciting. At the moment, Tommi Femrite is my hero!

I don't know anyone else who could have written such an enthralling book on intercession for the Seven Mountains. Tommi's first credential is her recognized gift and office of intercessor. Among other things, she has served my wife Doris and me as one of our close circle of intercessors for many, many years. She is in high demand as a teacher and conference speaker on the subject throughout the United States and in many other nations as well. Her vast field experience has taught her the rules of engaging the enemy, and she has published key books on intercession.

Tommi's second credential is her thorough understanding of the dynamics of the workplace both in theory and in practice. As you read this book, you will see how she grasps and applies what the Spirit is saying to the churches about things like the church in the workplace, the dominion mandate, and the 7M™ template. She is thoroughly equipped to write the textbook you have in your hands.

In this foreword, I would like to pick up where Tommi leaves off in her last chapter, "Marching Orders." There she describes the process through which God led her to establish Apostolic Intercessors Network, or AIN. I believe that this is one of the most important innovations that the body of Christ has seen in a long time. The term I like to use for this new type of ministry is "professional-level intercession." I favor the adjective "professional" because it helps move the scenario outside of the Religion Mountain into the other six mountains of the workplace.

Let me tell you why professional-level intercession is needed from a personal perspective. I have spent my career as a leader in the Religion Mountain. However, within the past ten years or so I have gained a fairly competent understanding of the nature and characteristics of the other mountains as you would see if you read my book, *The Church in the Workplace*. We now understand that God wants His kingdom-minded people to rise to positions of influence in whatever mountain He has placed them. It is good to keep in mind that, whereas influence in the Religion Mountain is attained through spirituality, this is not true of the other six mountains. There, influence is attained primarily by success.

Let's pretend that a kingdom-minded leader in the Business Mountain has been enjoying success by seeing revenue increasing every year for the past five years. Then suddenly, for some unknown reason, it stops. What could be going wrong? It could well be that Satan and his demonic forces of darkness had just begun taking notice. If you are low in influence in your mountain, Satan probably isn't paying much attention to you. But as soon as you get to a certain point, you become a target. In this case, demonic forces might have succeeded in forming a spiritual stronghold over the business. If I suggested this to the leader, he or she might have agreed. The next question: "What do I do about it?" My answer would be, "You probably need strategic intercession," and in most cases the leader would agree to that as well. But then the next question: "Where do I get the intercession I need?"

Up until recently, I confess that I didn't have a good answer for that question. I might say, "Ask God, and He will give intercessors to you." That may be a good Religion Mountain suggestion, but it wouldn't fly in most parts of the workplace. Or I could say, "Ask your pastor, and he or she can help you." Suppose the pastor is an old school Baptist or Presbyterian or Lutheran who knows virtually nothing about warfare intercession? They might reply, "Oh, I'll put you on our church prayer list." That's a kindly gesture, but hardly what our business leader needs. It was a discomforting situation both for the leader and for me.

But then along comes Tommi Femrite with a definitive solution to the problem. I'm watching her closely because I'm on her Board of Directors. Tommi suggests that, in order to conform to the workplace culture, we start a new company (notice she didn't suggest a new ministry). This would be a for-profit company called Apostolic Intercessors Network (AIN), and it would provide professional-level intercession for those like the business leader I have been talking about. Finally I have a sensible answer. I now can say to my hypothetical friend: "Get in touch with Tommi Femrite and AIN!"

When the call comes, Tommi will arrange for her or one of her trained colleagues to make a one-day on-site visit to analyze the spiritual condition of the business first hand. The business pays all expenses plus a consultation fee. At the end of the day she will typically work with the leader to come up with an intercession team which she describes in Chapter 12, "Recruiting an Army," AIN has enlisted a substantial number of experienced strategic intercessors, many of whom have specialties just like MD's have different specialties within the medical community. The business pays a monthly fee to AIN for the intercession team.

Does this work? I have a thick file of typewritten testimonies from AIN clients in all of the mountains describing the before and after effect of professional-level intercession on their enterprise, whatever it might be. I believe that God has raised up Tommi Femrite and her AIN colleagues for a time like this. As you read this book, you will be fascinated by seeing all the pieces come together for launching strategic intercession into the Seven Mountains, empowering God's people to transform their segment of society for the kingdom of God!

—C. Peter Wagner
Vice President and Apostolic Ambassador
Global Spheres, Inc.

PART 1

We Need an Army

Chapter 1

SPIDERS IN THE ROOM

*I*AM ABSOLUTELY DESPERATE. *I need you to pray.*"

The words took me by surprise as I answered the phone. I had never met the young woman on the other end. She introduced herself as Rebecca* and said she was an American citizen serving with a ministry in a former Communist Bloc country.

"I work with orphans," she explained, "and the ministry I'm with desperately wants to help the orphans by building homes and schools where they can grow up in a healthy environment and break the cycle of hopelessness. But the Communist government..."

Her voice trailed off for a moment. Then she began to share with me the horrific conditions these abandoned children had endured for generations. Under the Communist regime the nation's orphanage population swelled uncontrollably when, in 1966, the government banned abortion and began rewarding couples for each child they produced. Mothers of five or more received significant benefits, while those who birthed at least ten children were honored by the state as "heroine mothers." Yet the plan tragically backfired, as it became common practice for parents to abandon their children once they reaped the immediate benefits.

While relocating peasants into urban centers and building a government palace larger than the Pentagon, the President established a culture that viewed these orphans as property rather than people, and every state-run orphanage throughout this Communist country reflected this. In these orphanages, infants were bound tightly, placed in boxlike containers, and left to themselves for most of the day. Malnourished toddlers and even older children had ropes tied around their ankles to a bedpost. From morning until night, they were confined to the tiny area around their bed, where they did everything—ate, slept, and, yes, even relieved themselves. As they grew, many of these children became

---

* I have changed some of the details of Rebecca's story—including her name—to protect her ministry.

victims of sexual abuse. And by the time they reached their teen years, most would fall further into the self-perpetuating cycle of despair. Young girls would become pregnant from the first boy who paid them any attention, and their babies would be placed into the same orphanage while they were kicked out onto the street with no education or skills to integrate into society. And so the cycle continued.

When the Iron Curtain fell and the country's president died, the Western world was exposed to the atrocities affecting these 140,000-plus innocent children—or what one UNICEF leader called a "lost generation." Rebecca was one who took notice and, heartbroken over the orphans' condition, set out to change their lives. She told me about the ministry's vision to build homes on a property where couples from around the world could come and live, committing to spend ten to twenty years of their lives raising their adopted children from birth until adulthood. It was more than just a noble vision; it was the heart of God.

"I don't know how I'm going to do this," I eventually said to her, "but I promise you, I will bring a team."

AN OFFICIAL VISIT

Within a week, I had assembled a team of intercessors to travel to this country for the purpose of supporting Rebecca and praying with her in person. We weren't there to simply offer moral support; we wanted to clear the way for her in the spiritual realm so that God's will for bringing hope into these orphans' lives could come to fruition. After visiting a couple of orphanages and seeing firsthand how, despite slight improvements, living conditions for these children remained appalling, we instantly recognized the long-standing and deep-rooted issues ruling the territory. Our group prayed fervently against the religious spirit that ruled the church and the Herod-like spirit that dominated the government. These demonic forces had actually joined the two spirits together to oppress and abuse the people. We sensed we were to visit some of the government buildings to break the strongholds of injustice and declare freedom and favor for Rebecca's ministry. Our plan was simply to walk into these locations, pray briefly, and walk out. But God had another plan.

On the last full day of our trip, we headed to the state capital. When we arrived at the massive capitol building, I volunteered to distract the guards so the rest of my team, accompanied by Rebecca, could pray at the entranceway. Days earlier, the Lord had miraculously put us face-to-face with a high-ranking secretariat in Rebecca's hometown who had repeatedly blocked any attempts by Rebecca's ministry to begin their building program. We watched this woman transform within minutes from carrying a stone-cold professional countenance to pouring out her heart and weeping as we prayed for her. The divine appointment had given me the confidence to approach these guards and ask for the moon—or, in this case, a visit with the governor. I'll admit, I didn't expect this request to be granted, but it was at least worth a shot.

"What are you doing?" one of the guards asked sternly with his thick accent. It was hard not to stare at the massive M-16 strapped over his shoulder. Yet rather than stumble over my words, I found myself boldly announcing our arrival.

"We've come to see the governor."

"Who are you?" he asked.

"We're an official delegation from the United States, and we've come to see the governor."

"The governor is not available," he said with a straight face. "He is gone, and he'll be back tomorrow."

At this point, my only intent was to continue stalling the guards so the rest of my team could finish our prayer assignment in that strategic place.

"We can't come back tomorrow. We're leaving," I told the guard. "We have to see the governor today. It *has* to happen today." Meanwhile, my mind was pondering if I was crazy for being so bold with an armed man who clearly wasn't amused by me.

A phone call or two later, the guards escorted our entire team into a conference room, where we were seated at a long conference table and then left to ourselves.

"What are we going to say when they ask who we are?" one member of the group asked, breaking the room's penetrating silence.

"We'll tell them the truth," I answered, "that we're an official delegation from the United States."

"Yes, but what are we going to say when they ask what we're here for?"

Again, I said we would tell the truth—that we wanted to bring greetings to the governor.

The team members continued to ask a string of "Well, what if..." questions until it occurred to me that the room might be bugged. After scanning the room, I cut the questioning short by looking to the team and stiffly announcing, "You know, I think we should look out for some spiders in the room."

They got the point. Within minutes, a man entered the room and asked us a series of questions—the exact same ones my team members had been asking me. My answers were verbatim to my previous ones. I can only assume the official saw my truthfulness because moments later, our team was in the governor's office, shaking hands with him. An imposing man, the bald-headed, mustached governor wore a dark winter coat and equally drab tie. He invited us to sit down and, after some cordial formalities, asked us what our problem was that we wanted to discuss with him.

"We didn't come with a problem, but instead a blessing from our nation," I assured him. I shared that his country had been in the American news lately and that we were there to encourage him in his role of running the state, realizing that it was an extremely difficult job. "We're here to tell you that we know your job has been difficult with the orphanages, and we're so grateful for all the work that you've done. We know you are a man of integrity and that you will lead your state with integrity."

Suddenly the walls around the governor's heart fell. He leaned forward, smiled, and asked what he could do for us. When I told him that we truly didn't want anything from him, it still took him a while to believe it.

"You have to want something," he said. "Everyone who comes to my office wants *something*."

As we continued to shower the governor with verbal blessings, we interceded and asked the Lord what He wanted us to say and do. After all, we had never expected to be in this man's office, speaking with him face-to-face, in the first place!

The governor eventually gathered from our conversation that Rebecca lived in his state, so he asked what she was doing. As she shared about love for children and her work with orphans, suddenly a light went on in his mind.

"Yes...yes! The ambassador told me I was supposed to meet with you. Why did the ambassador want me to meet with you?"

It was the open door Rebecca had been waiting and praying for. She explained that she had been trying for two years to get an international phone line so those outside the country could contact her for physical and financial support but that her multiple requests on behalf of the ministry had yet to be answered. Since she still didn't have a line, she had no way of communicating with the donors and supporters abroad, which was directly affecting her work with the orphanages.

"You will have a telephone within the week," the governor replied. "If not, contact me immediately."

SHIFTING SOCIETY

I went ten years without seeing or hearing from Rebecca again. But after reconnecting with her not long ago, I discovered that during that time, she helped build five homes on the ministry property. Each home now has a strong Christian couple—just as she envisioned and prayed for— who has committed to remain there and raise their adopted children until they are old enough to live on their own. Rebecca oversaw the construction of an elementary school and recently began work on a high school. She has also personally adopted nine children and continues to nurture them.

In ten years, Rebecca has changed a nation. By rescuing children from a broken orphanage system that produces a cycle of drug use, alcoholism, teen pregnancy, depression, and further abuse, she has changed the course of countless lives. Her efforts to educate, care for, and love these precious children have not only planted seeds of hope where there were none before, but they have also affected multiple generations. And as those generations have been transformed, so has the entire society around her.

Because of Rebecca's tireless and faithful work, I believe the kingdom of God is expanding forcefully in this nation. But I also believe prayer had more to do with that than we'll ever know. During our brief stay, God miraculously opened doors through the power of prayer. And for ten years, Rebecca had a network of intercessors praying regularly for her and the entire ministry. These weren't just the members of our team that visited her; Rebecca had prayer warriors stationed literally around the world. Every orphan she came across was saturated with the prayers of believers they will likely never meet on this earth. Every divinely appointed family that committed to become adopted parents was a result of hours of spiritual breakthrough in the heavenly realm.

Rebecca changed a culture with her actions; those praying for her changed a culture with their intercession. What if we could see the same societal transformation here in the United States? What if our generation and those to come could witness kingdom results like never before?

I believe we can. And I believe part of the strategy to see such a revolution is in this book. But just as Rebecca spent time learning the country's culture and recognizing the reality of the obstacles she had to overcome, we must be honest with recognizing and assessing the true condition of our land.

Think for a moment about the current woes of our culture. Despite the increased emphasis American society has placed on raising children, only 63 percent of them grow up with both their biological parents—the lowest figure in the Western world.[1] The latest statistics show that 1.3 million abortions are performed each year in our nation (and that's only those that are legal and reported), while approximately half of all marriages here end in divorce.[2, 3] In a country birthed in gratitude for God's mercy and founded upon His Word, teachers are now arrested and students suspended for praying in schools. Politicians are mocked and rebuked for uttering Jesus' name in public, and our current president has already declared that America is no longer a Christian nation. Our biggest newspapers, magazines, television networks, and online media outlets simply further this by spewing vitriolic "editorials" announcing the death of Christianity, evangelicalism, the church, and God Himself. Meanwhile, pornography has become a cultural norm for entertainment, as the sex industry makes more than $13 billion a year—more than all of the major sports leagues *combined*.[4] And in the business world, we are no longer surprised when a Fortune 500 company goes belly-up from yet another Wall Street Ponzi scheme or leadership scandal.

Clearly, we need societal transformation. In every facet of America that I just mentioned—religion, family, education, government, media, arts and entertainment, and business—we have drifted farther and farther away from following God's standards. To say we are a secular nation is nothing new. Yet equally tragic is the dwindling role of the American church in recent generations and its inability to correct our course. Simply put, the church has lost ground. And worse still, it is painfully obvious that ungodly forces are in command.

As Christians, we know that ultimately God is sovereign and in control. He "removes kings and establishes kings" (Dan. 2:21). He "reigns over the nations" while He "sits on His holy throne" (Ps. 47:8). As Job declared, "He makes nations great, then destroys them; He enlarges the nations, then leads them away" (Job 12:23). As adopted sons and daughters into the King's royal line, believers have a role in shaping these nations that rise and fall. God's plan has always been for us to have kingdom dominion and rule over every part of the world, so that *His* kingdom might fully inhabit the earth.

Yet when we look at the various areas of American society today, we must ask ourselves, *Who is ruling?*

Sadly, it's not us.

A DIFFERENT KINGDOM

This is not a book written to trace the history of exactly how Christians lost cultural ground. Nor is it a book that will offer fifty reasons why our current condition proves we are living in End Times. I would submit that both are secondary to the bigger issue that we'll address throughout these pages: the kingdom of God.

The truth is, humans can devise ingenious solutions and implement proven programs to solve our cultural problems, but unless God's power is allowed to take full force, we will gain little ground. We need societal transformation—that is undeniable. But true cultural change that yields lasting fruit can't occur unless the kingdom of God is allowed to reign. The goal for Christians is not to dominate society; it is to bring about God's kingdom on earth. When Jesus prayed, "Your Kingdom come. Your will be done, on earth as it is in heaven" (Matt. 6:10), in one brief sentence He unveiled the secret to true transforming power. When the kingdom of God truly rules on earth, it doesn't matter who sits on what worldly thrones because those ruling and serving throughout the land know which King ultimately holds all power.

If you have a vision to see not only the United States but *all* the nations of the world fully inhabited by the kingdom of God, this is the book for you. In these pages, I believe you will find the key to transforming whatever sphere of society in which you operate. You'll also be encouraged by the powerful stories I share of how regular people are doing remarkable things to change the course of culture. We are in remarkable times. And, as history proves, remarkable times call for remarkable people. I believe it is time for the Rebeccas of the world to rise up and change the face of this earth.

CHAPTER 1 NOTES

1. David Popenoe and Barbara Dafoe Whitehead, "The State of Our Unions 2005: The Social Health of Marriage in America," The National Marriage Project: Rutgers, The State University of New Jersey, 2005, http://www.virginia.edu/marriageproject/pdfs/SOOU2005.pdf (accessed August 25, 2009).

2. Lawrence B. Finer and Stanley K. Henshaw, "Estimates of U.S. Abortion Incidence, 2001–2003," Guttmacher Institute, August 3, 2006, http://www.guttmacher.org/pubs/2006/08/03/ab_incidence.pdf (accessed August 22, 2009).

3. Centers for Disease Control and Prevention, "Marriage and Divorce," http://www.cdc.gov/nchs/fastats/divorce.htm (accessed August 22, 2009).

4. *ABC Primetime*, "Porn Profits: Corporate America's Secret," May 27, 2004, http://abcnews.go.com/Primetime/story?id=132370&page=1 (accessed August 25, 2009).

Chapter 2

MOUNTAIN CLIMBING 101:
RULING THE MOUNTAIN

I F YOU LIVE in Tibet, you know a thing or two about mountains. Often called the "Roof of the World," the East Asian region is the highest on earth, with an average elevation of more than sixteen thousand feet. To the south stand the renowned Himalayas, up north are the Kunlan Mountains, and on the west side lies the Karakoram Range. Simply put, it's hard to go anywhere without climbing a little.

In 1999, I led a team on a prayer journey to Lhasa, the capital of Tibet, where I experienced firsthand a climbing ritual most Tibetan Buddhists have followed for hundreds of years. When at the base of a mountain, they will often pick up a rock and, upon reaching the summit, place the rock as a marker that they have made it to the top. In fact, you can often tell how many people have succeeded in a climb based on the number of rocks assembled at the peak. Tibetan Buddhists take things a step further by attaching a "prayer flag" to a pole and erecting it in the pile of marking rocks. The multicolored banners attached to this flagpole aren't just for decoration; they are adorned with Buddhist "scriptures," if you will—sacred symbols and mantras that Tibetans believe spread goodwill, harmony, and compassion through all the natural elements.

Both the pile of rocks and the prayer flags make a declaration. For anyone standing at the base of a mountain looking up at its majestic, intimidating slope, they declare who has "conquered" the mountain. And even though Tibetan Buddhists view the surrounding mountains as more honorable than conquerable, this sense of ruling and reigning is still understood by even the least spiritually minded climbers in the land. Simply put, whoever ascends to the top of the mountain conquers—and therefore rules—the mountain.

It is no different in society. Like the physical mountains of Tibet, culture's "mountains" have been around for a long, long time. Throughout history, kings and dictators have always tried to conquer a mountain. Painters, composers, and rock stars have ascended another type of mountain. Popes and sheiks have climbed to the top of yet another. Again, the principle has remained since the beginning of every culture's existence: ascend to the top of a mountain, and you will rule it.

TWO PLACES, ONE MESSAGE

In August 1975, God spoke to two men who stood hundreds of miles apart amid the same mountain range. While staying at a cabin in the Rocky Mountains of Colorado, Youth With a Mission founder Loren Cunningham received from the Lord what he calls a "list of things I had never thought about before."[1] He jotted these down on a yellow notepad and felt impressed to eventually share them with his good friend, Bill Bright, the founder of Campus Crusade for Christ. Later that day, a local ranger notified Cunningham of a phone call waiting for him back at the ranger's station. He hiked the seven miles to the station, only to find that it was the friend he had just been thinking about. Unknown to Cunningham, Bright and his wife were staying in Boulder, Colorado, and the phone call was an invitation for Cunningham and his wife to come over and meet with them.

As the two men greeted each other the next day, Cunningham was about to pull out his yellow notepad when Bright said God had shown him a few things a day earlier. To their surprise, they discovered the Lord had given the *exact* same message to each man within a twenty-four-hour period—a message each felt he was supposed to share with the other. In their revelation, God had told both that there were seven "spheres," or mountains, that were the foundations of every society: religion, family, education, government, media, arts and entertainment, and business. Whoever could take those mountains could take a nation. Just as Caleb had made the request of Joshua to "give me this mountain" (Josh. 14:12, KJV), Cunningham and Bright both believed missionaries could make the same request of the Lord for the nations they were pursuing with the gospel.

Since then, this strategic list has been renamed using different terms, all reflecting the same basic principle. Some have called it the seven areas of concentration. Others refer to it as the seven chief categories of society. Many stay true to Cunningham and Bright's original terms, labeling it the seven spheres of influence or the seven "mind-molders" of culture. Still others dub it the seven apostolic spheres, the seven gates, or the Seven Mountains (which today seems to be the most commonly used term).

All are variations on the same theme that underscores the importance these mountains play in shaping the landscape of every culture. Yet I support Peter Wagner's stance that we, as a body, should use the same terminology. When it comes to advancing God's kingdom throughout society, Wagner believes that "a key factor is language and terminology." Yet the discrepancy of terms signals to him "a weak point in our current spiritual army. If we fail to talk the same language and use the same terminology, we will never be as strong and powerful as we hope to be."[2]

I have the utmost respect for Cunningham and Bright, two contemporary giants of the faith who both accomplished monumental things for the body of Christ. That said, I believe the full scope of this "Seven Mountain strategy," as it became called, was not revealed or understood until recent years. Cunningham and Bright were both evangelists and therefore perceived this revelation through a mission-minded grid. As a result, the church has for the most part applied the Seven Mountain strategy strictly to evangelistic efforts, at the cost of excluding all other avenues in which the church should operate. What we needed was an understanding of how this powerful revelation applied to *every* facet of society.

Let's Talk Strategy

The first time I heard Lance Wallnau speak was in 2004. Within fifteen minutes of listening to him talk about the Seven Mountains, I knew he was on to something. Wallnau not only grasped the premise of Cunningham and Bright's Seven Mountain principle, he had keen insight on how it applied to everyday living—in a relevant, tangible form—for any Christian serving on any of the mountains. The problem was that his understanding ran so deep, and his delivery so powerful and rapid, that trying to soak it in was like drinking water from a fire hydrant.

A former pastor-turned-businessman, Wallnau opened my eyes—and undoubtedly thousands of others' as well—by breaking down this Seven Mountain strategy into bite-sized pieces. Ultimately, the spiritual principle behind applying this strategy to culture is the same as it is on the mountains of Tibet—the same as it has been throughout the history of cultures. "If the world is to be won," writes Wallnau, "these are the mountains that mold the culture and the minds of men. Whoever controls these mountains controls the direction of the world and the harvest therein."[3]

To control cities, regions, and nations, we have to control the Seven Mountains that shape culture. Whether the goal is to take New York City, Singapore, Moscow, London, or Padukah, Kentucky, the strategy is the same. Possess the Seven Mountains and you will possess the keys to a culture. But let me state again something that will be reinforced throughout this book: the end goal is not controlling these different parts of society for the sake of control or power but to see God's kingdom reign throughout the earth, just as it is in heaven. The kingdom of God encompasses all Seven Mountains. That means God already has a strategy for each mountain in every culture around the world. Like a basketball coach waiting for his team to execute the play he's designed, knowing it will bring about victory, God is waiting for us to apply His divine strategy in every area of every society on the face of this earth. And He knows we can bring about His victorious kingdom!

WHAT HAS TAKEN SO LONG?

Since the moment mankind fell, the transformation of society has always been on the heart of God. He has relentlessly pursued it yet has remained infinitely patient with the vessels of transformation He has chosen to use: His people. If expanding God's kingdom rule on earth is only a matter of applying His strategy, then why haven't we as Christians done this sooner? What has taken so long for us to transform society to mirror this glorious kingdom?

The sad truth is that we have tried to do this, yet we have only succeeded in limited spurts. Think of some of the most renowned movements in church history. The Crusades. The Reformation. The First and Second Great Awakenings. The Welsh Revival, Azusa Street Revival, and other similar revivals. These all shaped entire communities, cities, and countries alike. To a degree, each left a lasting impact. Yet as I highlighted in the last chapter, any thorough look at American society today reveals that the impression from these glorious eras has largely become worn, faded, and forgotten. The same is true in countless nations around the world where Christianity is promoted more as a religion than a relationship with Jesus Christ.

Despite a rapidly expanding Muslim population, by sheer numbers Christianity is still the largest religion in the world, with more than 2.1 billion followers. (Islam ranks second with 1.5 billion.)[4] You would think, then, that believers worldwide would have more influence in every vein of society than we do. But numbers don't determine rulers. For generations, American Jews—numbering a mere 1.7 percent of the US population (5.2 million out of 304 million)—have ruled the mountains of arts and entertainment, business, and media.[5, 6] To this day, they continue to prove one of the fundamental truths of the Seven Mountains: it only takes one person to reach a mountain's summit and claim it as his.

While Christians have been content to focus almost exclusively on the mountain of religion and largely ignore the other six, countless Jews, Muslims, Buddhists, Hindus, atheists, and agnostics have seized every opportunity to gain ground in these key culture areas—including the very mountain the church has tried so hard to protect! If Christians truly ruled the mountain of religion, then why are some of our church leaders involved in adultery, homosexuality, pornography, drugs, and alcohol? Why is abortion a non-issue in many Christian circles? Why have so many of us abandoned our calling to care for the poor? All of these issues shed light on Christians' true lack of influence, despite our majority status. Instead of encouraging believers to venture out into every mountain of society, the church has reinforced a "hunker down" mentality upon the mountain of religion—all while failing to protect its sacred territory. This is not only true in recent generations, but is a pattern that has been repeated since the church underwent one of its greatest and most damaging shifts.

THE GREAT CHURCH SHIFT

In A.D. 312, Constantine I was the first Roman emperor to become a Christian. The following year, he put an end to the persecution of believers by not only announcing toleration for Christianity, but also declaring it the Roman Empire's official religion. Most scholars agree that his Edict of Milan did more to shape the church in the following 1,700 years (and continues to!) than possibly any other humanly created influence. Whereas believers before had to congregate secretly while daily facing the possibility of dying for their faith, Constantine suddenly made Christianity a majority religion. In the first three hundred years of its existence, the church gained strength, power, and unity through the persecution of believers, just as Jesus had promised. But with this sudden declaration, being a follower of Jesus Christ became *en vogue*.

This wasn't necessarily a good thing.

Constantine quickly created a division within the church between what became known as "clergy" (those who do ministry) and "laity" (those who are ministered to). Rather than every member being an equal, contributing, and necessary part of the body of Christ, now only a select few were chosen to lead. These church leaders soon drew lines between holy and unholy, sacred and secular, spiritual and worldly. And in doing so, much of what God intended to be part of believers' natural domain was unfortunately cast aside as irrelevant, ungodly, and unfit for the newly established boundaries of "church." (It is no coincidence that the simultaneous cultural fixation with building churches, cathedrals, and houses of worship also ushered in the notion of *going* to church rather than *being* the church.)

As emperor of the most dominant worldly kingdom, Constantine clearly ruled the Government Mountain during his time. And though his influence was also profound on other mountains (e.g., business), his lasting impact on the Religion Mountain is undisputed. Unfortunately for true followers of Christ rather than those who cling to religion, this effect has created a division in the church ever since.

Peter Wagner describes the two sides of this split using a term familiar to most sociologists and psychologists. In the early part of the twentieth century, people began using the terms "nuclear family" and "extended family" to describe what was happening with human habitation patterns. Your nuclear family is your immediate family—your father, mother, sisters, and brothers—and your extended family is your broader family tree—your uncles, aunts, cousins, second cousins, and so on. In a similar way, Wagner uses the terms "nuclear church" and the "extended church" to describe how the church typically functions.[7] For hundreds of years, we have operated under the principle that the nuclear church is those who gather on Sundays, while the extended church is the people of God throughout the rest of the week—most of whom labor in the territories that make up the other six mountains of society. Working in tandem with Constantine's clergy/laity model, this has established the mentality that says those in ministry are the truly spiritual ones, doing the important work that yields eternal fruit that will be rewarded in heaven. Those of us who work in the secular arena, on the other hand, are somehow considered defiled, less holy, or not as spiritual, and therefore our work is viewed as far less significant.

The gap between the nuclear and extended church is huge, yet sadly few churches are helping the situation. We create programs to minister to children, youth, college students, single adults, married adults, senior adults, even entire families...and yet aside from the occasional busi-nessmen's breakfast, we have done a lousy job of ministering to those in the workplace. That isn't just strange; given that 95 percent of us offi-cially *work* in the workplace, it is truly pitiful.

God makes no distinction between the believers who make up what we often call "church" (what people say they attend on Sundays) and those who comprise the workforce. In His eyes, they are all part of His church. The nuclear church and the extended church *is* the church! Likewise, the Bible never refers to the church as a building or service, but instead as a people of God—*ekklesia*. You and I do not *go* to church; we *are* the church. Just because most of us spend the overwhelming majority of our time in the workplace of the non-religion mountains does not mean we are any less of the church. We are the church wher-ever we go, in whatever we do.

WARNING: CONSTRUCTION AHEAD

To begin to see the church more like God does, and to adopt a more cohesive paradigm of the church, we must first overcome a few long-standing roadblocks.

First, we need to dispel the notion that clergy is sacred and laity is secular. Constantine's impact on developing the faulty mind-set that says priests and pastors are exclusively involved in superior spiritual work cannot be overemphasized. We have held on to this fallacy far too long, and it has resulted in a church that is largely ineffective and power-less beyond its "natural territory" of the Religion Mountain. Thankfully, we are now seeing more signs of a Spirit-empowered church ascending the other mountains with force, which is why I believe this book is cru-cial for these times. In fact, one of my main purposes for writing it is to remind those laboring in the secular arena they are not alone. The Holy Spirit is on the move, working to redefine our understanding of what it means to reign and rule on every mountain in society. Yet one of the first places we must make a paradigm shift is in how we view the work of pastors, ministers, and clergy compared to the rest of us.

To align our vision for the church with God's, we must also rid ourselves of the mentality that believes all spiritual activity origi-nates within the four walls of a church building. Once again, the shift that occurred during the Constantine era drastically transformed our understanding of church. We must get beyond the stronghold of the past 1,700 years that says we enter a "sacred" building, offer a sacrifice, and become cleansed and made right with God just as the Israelites would in the Temple. Jesus Christ's new body on earth—His church—is living, breathing, and cannot nor should not be contained in a room or building. When we limit "spiritual activity" to a concrete structure we call church, we essentially deny the power of Christ's work on the cross and His new creation through resurrection. Again, we don't *go* to church, sit in church, work in a church, visit a church, or attend church; we *are* the church. That means our activity is just as spiritual, sacred, and potentially Spirit-empowered in an office cubicle, courtroom, classroom, or living room as it is in a sanctuary. To think otherwise is to deny the power of the Holy Spirit as God indwelling us.

Along these lines, we must also recognize that God's design for the church, as outlined through the fivefold ministry Paul described in his letter to the church in Ephesus, is not to be contained within the nuclear church sphere. In Ephesians 4:11, Paul writes, "And He gave some as apostles, and some as prophets, and some as evangelists, and some as pastors and teachers." The fivefold ministry gifts were never intended to be kept within the nuclear church but are designed by God to function in every area of society. It is time for the church at large to recognize, encourage, and equip those who are gifted specifically to ascend the highest of heights on each mountain. Let's undergird those boardroom pastors, newsroom evangelists, and prophetic policemen!

Finally, to become a unified, power-filled church as Jesus desires, we must heal the breach between workplace leaders and ministry leaders. We can talk theoretically all day about the nuclear and extended church, but where the rubber meets the road is in people and relationships. And for generation after generation, both "sides" (I cringe even using that word) have felt wounded or misunderstood by the other. Church leaders have often been hurt by overeager, visionary, type-A workplace leaders. Pastors report that those leading in the marketplace rarely know how to truly serve in ministry, and they commonly judge these business leaders as controlling and "worldly."

On the flip side, those leading in the workforce—especially the remarkably successful ones—share a common feeling of being used and abused by ministries and churches who treat them as walking checkbooks for donations. To add insult to injury, many have witnessed church leaders mishandle finances or display lousy stewardship skills, which can often lead them to buy into the notion that pastors are irrelevant and disconnected from the "real world." Other business leaders have found their pastors unwilling to receive any wisdom, advice, or leadership insight they might offer on how to prosper and succeed.

We cannot forget that both sets of leaders make up the church. Just as important, both are needed for the church to rule over any of the non-religion mountains. If we want to experience the transference of wealth that often sparks citywide and nationwide transformation, we need to build bridges and bring healing to these breaches. Clearly, the Religion Mountain alone has not been able to transform the world. Every mountain must be inhabited and ruled by the church for it to rise to the position God intends.

Doing this requires connectivity between the mountains. Each mountain needs the other. Each mountain must remain linked with the others. Sadly, what many Christians don't understand is that we the church already have an advantage over the world in creating this cohesive unit. God has equipped the church with a powerful tool like none other that instantly connects each of the Seven Mountains. Now let's discover what that tool is.

CHAPTER 2 NOTES

1. Os Hillman and Kelle Hughes, "Interview With Loren Cunningham," November 19, 2007, http://www.reclaim7mountains.com/apps/articles/default.asp?articleid=40087&columnid=4347 (accessed September 12, 2009).

2. Personal email from C. Peter Wagner, March 22, 2010.

3. Lance Wallnau, "A Prophetic, Biblical, and Personal Call to the Marketplace," privately circulated paper.

4. Adherents.com, "Major Religions of the World Ranked By Number of Adherents," http://www.adherents.com/Religions_By_Adherents.html (accessed August 19, 2009).

5. The Pew Forum on Religion and Public Life, "U.S. Religious Landscape Survey," http://religions.pewforum.org/affiliations (accessed July 10, 2010).

6. U.S. Census Bureau, "USA Statistics in Brief—Population by Sex and Age," 2008, http://www.census.gov/compendia/statab/2010/files/pop.html#footnote1 (accessed July 10, 2010).

7. C. Peter Wagner, The Church in the Workplace: How God's People Can Transform Society (Ventura, CA: Regal Books, 2006).

Chapter 3

THE TIE THAT BINDS US ALL

I LIVE IN COLORADO Springs, Colorado, at the foothills of the majestic Rocky Mountains. Every morning when I awake in my house, I am blessed to look out the window and gaze upon mountains and valleys that appear as if they've been brush-stroked by a master artist. For anyone living in the area, the breathtaking landscape of Colorado's Front Range serves as a constant reminder of the awesome beauty found in God's creation.

But a few years ago I began to see these mountains from a different perspective. While in a season of understanding more about my calling as an intercessor, the Lord reminded me of something regarding mountains: they rarely stand alone. That is certainly the case in Colorado, which serves as one of the entryways to the three thousand-mile-stretching Rockies. A mountain range, by definition, always involves a series of mountains connected by passes or valleys. Without these saddle terrains, a mountain range would not exist—it would simply be a single, gigantic mountain (or, in many cases, a massive plateau).

Likewise, a nation's society isn't made up of a single mountain but of seven distinct peaks, which we identified in the last chapter. In between those cultural mountains is a connective landscape that may not be as physical in nature but is just as powerful as those majestic formations: intercession. This powerful spiritual discipline is the natural bridge between each of these mountains, and those who are called and gifted for a lifestyle of prayer—intercessors—serve a vital role throughout the kingdom. Unfortunately, for generations this office has been largely ignored and misunderstood.

The word *intercede* is derived directly from the Latin words *inter* (meaning "between") and *cede* (meaning "to go"). By its very description, then, intercession is the act of going between, mediating, or joining. In judicial terms, interceding for someone is pleading for or requesting something on that person's behalf. When using the term in a more military sense, intercession is the act of intervening to create an alliance or treaty. In every facet of life, intercession serves a powerful purpose.

If you study any culture throughout history inhabited by true followers of Jesus who understood the power of prayer and intercession, you will discover the role intercession has always played in shaping society. In every case, all it took were a few people to stand in the gap of those cultural mountains and intercede. God spoke of this through the prophet Ezekiel more than 2,500 years ago: "I searched for a man among them who would build up the wall and *stand in the gap* before Me for the land, so that I would not destroy it; but I found no one" (Ezek. 22:30, emphasis added).

In every nation and culture, the Lord searches for those who will stand between the mountains of society and intercede for those believers ascending the sloped terrains. To intercede, even by the most secular of definitions, means "to mediate" or "to intervene between parties with a view to reconciling differences."[1] In court, a lawyer intercedes by entreating the judge in favor of his client. On this earth, God has called intercessors to stand in the gap for people, situations, and entire lands. These prayer warriors are crucial to the Lord's strategy to manifest His kingdom on earth. I'm guessing you have picked up this book because you can identify with this special role and calling. Maybe you have years of experience under your belt of rending the heavens. Maybe you are just starting the journey. Whatever the case may be, the bottom-line question is still this: When God looks in the mountains of your culture, will He find you? Will you be willing to stand in the gap and intercede for others?

A few years ago I sat down with my grandkids to watch the movie *Shrek* for the first time. One of my favorite scenes is when Shrek, a grouchy green ogre who loves his solitude, sets out to meet Lord Farquaad, a villainous ruler who has disrupted Shrek's peaceful existence by sending exiled fairy-tale characters to the ogre's swamp. Shrek gathers these famous characters together to ask a few questions but discovers the only one who will respond is a talkative, overeager donkey named, well…Donkey.

"All right, who knows where this Farquaad guy is?" Shrek asks the assembly.

"Oh, I do! I know where he is!" Donkey eagerly answers with his hoof raised.

"Does anyone *else* know where to find him?" Shrek inquires, hoping someone other than Donkey will reply. "Anyone at all?"

As various fairy-tale characters point at each other and duck away, Shrek is left with a donkey bouncing through the crowd like a Pogo stick, trying to get Shrek's attention. "Pick me! Pick me! Oh, I know! I know! Pick me!"

That is the way we should respond to God's inquiry: *Pick me! Pick me!* The Lord is looking for those who will stand in the gap, those who will intercede for the sake of His kingdom plans. And just as Shrek eventually realized he needed someone—even Donkey—to help him on his journey, the truth is that *someone* has to stand in the gap. God will find someone to step up to the task. I've resolved that someone might as well be me. How about you?

To Each His Own—Mountain, That Is

The truth is, you may not be called to intercede for every mountain, just as you aren't called to ascend every mountain. In all likelihood, you already have a proclivity to pray for a certain mountain because of the way God wired you. You may have expertise in a specific field. Or it is possible your past experiences, education, upbringing, or vocation make it obvious which mountain you are called to pray for most. Some people are drawn to more than one mountain. Whatever the case, the important thing is to know first that God's calling for you to stand in the gap brings freedom, not a heavy burden or sense of dread. While you may carry an intercessory burden for a particular mountain, true prayer warriors take to heart Christ's words when He said, "My yoke is easy and My burden is light" (Matt. 11:30).

Second, it is crucial that you understand why your standing in the gap is so important. Let's examine this for each mountain.

Religion Mountain

Upon the mountain of religion, people either worship in spirit and truth or they settle for religious ritual.[2] In the last chapter, I alluded to how the American church, despite Christians being most familiar with this mountain, has relinquished its territory by relying on ritual rather than relationship. As long as we cling tighter to man-made institutions than to the Holy Spirit, we will continue to lose ground on this vital landscape. And with entire generations now believing that truth is relative, church is irrelevant, and God is whoever you want Him to be, it is evident that we have failed as intercessors to stand in the gap for those warring on this mountain.

Family Mountain

Within the family either blessings or curses are passed on to successive generations.[3] What happens when no one will stand in the gap for this fundamental unit of every society? We can already see the results of this in Europe and are progressively watching it come to fruition in the United States with the emergence of same-sex marriage laws, abortion rights, and other major issues of our day that erode the family structure. In recent years, many Christians have assumed those on the Religion Mountain would defend the family, or that certainly those standing atop the Government Mountain would do *something*. But if we notice who currently rules those mountains' peaks (hint: it's not the church), it becomes evident that these domains are no longer kingdom-controlled but flesh-dominated. The truth is, we have expected someone else to do our fighting for us when in fact we are the ones who should have been praying. As the twentieth century rendition of an Edmund Burke quote fittingly says, "All that is necessary for the triumph of evil is that good men do nothing." Indeed, in our motionlessness, we have abdicated our authority, and the result is the constant assault on the family that rules our country today.

Education Mountain

Upon this mountain are those teaching either truths or lies about God and His creation.[4] Tragically, we have already seen the results of what happens when those called to pray for this mountain fail in their assignment. Our schools—once the hub of teaching God's ways to the next generation—now prohibit prayer and penalize those who stand up for biblical truth. They continue to be some of the main battlegrounds for the enemy's attempt to remove God from the public square. And all because we did not know how to war against the enemy.

When we relent from standing in the gap for our education system in prayer, we not only give the forces of evil license to enter in, but we also affect virtually every other mountain. Schools build up or tear down potential future leaders in media, government, business, religion, the arts and entertainment, and even the family. As intercessors, we are called to pray in and pray for these world changers. Tragically, when we don't, we forfeit entire generations.

Government Mountain

This high-profile mountain is where evil is either restrained or endorsed.[5] Behind every power player in Washington, DC, stands an army of intercessors in the closets of America. For every city councilman or town mayor, there is a host of those called to pray on his or her behalf. Yet like Peter, James, and John on the night of Christ's crucifixion, many of these prayer warriors have fallen asleep despite God's instructions to "watch and pray" (Matt. 26:41). The results—particularly in recent years—are obvious as we see some of our country's most vital lawmakers fall further into political scandal and dissension. When the law of a land becomes littered with polluted morals, it is no surprise that the culture of that land follows suit.

Media Mountain

The media's role is to interpret information through the lens of good or evil.[6] Yet most of us would rather criticize, judge, curse, or ignore the media rather than do the one thing it needs from us most: *pray*. Certainly the media has at times abused its power in recent years, just as it has in generations past. But that does not change the fact that God desires a mass-audience mouthpiece that can proclaim His good news, righteousness, and holiness throughout the land. Until we are willing to intercede on behalf of those still standing in hope amid the thousands of skeptics ascending this social mountain, we can expect the same spirit of hopelessness. Instead of getting our information from those who view through a kingdom lens and offer a Joshua- and Caleb-like report, we will constantly hear "a bad report of the land" from those who spread fear through their stories of giant-sized obstacles and "a land that devours its inhabitants" (Num. 13:32).

Arts and Entertainment Mountain

This societal arena, where values and virtue are celebrated or distorted, is often embodied in one word: *Hollywood*.[7] For years, Hollywood became the church's enemy *numero uno*, embodying everything unholy, God-mocking, and purely evil. As various cultural revolutions took place, every change for the worse in society was dubbed a product of "those Hollywood liberals."

While such God-abhorring, sin-glamorizing liberalism may still dominate Hollywood, the church must wake up and realize the enemy no longer just resides in a star-studded Los Angeles territory; its values have now been ingested into virtually every home across America through television, movies, music, the Internet, and so on. Though by themselves these are inherently neutral tools, they have been dominated by the enemy. And if we are to tear down these opposing strongholds, we must intercede on behalf of every warrior called to fight for holiness on this mountain. We need to stand behind every believer who, like a client I worked with, dreams of buying a movie production company to invade Hollywood and transform it with pure representations of the Master Artist. When others—even Christians—speak over them word curses ("There's no way they'll ever succeed in Tinseltown") or even opposition ("God, keep them from such a dark environment because I'm sure it will destroy them"), we must be the ones to secure their God-given assignment in prayer. Likewise, when an athletically gifted teenager feels called by God to play in the NBA and works tirelessly toward this goal, we must take to heart the seriousness of his vision and cover his journey with intercession.

Business Mountain

One of the most pivotal areas for the church in the coming years, the workplace holds the power over resources that are either consecrated for the kingdom of God or captured for the powers of darkness.[8] I will address this mountain specifically in later chapters, but for now I cannot stress enough the importance of God's kingdom being allowed to rule and reign upon the Business Mountain. Our God may own "the cattle on a thousand hills" (Ps. 50:10), but in recent seasons the enemy has worked hard to steal as much of the church's inheritance as possible. And as Wall Street's corrupt leaders continue to be exposed, the need for a revolution of righteousness in the business arena becomes more apparent. Until intercessors will step up and stand in the gap for those who desire to operate upon this mountain with integrity and holiness, we will continue to find the church robbed of the resources that rightfully belong to us.

RIGHT PLACE, RIGHT TIME

In the past fifty years, we have witnessed possibly the most rapid moral decline in history. The culture we inherited from our nation's forefathers is disintegrating before our eyes. And each of these mountains, now controlled by the forces of darkness, has played a part in this moral deterioration. Clearly, it is time to fight and take back these mountains of influence.

To take on a task of such magnitude without prayer, however, is nothing short of foolishness. Workplace influencers on these Seven Mountains need powerful, purposeful intercessors willing to pay the price in the heavenly realm to shape history on earth. Our prayers are not just lip service, nor are they wimpy petitions to God. The Lord has given us a true weapon for the assault that can make a significant difference in what is accomplished. Whether we believe it or not is irrelevant. Intercession *can* change the world. The key for God's people, then, is to realize that He strategically places intercessors to pray in the right place at the right time so that His kingdom comes and His will is done throughout the Seven Mountains.

I am amazed how the Lord, throughout history, has always orchestrated circumstances and put people in the right place at the right time so they can accomplish His kingdom purposes and plans. One of the most powerful examples of this is William Wilberforce. While only twenty-one years old and still a university student, the ever-popular Wilberforce was elected to Britain's Parliament and, using his remarkable oratory skills and natural charisma, was well on his way to political stardom. But in 1785, only five years later, the young legislator had such a radical encounter with God that he seriously contemplated abandoning his political post and pursuing a life devoted to serving God— which, in his eyes, meant retreating from the public eye.

He sought the advice of his college friend, William Pitt, who had since become Britain's prime minister, and John Newton, a leading Anglican priest of the day. While Pitt's advice was more of a political nature, Newton shared a spiritual truth that forever changed Wilberforce's life. Essentially, Newton reminded this struggling believer that God had equipped him to ascend the mountain of government and that the King of Kings could be served just as powerfully and effectively in that arena as on the Religion Mountain. The message stuck, and Wilberforce went on to stand up for biblical values in the face of a culture that, for almost three hundred years, had not only accepted but prospered under the dark shadow of the slave trade. His tireless efforts over a twenty-year span paved the way for a final vote in 1807 that officially abolished slavery and changed the course of history.

All because God placed one man in the right place at the right time.

Praying for Clean Oil

This happens just as frequently today. Not long ago I witnessed such a *kairos* situation—when God puts the right person in the right place at the right time—through a trio of clients. In 2000, I was leading a group of intercessors at an Ed Silvoso Harvest Evangelism event in Argentina and ran into a man from Texas whom I had met several years prior. He was serving at a church in Singapore at the time and was concerned about a couple in his congregation who worked in the oil and gas industry and needed significant prayer covering. Knowing I was an intercessor, he asked if I would commit to pray for them on a regular basis. Normally I would have taken time to think through and pray about making such a promise—especially since I had never met or even heard about this couple before. But something in my spirit instantly knew this was an assignment for me, so I agreed.

Years later, this couple moved from Singapore to Texas, and we arranged to meet for lunch in Dallas. I had interceded for them all that time, sending them prophetic insights and specific prayers when the Lord prompted me. But when we finally met face-to-face, they were surprised to find out that I—in their own words—"looked normal, acted normal, and spoke normal." We had a good laugh about that one, but the fact is, we intercessors have a reputation for acting strange—and unfortunately, we're all too often the ones who legitimize that perception!

My relationship with the couple grew after that meeting as they began to trust me more. One day, the husband called and asked me to pray for his company, which had been struggling for about a year and a half. Although two of his business partners were strong Christian men, the head partner was engaging in some under-the-table activity that put not only their entire business at risk, but also their lives in danger overseas. The three godly men were extremely concerned about the situation and asked for both my prayers and any insight I sensed from the Holy Spirit. As I began to work more closely and pray with them, I felt like they needed to start their own company. This was easier said than done, however, and God knew they needed a definite word from Him to move in this direction.

Only months later, the three men attended an International Coalition of Apostles (ICA) meeting focusing on kingdom progress in the workplace. Longtime successful businesswoman Linda Rios Brook spoke during one session and gave them the exact confirmation that these men needed to pull out of their business and start a new one. Within months they did just that, establishing an oil and gas company that was founded on and operates on godly principles. I worked with them as they created their business' mission statement and vision, and it was truly wonderful to see three leaders relying on God's voice and direction to guide their every move.

Their international company continued to grow, not despite but *because* of their kingdom-first mind-set. Any potential investor or client immediately knew what these men stood for upon seeing the company's mission statement, which said: "We are an association of people brought together for the glory of the kingdom of God, who gives us power to create wealth from the treasures of oil, gas, and other resources of the earth, to advance the purposes of God in the earth realm."

If you visited their offices, you'd also notice their vision painted on the window as you entered the front door: "With God working through our expertise, gifts, and faiths, we will co-labor to bring hope and transformation to our world." Talk about being forthright!

I believe God has established these men in just the right place at just the right time. Their impact on the Business Mountain could be profound, yet since their top priority isn't building their own kingdom but God's, their influence is sure to extend to other mountains as well. I also believe none of this would or could happen without them acknowledging the power of intercession. They have walked step-by-step with both me and my team of intercessors, refusing to move in the natural unless it first has been made clear in the spirit where God is leading them. In their minds, intercession is not a good luck charm to boost their bottom line; it is an integral part of everything, from their daily operations to their overall vision. And that is how business—or, for that matter, any of the other six societal arenas—should be approached.

THE WEAKEST LINK

Though such companies are still the exception rather than the rule in the corporate world today, God is on the move to establish powerhouse businesses and individuals in every sector of society who will not compromise when it comes to operating with divine purposes rather than worldly motives. What these individuals and groups must understand, however, is the same thing my three clients recognized early on: you cannot progress up your assignment mountain and hope to stay there without serious intercession.

Not long ago, millions of TV viewers tuned into a game show each week called *The Weakest Link*. Contestants would answer as many trivia questions within a certain time frame as possible, and after each round, would then vote on who among their group was the "weakest link" for either missing questions or taking too long to answer them. When a contestant was voted off, the notoriously curt host would announce in her British accent, "You...are the weakest link!"

It is always the weakest link in a chain that causes a break. As the saying goes, "You are only as strong as your weakest link." That has been widely accepted in business partnerships, customer service, and sports teams. But why have we not considered how it also applies to the church's decline of influence in society? Perhaps the weakest link— or in many cases, *missing* link—for those kingdom-minded workplace influencers scaling culture's Seven Mountains is intercession. Perhaps we have fallen off these mountains not because of our skill sets, talents, money, or innovation, but simply because we failed to cover our every step with prayer.

It is time those scaling the slopes get the spiritual protection they need to break through to the next level instead of succumbing to the enemy's attacks. Ezekiel 22:30, which we looked at earlier in this chapter, shows us that God is still on the lookout for those who will "stand in the gap before Me for the land." He is searching for those who will do what Aaron and Hur did for Moses when the Israelites fought the Amalekites: "But Moses' hands were heavy. Then they took a stone and put it under him, and he sat on it; and Aaron and Hur supported his hands, one on one side and one on the other. Thus his hands were steady until the sun set" (Exod. 17:12).

What was so important about Aaron and Hur standing alongside Moses? Simply put, it was life or death for the nation of Israel. Whenever Moses raised his hands and held up the staff God had given him, the Israelites would win; and whenever he lowered his hands, they would begin to lose the battle. For generations, the church has endured attack after attack from the enemy with no one standing up to the opposition, raising the emblem of God, and declaring victory. We have failed to realize that warring with the enemy is often a life-or-death scenario. Notice that Moses stood on a hill and looked down on the battlefield. Whenever we intercede, we take the heavenly position, which allows us to see from a higher viewpoint and strategize more effectively as we see the fighting unfold. (More on that in chapter 8.)

Just as Aaron and Hur helped Moses, intercessors must come alongside workplace influencers to engage the enemy and declare the kingdom victory of God. We have spent far too many years watching those on the front lines fall in defeat and lose ground to the enemy. It is time for intercessors to understand their crucial place in the war for our culture and for workplace influencers to realize the necessity of intercessors. When powerful prayer warriors are allowed to fight alongside those ascending the cultural mountains, it allows these instrumental leaders the time and energy to hear from God on how they should lead their organizations more effectively.

By working together in the alignment the Lord intended, we can render the enemy's weapons ineffective, thwart demonic tactics, and successfully reach the summit to declare God's kingdom victorious. Yes, intercession is that powerful. It is a weapon that can transform every situation and change the outcome. It makes all the difference. And in the next chapter, we will start to unveil exactly how it can have such a drastic effect in your surroundings.

CHAPTER 3 NOTES

1. *Merriam-Webster's Online Dictionary*, s.v. "intercede," http://www.merriam-webster.com/dictionary/intercede (accessed September 18, 2009).

2. Adapted from "Reclaiming the Seven Mountains of Culture" by Os Hillman, http://www.youtube.com/watch?v=wQtB-AF41p8 (accessed September 20, 2009). Used by permission.

3. Ibid.

4. Ibid.

5. Ibid.

6. Ibid.

7. Ibid.

8. Ibid.

Chapter 4

THAT'S WHY WE PRAY

YOU DON'T WANT to mess with the IRS. Texans may have trademarked a slogan about messing with their state, but there are few things that create as much fear in the average American as a call from the Internal Revenue Service. So when a client of mine got just that, it felt like the world was crumbling all around him.

Matthew was meeting with my team of intercessors, but at the time he had yet to sign on as an official client. He was an active investor and had been contacted by the IRS, which claimed he owed them $130,000—certainly not chump change. Matthew's CPA had already met twice with an IRS representative, who seemed to have little compassion and was unyielding in his belief that Matthew was in the wrong. With the situation still unresolved and things looking bleaker by the moment, the CPA and IRS agent were scheduled to meet again in three days, upon which time Matthew would receive official word of how much money he owed.

"Please pray for favor," he asked us. "Pray that the whole ordeal will finally be resolved—and that I won't owe them as much as they say I do."

The panic in his eyes was obvious. Whether out of desperation or faith, he ended up hiring us to intercede on his behalf not only for those three days but throughout the months-long audit. We did just that, crying out to the Father for extreme favor and standing in the gap for our brother, who sincerely believed he had done nothing wrong, illegal, or anything that would justify such a severe penalty.

When the meeting occurred three days later, a different IRS representative arrived, which at least lowered Matthew's stress level, though not his anxiety. The new official seemed sincerely concerned about the situation and sat down with Matthew to once again go over his books. The longer they spent culling through the numbers, the more this man shook his head.

"Something is terribly wrong here," he said.

Taking a deep breath, Matthew instantly seemed to lose hope. *I thought the intercessors were praying!*

"Sir, something is terribly wrong," the man again stated, then followed it up with something that caught Matthew completely off guard: "It looks like we owe *you* money."

Within a few weeks, Matthew received an unexpected check for $40,000 from the IRS!

The world is full of countless stories like this that underscore the power of prayer. God has forever been in the business of moving mountains for His praying people. He has equipped us with tools to rend the heavens, yet most often He is waiting for us to use them so He can begin moving on our behalf. Unfortunately, too many once-powerful intercessors render themselves useless by abandoning hope (and yes, faith too) when certain prayers seemingly go unanswered for too long. There are many factors behind these intercessory dropouts, but I believe one of the main ones that can sidetrack prayer warriors is forgetting the basic truths of what prayer actually does. At times, situations (or the enemy) can blind us to the reality of prayer's effects. Before going any further in discussing how to intercede for those on the Seven Mountains, let's address in general what happens when we pray.

Ten Effects of Prayer

When we stand in the gap and pray for others, it…

1. *Inspires decisions.* Many people arrive at the place of total dependency on the Lord only when they reach the end of their rope. Prior to that, they stay in control, yielding only partially to the Lord's sovereignty and still calling the shots. I can't begin to count the number of people over the years who have asked me to pray for them simply because they were frozen in making a decision. They needed an answer—fast! Prayer sparks solutions; it is the fertile ground for birthing decisions.

2. *Creates a climate for wise decision-making.* Just making a decision does not cut it. Those in the business world know this especially well. What seems like the best choice at the time can end up costing a company, nation, family, or individual a lifetime of regret. The key is making a wise decision that bears maximum fruit both today and in future generations. This is why it is essential to intercede for wisdom on behalf of others. It is possible that those you pray for will continue to rely on their own strength to make decisions. But believers who understand the powerful nature of prayer will recognize their need to have intercessors

surrounding them. After all, prayer is the greatest incubator in which we can receive divine, heaven-sent wisdom straight from the Holy Spirit. I doubt there are many who would turn that down!

3. *Helps them focus on their priorities.* In Mark 1:35–38, we find Jesus relying on prayer to set first things first: "In the early morning, while it was still dark, Jesus got up, left the house, and went away to a secluded place, and was praying there. Simon and his companions searched for Him; they found Him, and said to Him, 'Everyone is looking for You.' He said to them, 'Let us go somewhere else to the towns nearby, so that I may preach there also; *for that is what I came for*'" (emphasis added).

We know Jesus was the ultimate intercessor and prayer instructor. We also know He did nothing by Himself but only acted upon what He saw the Father doing. (See John 5:19.) The passage in Mark offers us a wonderful glimpse into the personal prayer life of Jesus, as even the Son of God had to converse with His Father in private prayer to refocus on what mattered most.

We live at a breakneck pace in today's culture, regardless of what mountain we are on. It's easy to continue running the race and, over time, forget why we are running in the first place. By standing in the gap in prayer for individuals, we can push the pause button on a frantic lifestyle and deliver a Holy Spirit–inspired, prophetic word that pierces the heart. For some, that is what's required to spark a hunger to commune with their heavenly Father and allow Him to establish their priorities for the day, week, month, year—whatever the season. Others may simply wonder where they should start, and it is through seeking God in prayer that we can deliver "a word spoken in due season" (Prov. 15:23, KJV) to help them prioritize things.

4. *Prevents anxiety.* One of the biggest misuses of time and energy, anxiety runs rampant in American society today. In fact, anxiety-related disorders are the most common mental illness in the country, affecting a whopping 40 million adults (or 18 percent of the US population). These disorders aren't just mentally taxing but cost the nation more than $42 billion each year. That's partly because those suffering from anxiety disorders are three to five times more likely to visit a doctor than those who do not suffer from the illness—and six times more likely to be hospitalized.[1]

What an effective weapon the enemy created to thwart potential kingdom-bearers! Philippians 4:6 tells us, "Be anxious for nothing, but in everything by prayer and supplication with thanksgiving let your requests be made known to God." My favorite part of this passage, however, is the next verse—one all too often forgotten: "And the peace of God, which surpasses all comprehension, will guard your hearts and your minds in Christ Jesus" (v. 7).

It's one thing to be told to settle down and not worry (which is essentially all anxiety is). It's another to be told *how* to not fall prey to anxiety. Yet that is exactly what Paul did in writing to the Philippians, reminding them that prayer not only prevents and deflects anxiety, but also establishes the very peace of God. When God's peaceful presence is established through intercession, a protective covering is formed in the spirit realm, much like the mind-insulating "helmet of salvation" Paul mentions in another letter (Eph. 6:17). This covering guards both the heart and mind, making decision-making and prioritizing even easier.

5. *Releases favor with key people.* Though it rings true in all aspects of society, there is an old adage that is known all too well for those involved in business: "It's not what you know, it's *who* you know." Having favor with the right people can open doors that otherwise would remain shut. Nehemiah understood this in his day, and it was through prayer that he experienced remarkable favor to accomplish the Lord's kingdom purposes. Yet his was not just any kind of favor; it was favor with Artaxerxes, the king of Persia:

> Then the king said to me, "What would you request?" So I prayed to the God of heaven. I said to the king, "If it please the king, and if your servant has found favor before you, send me to Judah, to the city of my fathers' tombs, that I may rebuild it." Then the king said to me, the queen sitting beside him, "How long will your journey be, and when will you return?" So it pleased the king to send me, and I gave him a definite time. And I said to the king, "If it please the king, let letters be given me for the governors of the provinces beyond the River, that they may allow me to pass through until I come to Judah, and a letter to Asaph the keeper of the king's forest, that he may give me timber to make beams for the gates of the fortress which is by the temple, for the wall of the city and for the house to which I will go." And the king granted them to me because the good hand of my God was on me.
>
> —NEHEMIAH 2:4–8

Nehemiah went from being the king's cupbearer to essentially filling the role of a Judean governor and leading the movement to rebuild the walls of Jerusalem. Artaxerxes even granted Nehemiah all the paperwork to not only prove to other provincial leaders he had been sent by the king, but also to require their help. Now *that's* favor!

In the first chapter, I told the story of Rebecca, the American working with orphans in a former Communist Bloc nation. She labored for more than two years in a city, where her ministry's plans to build homes and schools for children were continuously blocked by government red tape. One of those most responsible for this was a high-ranking official named Fredrika. She served as the secretariat and had a reputation for "changing the rules" or increasing the requirements to gain permits, licenses, and other government-issued documents. Our divine appointment with her, however, broke down seemingly immovable walls between Rebecca and Fredrika, and the two now have a close relationship. Fredrika not only works with the city mayor, but her connections with state and national government have paved the way for favor that allows Rebecca to move in greater freedom.

In both Nehemiah and Rebecca's cases, the key to releasing God's purposes wasn't just general favor; it was favor with key people. Yet before such specific favor was ever granted, both sought God through prayer. We can't expect favor from key people to automatically happen with some offhand, "God, could You help me out?" prayer. That is why our standing in the gap is so crucial for some people. We may be the only prayer—literally—for them to find such favor.

6. *Opens doors.* This is connected closely with the previous effect of prayer, simply because favor is often manifested through new opportunities. We seek favor from certain "gatekeepers" (those key people) so that they might open doors of opportunity for us. Yet as you stand in the gap on behalf of someone else, let me offer a reminder regarding open doors. I have met with countless people who fasted and prayed for divine openings—a sudden opportunity involving a job, client, spouse, business deal, and the like—yet even when those doors were opened, they hesitated and wondered if they were actually supposed to walk through them. Don't just pray for open doors; pray also for the wisdom to know when or how to walk through them. Imagine how frustrating it would be to hear that the person for whom you have been interceding found a door of opportunity suddenly opened—but failed to walk through it. Opportunity may knock, but wisdom responds.

7. *Releases divine power to push back evil forces that can keep doors closed.* Just because a door you have asked God to open suddenly opens doesn't mean it will stay open. Some doors are closed not by God but by evil powers. When we pray, we engage those evil powers and declare the strength and victory of the Lord. Our prayers are a declaration of breakthrough.

One of the people I regularly pray for spent years working with Enron. He had tremendous success developing computer software for the corporation, which had paid him in stocks. When I first met Steve, the value of these stocks was so high that he did not have to work another day in his life. Shortly before the Enron fall, however, Steve felt a check in his spirit about being connected to the company and, prompted by the Holy Spirit, decided to resign and give Enron the rights to the programs he had created. He walked away and started his own company. The move was not easy, and his new enterprise continued to encounter roadblocks because of his past connections with the corporation. When he asked for my help in interceding for both him and his company, I began to pray to sever every preexisting unholy alliance that was preventing Steve from succeeding. Officially disconnecting from Enron eventually cost him a significant amount of money, yet not long after he did, the scandal broke. Though Steve's personal stocks plummeted, he continued to walk in integrity, and his company is now prospering. I believe this is directly related to a breakthrough in the spirit, prompted by our prayers that called for all doors shut by the Enron collapse to be opened.

8. *Adds spiritual meaning and significance to their labor.* No one wants to live in a clock-in, clock-out mentality. We all want to find purpose, meaning, and significance in what we do. When we engage the Holy Spirit in prayer on behalf of another person, we can press in so they will find all of this through a higher purpose for their actions. What was once menial work can become an opportunity to glorify God and worship Him with their hands, feet, mind, and attitude. Though this element of prayer is often overlooked or seen as trivial, it is no less miraculous and awe-inspiring. Through prayer, God can transform *any* task or situation into an earthly portal primed for kingdom invasion.

9. *Shifts their perspective from serving people to serving God.* Do the people you are praying for sometimes put more weight in others' words than in God's? Are they stuck in a cycle of desperately trying to please their spouse, child, parent, co-worker, boss, or pastor? Despite good

intentions, do they often find God slipping to the bottom of their list of priorities? If you can answer yes to any of those questions, then your standing in the gap for them is invaluable right now—more than they will probably ever know. While putting others ahead of yourself might sound noble and selfless, it is ultimately meaningless if it is not a by-product of serving the Lord. Your intercession can shift their focus back on the only One completely worthy of everything they could ever offer in service. As they connect with Him, sense His heart, and hear His thoughts, then they can truly serve others in power.

10. *Stirs up Holy Spirit activity.* God has a habit of showing up in situations that have been saturated in prayer. He is certainly not limited to our heaven-bent requests, petitions, and pleas, but it doesn't take a Bible scholar to know God's heart has always been moved by those whose cries align with His kingdom purposes. Our prayers have the power to stir up the heavens and create an atmosphere in which the Holy Spirit has complete freedom to move in power. I don't know about you, but that is the kind of "activity" I always prefer!

ARE YOU SMARTER THAN A DUMB BOMB?

My husband used to be a fighter pilot. When he fought in the Vietnam War, part of his assignment was to fly over enemy territory and drop bombs on specified targets. Military technology at that time was nowhere near what it is today, and often fighter pilots would release as many bombs as possible over a target, knowing that only a few would probably hit the mark. These "dumb bombs," as they were then called, could veer off course for a variety of reasons—wind, temperature, altitude, aircraft speed, accuracy of the pilot, to name a few.

Today these are more commonly referred to as gravity bombs since this more accurately describes the ballistic trajectory they follow. The original term had nothing to do with intelligence, but simply referred to that fact that "dumb bombs" lacked a guidance system. Bombs that are equipped with these homing devices, on the other hand, are called "smart bombs" and are in the vast majority today. These amazing weapons have changed the nature of warfare. Instead of releasing dozens of bombs with hopes of only a few connecting, fighter pilots can drop a single smart bomb and even direct it after its release. In fact, smart bombs are so accurate now, they can hit a target as small as a window or a chimney from miles in the air. Now that's precise!

That is how God wants our prayers to be. He is looking for intercessors who truly understand the effects prayer can have in transforming every situation. He wants those who are willing to fight in the heavenly realm to be skilled warriors who are masters of their weapon because they have put in the blood, sweat, tears, and time to prepare for battle. He wants spiritual snipers—those who can strike with pinpoint accuracy— not believers who casually lob up spiritual thoughts from time to time in hopes of someday hitting the mark.

The truth is, we are equipped with the most powerful weapon of war the earth has ever known. Prayer has the potential to cause more damage on the forces of darkness than any nuclear weapon invented. Sadly, many believers do not realize this, while others who do fail to take action. That is why your role as an intercessor in the Seven Mountains of society is not just important for these times, it is critical. You wield a weapon that can inspire and create wise decisions, renew people's focus on what really matters, ward off fear and anxiety, open doors of opportunity and prompt unexpected favor with key individuals, dispel evil forces from thwarting divine appointments, add purpose to everyday life, shift hearts toward serving God, and create an environment for the Holy Spirit to move. As hard as it may be to believe, that barely scratches the surface of what prayer can do.

Like an army in preparation for battle, intercessors around the world are awakening to a new sense of purpose in their calling to stand as prayer warriors. In the first part of this book we have established the clear need for such an army to arise and stand in the gap for those ascending the mountains of culture. Now let's dive into the plan of attack—and why we have not already begun our assault.

CHAPTER 4 NOTES

1. Anxiety Disorders Association of America, "Facts & Statistics," http://www.adaa.org/about-adaa/press-room/facts-statistics (accessed September 30, 2009).

PART 2

Here's How We Fight

Chapter 5

ENEMY TACTICS

GOD WANTS THE church to rule and reign on every mountain of society. His desire is to see the earth become a mirror reflection of His heavenly kingdom. So that we might overcome the forces of darkness that currently rule the mountains of this world, He has equipped His children with a heavenly weapon strong enough to demolish any stronghold or fortress established on those mountains. (See 2 Corinthians 10:4.) We have the means to take back the enemy-possessed land with God's *dunamis*, miracle-producing power. But if prayer is truly the most potent weapon in the world, then let me pose the obvious question: Why haven't we already invaded the mountains with it? Why have we not launched an all-out assault on the demonic realm within the land, knowing that the victory is ours for the taking?

The answer is not simple, nor is it always obvious. Yet in getting to the core of why we have failed to invade the Seven Mountains of society, not only will we expose the enemy's strategy for keeping us on the defensive (which, we must admit, has been successful to this point), but we can also begin to unfold God's strategy to once again put us on the offensive—for good. And like an army general analyzing his previous losses to gain the next victory, we must face up to and examine the mistakes we, as a church, have made in the past.

NEVER UNDERESTIMATE THE ENEMY

As perhaps one of the most scrutinized military ventures of World War II, Operation Market Garden was supposed to be the Allied forces' final blow to the weakening German presence in Europe. Fought in both the Netherlands and Germany, the operation became the largest airborne offensive of all time—and also a moment of tactical failure history will never forget.

By September 1944, the Allies had advanced through Europe and appeared well on their way to the heart of the Axis powers in Berlin. For

a final surge, Supreme Allied Commander Dwight D. Eisenhower had
to decide between strategies devised by two of his top leaders, British
Field Marshal Bernard Montgomery and US General George S. Patton.
Faced with rising political pressure and given an assurance of victory
by Montgomery, Eisenhower opted for the Englishman's "Operation
Market Garden," which involved taking control of key bridges across
the Meuse River and two areas of the Rhine.

At the heart of Montgomery's bold plan was dropping paratroopers
behind enemy lines who would seize a series of bridges and eventually
team up with progressing ground forces. The operation began almost
flawlessly, with the initial Allied troops landing precisely in their drop
zones and encountering minimal resistance. Not long after, however, a
paratrooper regiment failed to take a 650-yard bridge at Nijmegen in the
Netherlands. This seemingly small, unexpected blip eventually enabled
the Germans to not only maintain the support lines they needed to ward
off other attacks, but also to regroup with stronger force. Meanwhile,
similar problems took place on a bridge at Arnhem, in the lower Rhine,
where another British airborne division met more resistance than antici-
pated. What should have been the final objective of the operation ended
up being a costly battle lost to German troops who refused to give up
the bridge's southern end.

The operation and ensuing battles were far more involved than my
simplified description of what transpired between September 17–25,
1944. But in hindsight, war buffs and historians can now offer a long
list of reasons Montgomery's multidimensional plan failed. At the top is
one I find most fascinating: a breakdown in communication. The battle
for the Nijmegen wasn't necessarily lost due to lack of preparation, but
because of a miscommunication that caused the paratrooper regiment to
delay engaging German troops until late in the day. Had they attacked
earlier, the British military would have faced only a dozen German soldiers; but in waiting, they gave an entire battalion time to arrive to bolster the enemy's defense. Historians later revealed that after the landing,
the Allied troops' radios were actually on different frequencies.

Montgomery also assumed his British forces would break through
enemy lines within a day or two. In reality, it took almost ten days,
during which time troops ran out of ammunition and supplies because
of Montgomery's miscalculations. Likewise, his faulty assessment of the
enemy's strength at certain points—including Arnhem—resulted in a
death toll of more than 15,000.[1]

Are you seeing the powerful spiritual connections woven throughout this true-to-life story? At its heart, intercession is pure communication—with God *and* with the forces of darkness. Though we will address this later in further detail, intercession is all about declaring to the enemy what God has already communicated to us. It is reminding Satan of his defeat as we stand in the gap and announce victory. Think about this: what physical structure "stands in the gap" to connect two things? A bridge. And the entire Operation Market Garden—what could have been the greatest victory for the Allies—hinged upon bridges. In fact, in *A Bridge Too Far*, the 1976 movie based on the operation, one of the top British commanders offers this prophetic line: "We shall seize the bridges—it's all a question of bridges—with thunderclap surprise, and hold them until they can be secured."[2]

Because of a breakdown in communication (intercession), those fighting for freedom were unable to hold the bridges (the key points of intercession, or the intercessors), which led to an inability to further support those fighting on the frontlines (the mountains of culture). Just as the Allied forces were unable to take over the enemy forces ruling the land without pure communication and control of the bridges, we will never win the war for the Seven Mountains of society if we are not positioned in the connecting places between those mountains and are not interceding *on the same frequency*. Being on the same wavelength takes tuning in to the same source—in our case, the Holy Spirit. God is always talking, giving us directions and strategies for overcoming the forces that inhabit the land. Are we listening? Have we trained our ears to be acute in receiving His plans for attack?

DIVIDE AND CONQUER

The enemy is well aware how vital communication is to our victory and his imminent defeat. After all, Satan is "the prince of the power of the air" (Eph. 2:2). That's why one of his most common (and effective, mind you) tactics is to break down communication lines. Whenever these wires are mangled, disrupted, or cut, we can expect confusion to be in the air.

In 1995, I visited Arnhem, where the famous battle took place during Operation Market Garden. More than fifty years after the Allied forces' costly defeat, the same spirit of confusion ruled the land. I arrived at a conference with a group of twelve intercessors, and from the get-go we encountered one cross-wired incident after another—to the point of having to laugh through our frustration.

Our host instructed us to check into our hotel and gave us our room number: 415. I don't think I was alone in presuming it would be on the fourth floor, but I eventually discovered it was actually on the second. Others in our group were in room number 320—which, against all logic, was located on the first floor. Shortly after arriving, the team leaders received a written schedule with a list of the conference speakers, as well as the times and places for each session. There was a problem, however: the entire schedule had been changed at the last minute, and none of us were notified, which left us in the dark throughout the conference. In addition, the maps we received were inaccurate, and because all twelve intercessory team leaders were from different parts of the world, we interpreted them differently—which, of course, resulted in us often getting lost. Surely the walkie-talkies that the conference leaders provided us would help us find our way, right? Of course not. Though we were supposed to have a designated channel used only for intercessory teams and the conference's leader, somehow the channel got crossed with another frequency, and we ended up hearing every notification—from housekeeping to conversations that had nothing to do with intercession.

The confusion throughout our time there was so astounding and overtly spiritual, it didn't take an intercessor to discern that miscommunication was still in the land. Neither does it take a rocket scientist to recognize that the fruit of miscommunication is division. Satan wants nothing more than to keep the church divided over linguistic misunderstandings and misinterpretations. He loves to create language barriers, especially when we are speaking in the same tongue. How often have a group of believers—a church, a network of churches, or entire denominations—split because they have majored on the minors when it comes to scriptural interpretation, theology, and eschatology? The more our enemy can wreak havoc among us with such "miscommunication," the less unified we are.

TOGETHER AS ONE

In the historical epic *Gladiator*, Russell Crowe's character, General Maximus Decimus Meridius, is a legendary Roman war hero betrayed by the emperor's son and forced to live through both the murder of his family and years of slavery. Maximus uses his remarkable combat skills to work his way up through the ranks as a gladiator until one day he is thrown into Rome's main coliseum with a group of fellow gladiators who must fend off a far more powerful (and unfairly equipped) horde of attackers. As the former general stands with the other slaves, facing what appears to be certain death, he uses his natural leadership skills to bring these gladiators—known for their rugged individualism—together.

"Whatever comes out of these gates, we stand a better chance of survival if we work together," he says to them. "Do you understand? If we stay together, we survive."

The group huddles together and, with Maximus directing their every move, manages to defeat one chariot-driving enemy after another. Those who break from the pack quickly perish; yet those who stay connected via Maximus's verbal cues survive and, to the bloodthirsty crowd's amazement, emerge victorious.[3]

David, a fellow warrior-general, wrote of "how good and how pleasant it is for brothers to dwell together in unity" (Ps. 133:1). He understood the power of coming together. Yet just as crucial as physically gathering is remaining unified through communication, as Maximus's band of gladiators proved. For them, it was literally a matter of life or death; for us, it may not be that different when considering what is at stake in the spirit.

From the very beginning, God has recognized this power of clear communication among a unified people. In Genesis 11:6, while watching the people of the earth pridefully attempt to make a name for themselves by constructing a tower, He remarked: "Behold, they are one people, and they all have the same language. And this is what they began to do, and now nothing which they purpose to do will be impossible for them."

Thousands of years later, Jesus recognized the same power and, in one of the most intimate prayers recorded in Scripture between the Son and the Father, prayed "that they may all be one" (John 17:21). If our unification is that important to Jesus, you can be assured it matters to our enemy, who lives in constant fear that one day we may finally come to such complete unity that we reflect the perfect union expressed among the Father, Son, and Holy Spirit. When we mirror that kind of harmony, we will walk in a power the world has not seen since the early church turned cultures upside down, ruined governments, and shook the nations. When we become attuned to the same frequency of the Holy Spirit's guidance, we will refine entire education systems, reawaken the arts, redirect the media, reallocate businesses, reassemble governments, reunite families, and reclaim pure religion.

As inspiring as that sounds to believers, we still have many territories to inhabit—and possess—before claiming the land as ours. Disunity may be one of the major reasons we have yet to invade the mountains of society, but there are many more. Let's examine some of these other reasons for the sake of identifying the enemy's tactics that keep us on the defense rather than the offense.

IGNORANCE

A businessman I once heard spoke about the value of keeping clients and employees informed: "You don't want to treat them like mushrooms— covered in manure and left in the dark." Yet Satan has done a remarkable job of this when it comes to blinding believers to the church's real lack of influence on the Seven Mountains. We have convinced ourselves that, despite a cultural shift in the moral climate of our nation, Christians still remain the dominant players on the mountain of religion. In the Bible Belt, for example, it is assumed that since there is a church on every corner, *surely* God is present and moving throughout the land. The truth is, if you don't know a problem even exists, how can you be expected to fight for a solution to that problem? As long as we remain ignorant of the reality of what is going on, we will be content to do nothing.

One of the greatest examples of this in the past twenty years is found in Rwanda. Only in the last few years has the Western world begun to understand the atrocities that took place during the 1994 genocide. Within a mere hundred days, extremist Hutus throughout the country killed approximately eight hundred thousand Tutsis and moderate Hutus. Sparked by a thirty-thousand-member militia group that called itself the Interahamwe (meaning "those who attack together"), the violence erupted overnight and pitted neighbor against neighbor, with many Hutus forced at gunpoint by military officials to slaughter their Tutsi relatives or friends.[4]

What many people overlook is that Rwanda was not a nation full of savages and criminals, as many Americans foolishly think of lesser-known African countries. Rwanda had actually been the pride of the continent, with more than 90 percent of its population considering themselves Christian. This was no guerilla warfare; it was literally a case of Christians slaughtering Christians in cold blood—which makes it even more unbelievable.

I set foot in Rwanda only three years following the genocide, and to this day it remains the most difficult trip I have ever been on, both emotionally and spiritually. Never before had I encountered such a thick residue of pure evil across an entire land. I heard stories of children who were given weapons and instructed to "play" with a man until he died. One eight-year-old girl had her throat sliced with a machete during a massacre of thousands, then spent five days trying to climb out from under the bodies piled on her. Another man lay in a heap of bodies, unable to move for days, and was nursed back to life by a rat (he called it his "angel rat") that brought him bits of flesh from the dead bodies around him.

On one occasion I visited a church where hundreds of worshipers had been massacred during the first weeks of the genocide. When I entered the windowless building, my eyes had trouble adjusting to the darkness, and I stumbled around trying to find something to hold onto or lean against. I was gradually able to make out some overturned wooden benches a few feet ahead and what appeared to be Bibles lying on the floor. As I made my way over to them, I continued to stagger until it suddenly hit me as my eyes fully adjusted: I was stepping on bodies. The horror and shock of the situation seemed to awaken every sense in me, and I was instantly overcome with the smell of rotting flesh.

I ran out of the building and began to weep. My tears were not only from the trauma, nor were they just for those victims. I realized this had happened in countless churches throughout the country—and with the outside world ignoring the cries of horror. What had always been recognized as places of refuge in the country overnight became sites of mass murder in the grisliest fashion. The flame of the Rwandan church had been snuffed out within a matter of days. Yet the Western world would not even stop to pay attention, much less offer help. Even the United Nations washed its hands of the matter and left the country after ten of its peacekeepers were killed.

For those hundred days, the forces of darkness ruled Rwanda. Yet even in the years following, those forces continued to reign elsewhere by successfully keeping millions of Americans—including countless Christians—in the dark. To this day, there are believers throughout the country who have no idea such unspeakable events ever happened. Obviously, Satan prefers it to stay that way knowing the longer he is able to keep us ignorant to the progressing forces of evil, the longer we remain inactive, apathetic, and ineffective.

SELF-CENTEREDNESS

Another of Satan's tactics to keep the church—and specifically the American church—from invading the Seven Mountains of culture is one with which this country has become all too familiar. The United States of America was built upon the bedrock of personal freedom. Today, that foundation has become a culture of hyper-individualism. In today's world of iPads, iPhones, iPods, MySpace, and YouTube, it's all about personal preference, personal space, and personal gain.

Obviously, people still have an inherent need for community; yet even in this, our culture has adopted a sense of community on individualistic terms. We occasionally gather around similar passions, marital statuses, social classes, and worship preferences—and then when we are tired of being around others, we close our garage doors and shut out the world. When I was growing up, most houses had a front porch, or at least an area for congregating with neighbors outside your front door. But have you ever noticed where the "porch" is placed on most houses these days? It is now the backyard deck, surrounded with a backyard privacy fence high enough to keep out any neighbors.

Sadly, the church has been guilty of the same isolationism on a broader scale. We have been content to separate ourselves from the "secular" world on the mountain of religion while developing a bad case of the "us four and no more" syndrome. As our cultural core of individualism has slowly morphed into isolationism, it has yielded a sense of territorialism among believers for establishing God's kingdom in our cities and communities. Churches continue to compete with each other for what I heard one pastor call "The Three Bs": buildings, budgets, and... well, backsides (he used another word).

I am a natural optimist, so I will be the first to say that today we are seeing an upsurge of churches come together in various regions. As I travel the country, I am delighted to find the walls of foolish spiritual territorialism coming down more as we rediscover Jesus' calling for us to be "one, just as We are one" (John 17:22). Yet we must still recognize both our past mistakes and Satan's success in keeping us segmented to the degree that we have failed to invade any of the major mountains.

APATHY

With extreme individualism and self-centeredness comes the natural by-product of apathy. There is perhaps no greater weapon for inaction than the heart that just doesn't care. Throughout my life, I have had several friends who entered into seasons of severe depression. (When you are around intercessors and intercessor types as much as I am, trust me, it is a common thing.) In almost every case, what began as a few days or weeks of "feeling blue" turned into unshakable heartache and a constant presence of sadness, which eventually became a supreme hopelessness saturating every aspect of life. When you reach that point, nothing seems to matter—and the stronghold of apathy keeps you bound to inaction (are you noticing a theme here?) and indifference.

Once the enemy has you in a place where you have convinced yourself that you don't care about anything or anyone, you lose all sense of ownership. And from Satan's standpoint, what is better than keeping Christians in a place where it does not matter if abortion laws are enacted, or schools incorporate Muslim history into curriculum, or the entertainment world continues to sink further into vulgarity? When we as the church are content to watch other mountains of our culture be dominated by evil while we hunker down on our own religious mountain, when we actually don't care about taking back our own communities or cities, then we have missed the kingdom perspective of the gospel. And sadly, we have also succumbed to the spirit of apathy.

RESIGNATION

Walking hand-in-hand with that spirit of apathy is the notion that it is not our responsibility as believers to save the world. This mentality believes that the earth is ultimately on a downward spiral that none of us can stop, so there is no point in trying to do so. I have heard countless people—Spirit-filled *Christians*, mind you—admit that with today's world "going to hell in a handbasket," there is nothing they can personally do to change things. All the inspirational stories and "you can make a difference" pep talks are great, they say, but essentially one person *can't* change the world, much less a city or community.

There are also those who subscribe to a *retirement* mentality when it comes to invading the cultural mountains and reclaiming them from the enemy. Years ago, my family lived near Sun City, Arizona, which is a major hotspot for retirees just outside of Phoenix. At that time, the suburban population was bursting at the seams, and the schooling system showed it. Schools were running two separate tracks: one for students who would come between 6 a.m. until 1 p.m., and another for those who went from 1 p.m. until 8 p.m. Sun City residents had the opportunity to approve a bill that would begin construction on an additional campus and stop these schools from having to create a third track. Unfortunately, the overwhelming majority of the senior adult residents voted against the legislation, arguing that since we have already done our part to raise our children, this is now the responsibility of others.

We, as the church, have done the same thing in fighting for the mountains of our society. We say, *I already prayed my kids through; it's someone else's turn to pray.* Or, *I paid my dues in the business world, so let all those young go-getters deal with all that craziness.*

I want to scream when I hear these kinds of outlooks—all of which, by the way, are fruits of a spirit of resignation. If there is anyone who *can* change situations, laws, systems, minds, hearts, environments, cultures, cities, regions, nations, and anything else we can think of, it is the follower of Christ—not because of that individual, but because of God. Our God is omnipotent—all-powerful. He can turn any form of darkness into light with one word. His very nature is one of redeeming and resurrecting that which was lost, broken, decrepit, and dead. And as His representatives on earth, if there is anyone who *must* change the world with the power He has given, it's us!

PRESUMPTUOUSNESS

Unfortunately, the church has fallen prey to another of Satan's tricks in keeping us from invading culture with this power. Rather than remaining humble, wise, and ever reliant upon the Holy Spirit as our source of power, in our exuberance we have declared victory too soon over the mountain of religion—and in some circles of believers, even over other areas of society.

In World War II, the Germans did the same thing as they marched toward Russia during their 1941 conquest of the eastern European front. By late November, the Nazi offensive had steamrolled to within twenty miles of the Kremlin in Moscow and captured hundreds of thousands of Soviet soldiers along the way. German chancellor Adolf Hitler was well aware of his military's susceptibility to the harsh Russian winters (he had stressed the importance of capturing Moscow before winter), yet he was also confident enough of victory that his troops had gone prepared only for fall combat.

Bad mistake. By the first week of December, temperatures dropped below negative forty degrees Fahrenheit, and the snowy conditions left the unprepared Germans miserable. Not only were soldiers freezing from a lack of winter clothes, their machinery froze as well, putting a sudden halt to their attack. To make matters worse, the Russian opposition had burned all of their own crops as they retreated, forcing the Germans to extend their supply lines. By spring the following year, the Soviets were able to drive away the weakened Nazi forces.

I venture to say that American believers have similarly rested on their laurels for generations, presuming that we already won the cultural war. Today you would have to be a hermit to think this remains true, and yet like the Russian soldiers caught in the cold, we have been unprepared for the attack against us. The result is just as Satan would have it: a church whose weapons have been rendered useless by the cultural climate and who would rather return to the warm, cozy confines of "home"—namely, the "non-secular" mountain of religion.

RELIGIOUS SPIRIT

It is ironic, then, that the most deadly tactic the enemy has in his arsenal is the one that exists so rampantly on this "home front" of the Religion Mountain. The religious spirit, that ancient spirit rooted in pride, is our greatest enemy to invading the mountains of society and producing true kingdom change in this world. It is the number-one opponent to lasting revival. This is true personally and corporately, for businesses and families, for states and nations—on any of the mountains. The religious spirit always resists change, and since intercessors are often on the frontlines of declaring a shift throughout the land, they are often the prime targets for the religious spirit to operate against or even through them.

In 2 Timothy, Paul spells out what the religious spirit looks like in the flesh:

> People will be lovers of themselves, lovers of money, boastful, proud, abusive, disobedient to their parents, ungrateful, unholy, without love, unforgiving, slanderous, without self-control, brutal, not lovers of the good, treacherous, rash, conceited,

> lovers of pleasure rather than lovers of God—having a form of
> godliness but denying its power. Have nothing to do with them.
> —2 TIMOTHY 3:2–5, NIV

The religious spirit has a form of truth yet lacks the fullness of truth. It operates under the guise of Holy Spirit power, yet has no intimacy with the Father to produce such power. It is a spiritual vacuum that can distract believers from their true destiny and calling for months, years, and even lifetimes. As I heard Chuck Pierce say at a recent conference, "Religious spirits are sent to seduce you and cause you to wander in the wilderness." And tragically, that is exactly where countless believers have remained while under the influence of this spiritually poisonous power.

This book is not about the religious spirit, exactly what it is, how it operates, who it operates through, why it is so effective, or how to get rid of it. (To learn about these and a host of other topics related to the religious spirit, I suggest that you read my book *Conquering the Religious Spirit*.) Yet without a doubt, the most frequent question I am asked as I travel the globe and unveil the truth about the religious spirit is this: *How do I recognize the religious spirit in me?* None of us wants this spirit to influence or have power over us. We, in turn, want to be mighty influencers for God as we intercede for His kingdom to advance in our culture.

Before moving on, then, let me offer this helpful list of ten signs that indicate the religious spirit is at work.

1. *Silenced voice.* As if your mouth has been taped shut, you stop speaking and declaring words of life over yourself. Your passions, hopes, and dreams begin to die, and you no longer remind yourself of the prophetic words spoken over you.

2. *God's silence, displeasure, and judgment.* The religious spirit convinces you at times that God has forgotten you or is done speaking to you—that you have committed some sin so egregious that He no longer desires to communicate with you. Likewise, this spirit can lead you to believe God cannot use you or has given up on you entirely.

3. *Doubting God's calling.* Though ungodly, doubt is a natural human emotion most of us wrestle with from time to time. Yet when you begin to doubt the calling of God on your life and question His "life declarations" over you, it is likely the religious spirit is trying to steal your

vision. (Remember, even Jesus encountered this when Satan tried to tempt Him in the wilderness prior to the start of His ministry.)

4. *Perfectionist mentality.* Yes, we are called to be excellent at what we do for the Lord. But when everything you set your hands to *must* be perfect—and you will do anything to make it so—a religious spirit is at work.

5. *Approval-seeking service.* When you find yourself serving God for His approval, know that something is awry. *Maybe God will like me more if…*or *Maybe I will have a greater anointing if I….* These are the kind of thoughts that stem from a works-based, approval-seeking mentality— one that is disconnected with the pure heart motives that God desires.

6. *Control and manipulation.* Easy to recognize, control is nonetheless one of the most difficult things for religious people to forfeit. They will maneuver around situations or people—often deceptively—to maintain or increase their level of influence. They will also use shame, guilt, favors, and authority to manipulate others.

7. *Unteachable attitude.* Under the influence of the religious spirit, you often carry a know-it-all attitude. Your mind and heart become unteachable, which furthers a sense of arrogance and pride (which, by the way, can be manifest even through a pretense of false humility).

8. *No accountability, counsel, or oversight.* When you are right all the time, why would you need counsel or oversight? When the religious spirit is at work, it seems no one *really* has anything to offer you in terms of advice or wisdom, nor does it benefit you to be vulnerable or let others keep you in check.

9. *Fear of man.* The first part of Proverbs 29:25 says, "The fear of man brings a snare." Some of us fear others more than we fear God. We are afraid of what people will say or think about us. This is a trap the religious spirit will keep us in for as long as we allow fear to control us rather than perfect love. (See 1 John 4:18.)

10. *Twisted truth.* The religious spirit does not tell the truth, and even when it appears to be acting through someone in a truthful manner, you can be sure the bottom-line truth is being distorted. Let me reiterate: the religious spirit presents only a *form* of the truth without the fullness of truth or power. There is no such thing as a half-truth; something is either completely true or it is a lie. When the religious spirit is at work in you, however, even this fundamental principle is twisted.

WHY FOCUS ON THE ENEMY?

Christians will often approach me and ask why I spend time talking about the devil and his strategies. They believe that since Christ has already defeated the enemy, I am wasting my time and energy by giving the demonic realm any attention whatsoever. In fact, some will even add that I am actually empowering it by giving it more credence than it deserves.

Let me set the record straight if there is any doubt: Jesus has won. He is the lone victor in the final battle and does not split the spoils with the enemy. The script has already been written: He wins; Satan loses. But until the church wakes up and realizes that we are the enforcers of that victory in the here and now, bringing the kingdom of God to earth, then we will remain oblivious to the battle that continues to wage over souls, cities, and entire nations—a battle in which the enemy has been highly successful at getting God's soldiers to sit on the sidelines as injured reserves. As Dutch evangelist Corrie ten Boom once said, "It's a poor soldier indeed who does not recognize the enemy."[5]

I do not keep my focus on the darkness, and I certainly do not plan on empowering Satan's armies even the slightest bit. My primary focus has been and always will be the kingdom of God advancing on this earth. Yet for that kingdom to move forward, we can no longer afford to be duped into thinking there isn't a war to be fought. If Holy Spirit-filled Christians still can't see that we are currently in a war over this country's religions, families, education, government, media, arts and entertainment, and businesses, then I seriously wonder if they should not be asking God for a hefty dose of discernment. We are at war!

I have spent most of my life in and among military families. In all those years, I have yet to meet one who didn't understand the necessity of preparing for war. My husband, Ralph, a retired Air Force colonel, attended National War College and Air Command and Staff College, both of which are advanced education in the art of war. One of the main textbooks he studied was *The Art of War*, written by Sun Tzu, a Chinese general, military commander, and strategist in the sixth century B.C. The classic book, which covers such topics as waging war, planning offenses, tactical positioning, and maneuvering armies, is now actually used as a guidebook in businesses worldwide. Yet ask any military family about preparing for war, and my guess is you will find an understanding of the same concepts. When you eat, sleep, and live around the concept of war 24/7, it becomes a part of who you are.

I believe Christians must have the same approach and understanding when it comes to being in this world but not of it. (See John 17:14–16.) It is time we wake up and perceive that the heavenly war being fought over this world is already raging.

In this chapter, we spotlighted several of Satan's tactics in keeping us from invading and conquering the Seven Mountains of society. The sheer number of people that confront me on why I focus on these strategies shows me that at least one of them (ignorance, among others) is still effective. As intercessors, we must no longer allow these same devices to blind us to the reality of our situation or to minimize the power God has given us through prayer and intercession. The truth is, we *do* have the most potent weapon in the world that can change everything. But until we wise up on the various ways Satan distracts, removes, and destroys those who wield this weapon—particularly those standing in key areas of the cultural gaps—we will continue to be an army with unlimited potential yet minimal effectiveness, simply because we fail to recognize our own God-appointed power.

CHAPTER 5 NOTES

1. Wikipedia.org, "Operation Market Garden," http://en.wikipedia.org/wiki/Operation_Market_Garden (accessed July 31, 2011).

2. *A Bridge Too Far*, directed by Richard Attenborough (United Artists, 1977).

3. *Gladiator*, directed by Ridley Scott (DreamWorks Pictures, 2000).

4. *BBC News*, "Rwanda: How the Genocide Happened," May 17, 2011, http://news.bbc.co.uk/2/hi/africa/1288230.stm (accessed September 29, 2009).

5. Elizabeth Alves, *Becoming a Prayer Warrior* (Ventura, CA: Renew, 1998), 97.

Chapter 6

INVADE, FIGHT, CONQUER

THE WRITER OF Hebrews says, "No discipline seems pleasant at the time, but painful" (Heb. 12:11, NIV). And for millions of Americans, 2008 and 2009 hurt—bad. Plummeting stocks, a bottomed-out real estate market, and a credit crunch serious enough to bankrupt dozens of banks certainly left a mark on virtually every family. Some opted to learn—for the first time in their lives, mind you—the discipline of delayed satisfaction. Others were forced to take a crash course in financial discipline because of an unexpected job loss, salary reduction, or depleted retirement account. Either way, it wasn't as if people could not see the danger signs ahead.

In January 2008, the financial industry's prophets had already emerged to declare an imminent stock market crash. These doomsday voices did not know when it would come; they just knew it would come. By April 2008—a full five to six months prior to the bottom falling out— the Center for American Progress even offered the following economic snapshot:

> America's families are caught in a perfect storm. Massive amounts of debt, falling house prices, disappearing jobs, flat wages, lower benefits, and skyrocketing costs for the most important consumer items are quickly emptying the pockets of middle class America and bringing many families to the edge of financial ruin. The fact that policymakers have for years ignored large economic imbalances only exacerbates threats to the economic well-being of American working families.[1]

Though economists continued to analyze all the elements that led to this perfect storm, for the common American, it came down to one critical mistake: We put the cart before the horse. By 2008, the average household carried a record-high credit card debt of $8,565, up almost 15 percent from 2000.[2] Worse still, overall household debt—including mortgages and credit cards—represented 19 percent of most families' total assets, compared to 13 percent in 1980.[3]

Even if you cringe at the thought of budgets and bank statements, it does not take a financial expert to understand the problem. We became—and still are—a culture dependent upon money that does not exist, money we simply do not have. Credit is now a way of life in America. We buy today what we can't pay for tomorrow so that we will be able to borrow even more later. Best-selling author and financial expert Dave Ramsey thinks it is ludicrous: "What we've got is people... who are leveraged to their eyeballs, can't breathe and the scare, just the fear that they might lose their job has completely paralyzed them as consumers."[4] As he reminds his talk-show listeners daily, what Proverbs 22:7 says is absolute truth: "The borrower becomes the lender's slave."

How, then, did we get so out of control with our borrowing and spending—to the point that it caused a near-catastrophic global economic meltdown? We got ahead of ourselves. In fact, we convinced ourselves that we no longer needed to follow the natural order of things: save first, buy later. Our out-of-order lifestyles didn't just show a lack of discipline with money, they also displayed a deep-seated misunderstanding of what it takes to gain financial victory. Like a football player showboating before he crosses into the end zone, we celebrated prematurely.

In the last chapter, we discussed the church's presumptuousness in viewing the mountain of religion as a battle already won. We also highlighted how Satan has used that strategy to dupe believers into being satisfied with the status quo. Yet what these modern-day characteristics of the American church also expose is a fundamental misunderstanding of how we should claim the cultural mountains for God's kingdom.

Before an army can take over a location, it must first invade that place. You can't legitimately claim a territory unless you have conquered it, and you can't conquer a territory unless you have invaded it in some form or fashion and then actually fought for it. We must first *invade* the cultural mountains, then fight for them. Then, and only then, can we begin to even think about conquering or claiming any sectors of culture. There is a universal order to the process: invade, then fight, then conquer—and ultimately occupy.

We have already discussed how the church does not rule the Seven Mountains of society, and even how we have relinquished control over the one mountain (religion) we presumed for generations to control by default. The sad truth today is that we have not even invaded most of the mountains yet. Sure, there are believers stationed on each mountain—this is according to God's masterful plan. Yet many of them remain unaware of the real reason they have been placed on those mountains and instead go about their business content to inadvertently serve the purposes of the ruling "lord" over that mountain, Satan.

As someone who has dedicated my life to mustering the troops for spiritual warfare, I am putting my foot down and saying, "No more!" I am not content to watch saints waste their talents, gifts, or even their lives without ever knowing they could have changed the course of the world by stepping up and challenging those who currently rule the mountains. God has given His church the tools, placed His foot soldiers in strategic locations throughout society, and stationed prayer warriors like you and me to stand in the gap. It is time we learn what it truly means to invade these mountains.

What's in a Word?

I was not an English major in college and have never been much of a wordsmith. Still, one word I always thought I understood well was *invade*. After all, my father flew anti-submarine warfare aircraft while serving thirty years in the US Navy. My husband served twenty-eight years in the Air Force, including flying fighter aircraft in the Vietnam War. I had heard the term used often since I was a little child. Yet it wasn't until a few years ago, when I decided to do some research, that I discovered the full scope of this powerful six-letter word. What I found amazed me.

Invade has at least seven different meanings:

1. *Invade: to enter forcefully as an enemy.* When we go into the mountains currently ruled by powers of darkness, often we are to enter with force as the direct opposition to those demonic powers. We are not supposed to walk in timidly or secretly or half-heartedly or doubtfully or hesitantly or fearfully or in any other non-invasive fashion. As Christians, we have no business negotiating with the enemy or being kind and gentle to those evil spirits. Once we are rid of the religious spirit in our own lives (which we identified in the last chapter), we can be truly forceful. To be forceful is to be vigorous and powerful—which, in turn, means having great power, authority, or influence. When you are powerful, you are mighty. And to the mightiest in the spirit goes the

victory. As John Hagee says, "You will never conquer, or change, what you refuse to confront."[5]

2. *Invade: to go into with hostile intent.* Christians are unfamiliar with being overtly hostile. We prefer to be known as the peacemakers (though, in fact, peace rarely comes without a battle). Even in our thought lives, we train ourselves to suppress anger and hatred and instead fill our minds with the orders of Philippians 4:8: "Whatever is true, whatever is noble, whatever is right, whatever is pure, whatever is lovely, whatever is admirable—if anything is excellent or praiseworthy—think about such things" (NIV).

Fair enough. But how many of us realize that we are to love what God loves and hate what God hates? God hates Satan. (I am well aware that is the no-brainer statement of all time.) So when it comes to invading those places inhabited by the enemy of our soul, we have full license to let loose on his forces with indignation. Peace rarely comes without a battle. This doesn't necessarily mean we go berserk by cursing the darkness and screaming at demons. But too many prayer "warriors" approach intercession as if they needed permission from the enemy to rebuke him. To be hostile means a person is unfriendly and inhospitable. There is no reason we should be hospitable to Satan. He "comes only to steal and kill and destroy" (John 10:10). We would not naturally welcome an axe-wielding serial killer into our house for a cup of coffee, so why do we treat the devil any differently?

We must take our cue from Jesus, who commanded the demons (who, let's not forget, were already trembling at the mention of His name) without all the bells and whistles. Jesus' mere presence indicated a hostile intent to the enemy. He was not there to be friendly or hospitable to any demons, nor did He merely *represent* opposition. No, Jesus was the very opposition that signaled sure defeat for Satan's armies.

As intercessors and warriors, we enter the mountains of society with the same fear-inducing presence because we represent this imminent defeat to the current rulers of the territory. As we come in the victorious name of Jesus, our arrival announces a changing of the guard. Which leads us to the next definition.

3. *Invade: to enter as if to take possession.* Let's get one thing straight: we are not visiting these mountains. We aren't going there to sightsee or scope out the territory for future journeys. We are there to take hold of each mountain. The key word in this meaning is *possession.* To possess is "to have as property; to occupy or control from within; to dominate

or cause to be dominated or influenced by an idea or feeling; to keep or maintain in a certain state of peace; to seize, take or gain; to make (someone) owner, holder or master of property."[6]

Notice that the idea of domination is a key part of possessing something. When we enter the Media Mountain, for example, we should never approach it saying, "Hey, Satan, don't mind me. I'll be out of your way just as soon as I'm through being a journalist and don't have to worry anymore about conveying truth to the masses. So as long as I'm here, feel free to have your way." No! Interceding for the Media Mountain means we enter the scene and declare to the darkness, "The kingdom of God will dominate you! In the name of Jesus, the one whom you fear, I am now here to take dominion."

4. *Invade: to enter and cause injury or destruction.* Once again, polite intercessors don't cut it when it comes to invading the mountains. Have you ever met a wimpy warrior? The mere word *warrior* invokes a sense of ferocity and strength. As true prayer warriors, we are there to do damage and cause serious harm—not to people but to demonic forces: "For our struggle is not against flesh and blood, but against the rulers, against the powers, against the world forces of this darkness, against the spiritual forces of wickedness in the heavenly places" (Eph. 6:12).

We invade the mountains to destroy these powers or, as the word is defined, "to put an end to; extinguish; render ineffective or useless; reduce to a useless form; or defeat completely."[7] I cannot think of a better job description for intercessors than that. Indeed, our task is to destroy the works of the enemy. What is interesting, however, is that two of the synonyms for destruction are *demolition* and *annihilation*. Both bring to mind images of a demolition site in which a building is reduced to a pile of rubble.

Several years ago, the primary way workers would tear down a building was by using a wrecking ball. A giant steel globe hung from a crane would smash through brick, concrete, doors, windows, pipes, and anything else in its way. Though the end result was a demolished building, the process was laborious, messy, and dangerous. Not only did those working around a wrecking ball risk injury, there were more than a few demolitions gone wrong in which a wrecking ball operator misjudged a swing and damaged a nearby building or structure.

Today, the wrecking ball has been largely replaced by long-reach excavators and, in the case of larger buildings, explosives. Controlled demolition, often known as an implosion, involves strategically placing several small explosives at the weakest spots within a structure. The goal is not for the building to explode but for it to implode and collapse under its own weight. Building implosions can do in seconds what used to take a wrecking ball days, weeks, or even months. In addition, the implosion process is safer for the surrounding environment and, despite the rubble, significantly cleaner than other methods.

As intercessors, we must learn to invade and attack the enemy's weak point with the same kind of precision—to the point that the enemy collapses upon itself. Just as an implosion reduces a building into fragments so tiny that restoration is impossible, we must reduce the powers of darkness to nothing. Our goal upon each mountain is to render the enemy permanently ineffective while causing the least damage possible to those around.

5. *Invade: to intrude upon.* This definition is self-explanatory. Though he currently rules the Seven Mountains, we do not need an invitation from Satan to enter the territory. Neither do we need his permission to wage war and eventually claim each mountain for the kingdom of God. We do not have to call first. There is no need to send an announcement or knock at the door when we arrive. We have full permission—from God—to just go on in. When the Creator of the universe says you can intrude all you want, it means you can intrude all you want.

6. *Invade: to encroach or infringe.* This is one of my favorite definitions of *invade* because of how accurately it captures our assignment as intercessors. To encroach means "to advance beyond established limits of property, domain, or rights of another in order to possess." Another definition of encroach says it is "to enter gradually and often stealthily on the territory, rights, or privileges of another, so that a foundation is barely noticed."[8]

You might recall that our first definition for *invade* was "to enter forcefully." So which are we supposed to do: enter forcefully or enter gradually and stealthily? The answer is both. At times, the Holy Spirit will guide us into blatant warfare with the enemy in which we loudly and boldly announce our arrival, then take over by dominant force. On other occasions, however, stealth is the key—not because our Commander cannot overwhelm the enemy, but because often the greatest damage is made using the element of surprise. Pearl Harbor. The Yom Kippur War. 9/11. These were all attacks that resulted in maximum damage because the targets were unprepared and caught off-guard. In the case of 9/11, the terrorists spent months training for their attack right under the American government's watch. They learned how to fly, observed airport patterns, and plotted their takeover of commercial aircrafts—all on American soil.

In the same way, we will ascend mountains that are currently under the watch of demonic forces. The higher up believers go on these mountains, the more noticeable they become. Think of it this way: as you rise in elevation on a mountain, the amount of land to scale decreases, and therefore there is less room for people. Naturally, the fewer people there are, the more obvious it becomes when some of them are enemies to the forces of darkness. The higher we climb, the easier targets we become for the enemy.

This is why conquering a mountain takes time and patience. It is a progressive work that, like a military operation, requires strategy. We must penetrate enemy lines and slowly enter the inner parts. At times, those who are "foot soldiers" on the mountains will be responsible for planting destructive devices in the spirit with the goal of causing the enemy to self-implode. As these soldiers move up the mountain, intercessors are responsible for covering their tracks, alerting them when the enemy catches wind of their presence, and fighting off the enemy in the spiritual realm. Though we will address this later in the book, for now it is important to realize that we cannot simply push back the darkness; it must be replaced with the light. As we push back the darkness, we must also push those foot soldiers—the carriers of God's light—higher up the mountain to stand in the places where darkness once ruled. This is how we encroach upon the enemy's territory.

7. *Invade: to make an invasion.* The final definition may seem to be the most obvious: an invasion is simply the "entrance of an army to take possession or overrun."[9] And yet as we invade the Seven Mountains of culture, we cannot forget that last word: *overrun.* Obviously, the goal is to overrun and overtake the enemy. But as powerful a weapon as intercession is, it is still possible for intercessors to be ones who end up trampled and overrun. The reason for this is rarely a matter of power, but instead is all about preparation. We must truly understand the weapons we use in warring with the enemy, and we must be skilled in using them.

ESTABLISHING DOMINION THROUGH APOSTOLIC-PROPHETIC INTERCESSION

Whenever one nation invades another, the goal is always the same: to establish dominion. Though the victor may not always overtake the other to the point of absorbing the land into its own boundaries, its objective is nonetheless to rule the territory. For example, from the late sixteenth century to the early twentieth century, the United Kingdom was the most powerful and far-reaching force in the world. At its peak, the British Empire exercised control over more than a quarter of the world's population and covered almost 13 million square miles.[10] The British enforced their rule in every corner of the world, yet their numerous conquered lands were not considered part of the central United Kingdom. Some of these acquired territories were self-governed, while others were under the command of a viceroy, yet all remained under the dominion of the British Empire.

Dominion is the undisputed spoils of those who invade, fight, and eventually conquer. For those of us who hope to invade the Seven Mountains of culture with intercession, we must not forget our single intent is to gain dominion. It is not merely to invade, though we must; nor is it to fight the enemy, though we certainly will. Both invading and fighting are essential. But as we begin to discuss more about how to invade and fight, we cannot forget the importance of "keeping the main thing the main thing." As I have said throughout this book, the main purpose behind everything we do as followers of Christ is to further His kingdom. As prayer warriors, that means we have been sent in the spirit to declare the dominion of His kingdom in every territory. Our task is to pave the way in the spirit for what should follow in the natural.

This is no small task, and it is why God is raising up an army of apostolic-prophetic intercessors in these times. In fact, apostolic-prophetic intercessors may be the missing link to taking the Seven Mountains.

By nature of their titles, an apostle is one who is "sent out on a special mission," while a prophet is one who "speaks for God under divine influence."[11] Within the context of prayer, this means intercessors are those prayer warriors who are sent out to declare the words of God. Like a messenger during the British Empire era sent by order of the king to declare British dominion over a territory, we bring a declaration of ownership from the King of Kings every time we invade enemy territory. Our apostolic intercession consists of proclamations, declarations, and decrees released with the objective to unlock God's kingdom purposes on earth. At the same time, our prophetic intercession includes calling forth what is presently dormant, lifeless, and bound into a state of freedom and life.

We cannot resort to an old mind-set of prayer if we hope to do this, however. I know far too many intercessors who, after all is said and done, approach prayer as if it involves nothing more than continually asking God for things. Many of these prayer warriors are not new believers, mind you, but mature Christians who have walked with the Lord for decades and devoted years of their lives to talking and hearing from God—yet they are still stuck in a single mode of begging God for Him to move. I call these "petition prayers," and although they have their place in the arsenal of every powerful prayer warrior, God is shifting us from petition prayers to apostolic-prophetic intercession.*

Let me use an example to highlight the stark difference between the two. I speak at conferences around the world, and almost everywhere I go, I encounter teams of intercessors who spend hours praying for the event before it begins. Often, though, I will discover that the main gist of their prayers has been petitioning the Lord for His presence: "God, we ask that Your presence be with us during the conference. As your servants, we cry out for You to come in power and might, to move through Your people and change lives. O God, we're calling out for You to show Yourself faithful."

A petition is simply asking someone for something. Yet when we spend all our time asking God for that which He has *already* granted us, we've missed the mark on the role and purpose of intercession. There

---

* This does not mean we abandon all petitioning—which is why I use the word shift. We must be flexible with the Holy Spirit's prompting as He leads us in intercession. The key is having the ability to change gears when He requires us. When you drive a manual transmission vehicle, for example, you do not stay in one gear the entire time—otherwise you ruin the transmission and engine. As the vehicle goes faster, you have to continue shifting up to the next gear; and as it slows down, you will eventually have to downshift. It is the same way with intercession. We must have the ability to shift from one type of intercession to another, according to what is necessary for that time and situation. Unfortunately, many intercessors cling to a single way of praying, and as a result, their "prayer engine," if you will, remains confined. (It's no wonder they also experience more frequently seasons of being worn out in prayer and feeling like the heavens are made of brass. They are stuck in first gear while the spiritual world races by them!)

is nothing inherently wrong about praying for more of God's presence. But the truth is, He has already said throughout His Word, "I will never desert you, nor will I ever forsake you" (Heb. 13:5; see also Deut. 31:6, 8; Josh. 1:5). Through Jesus, He has already declared, "My presence shall go with you, and I will give you rest" (Exod. 33:14). In fact, Jesus clearly stated, "Where two or three have gathered in My name, I am there in their midst" (Matt. 18:20).

Instead of asking for God's presence, we should be announcing it! In a case like this, we must shift from asking to making a declaration with prayers such as: "I declare that God Almighty, the great I AM, is here is this place. Lord, I welcome You in this place and declare in agreement with Your promises: You will never leave us nor forsake us. Where two or three have gathered in Your name, You are there. Faithful God, we eagerly await Your moving through us in power as we celebrate Your presence."

That is a big difference, isn't it? Apostolic-prophetic intercession begins with two premises. First, we have been given the authority by God to speak *His* words, not ours. Author and speaker Graham Cooke once stated that most believers tend to fall back into petition prayers—it's their default mode. Yet at its core, a petition is a formal request that originates in us rather than God.[12] It is time we reset our default method of prayer from petition that originates in us to proclamations and declarations that originate from the Lord and align us with Him.

The second major premise—one that prayer warriors often forget—is that we are already commissioned and sent by God. Paul uses the perfect illustration of this when he refers to us as ambassadors in his second letter to the Corinthians: "We are ambassadors for Christ, as though God were making an appeal through us" (2 Cor. 5:20). When an ambassador is sent to a foreign nation, he appears on behalf of his native country's ruler and is the representation of that ruler's kingdom. More accurately, an ambassador is the extension of the ruler and is given the authority to speak on his behalf. The ambassador comes with inherent power not because of anything he has done personally, but purely because he serves as the incarnate expression (i.e., the mouthpiece, the hands and feet) of the one who sent him.

This is our role as apostolic-prophetic intercessors. Jesus came as God incarnate, yet through Christ we have been adopted as sons of God and joint heirs to His kingdom (Gal. 3:26–29.) Since this is a foundational truth of our faith, we must stop praying as paupers and start interceding as ambassadors of the one true God. We have been given the authority: Jesus has commissioned us (Matt. 28:16–20) and empowered us with His Holy Spirit (Acts 2). We already know what to say because He has given us His message via the Word.

The only thing we lack, then, is the knowledge of how to wage war in the heavenly realm with our intercession. We know how to invade the Seven Mountains; now it is time to learn how to fight for them!

CHAPTER 6 NOTES

1. Christian E. Weller, "Economic Snapshot for April 2008," Center for American Progress, April 10, 2008, http://www.americanprogress.org/issues/2008/04/econ_snapshot.html (accessed July 31, 2011).

2. Ben Woolsey and Matt Schulz, "Credit Card Statistics, Industry Facts, Debt Statistics," CreditCard.com, http://www.creditcards.com/credit-card-news/credit-card-industry-facts-personal-debt-statistics-1276.php.

3. Gretchen Morgenson, "Given a Shovel, Americans Dig Deeper Into Debt," *New York Times,* July 20, 2008, http://www.nytimes.com/2008/07/20/business/20debt.html?_r=2&pagewanted=all&oref=slogin (accessed July 31, 2011).

4. Tess Vigeland, "Dave Ramsey on Our Love of Debt," *Marketplace,* a program of American Public Media, June 5, 2009, http://marketplace.publicradio.org/display/web/2009/06/05/mm_ramsey/ (accessed July 31, 2011).

5. John Hagee, *What Every Man Wants in a Woman* (Charisma House, Lake Mary, FL, 2005), 3.

6. *Webster's Talking Dictionary/Thesaurus,* CD-ROM, version 1.0b (Exceller Software Corporation), s.v. "possession."

7. Ibid., s.v. "destroy."

8. Ibid., s.v. "encroach."

9. Ibid., s.v. "invade."

10. Wikipedia.org, "British Empire," http://en.wikipedia.org/wiki/British_Empire

11. *Webster's New World College Dictionary,* 4th ed., s.v. "apostle," "prophet."

12. Aglow International, Aglow Worldwide Conference 2009, October 24, 2009.

Chapter 7

WEAPONS OF INVASION

A blow with a word strikes deeper than a blow with a sword.
—British scholar/clergyman Robert Burton

Handle them carefully, for words have more power than atom bombs.
—poet/author Pearl Strachan Hurd

If the word has the potency to revive and make us free, it has also the power to blind, imprison, and destroy.
—Novelist Ralph Ellison

A powerful agent is the right word. Whenever we come upon one of those intensely right words...the resulting effect is physical as well as spiritual, and electrically prompt.
—humorist/writer Mark Twain

Words are loaded pistols.
—French writer/philosopher Jean-Paul Sartre

THERE IS NO shortage in history of great men and women who have recognized the power of words. As far back as the sixth century B.C., King Solomon stated, "Death and life are in the power of the tongue" (Prov. 18:21). Years later, Jesus would tell us, "For by your words you will be justified, and by your words you will be condemned" (Matt. 12:37). James, the brother of Jesus, compared our words to both a fresh fountain and a wild forest fire (James 3). Indeed, words can be constructive or destructive, they can build up or tear down, and they can heal or injure.

Dutch Sheets, in his book *Authority in Prayer*, offers a brief yet comprehensive list of the various functions that words possess: "Wars are started with words. Love is communicated through words. Instruction and education are shared by words. Deception and confusion are propagated with words. Kingdoms are built with words. People are controlled by words. Lives are shattered by words. Worlds are created by words—the earth was and so is our personal world."[1]

Notice that this list begins with a phrase particularly appropriate for those who wish to invade the Seven Mountains of society with intercession: *Wars are started with words.* By now we know that ascending these mountains and engaging their ruling powers destines us for a showdown of great proportions. Although the war upon these prime territories can be expressed in the natural, the conflict begins in the spirit realm whenever intercessors take the initiative to face off with the enemy. At times the battles can be grueling engagements against long-standing strongholds, while other times they can be brief skirmishes in which prayer warriors show up, declare the name of Jesus, and watch the enemy flee. But in the majority of confrontations between light and darkness, the weapons of warfare are the same small yet infinitely powerful units of attack: words. So in this chapter, let's discover how to use them effectively as we intercede.

A Matter of Trust

Norma Johnson, founder of Beyond Restoration Ministries, recently wrote a series of articles that described the role and function of an intercessor. Most of what we do as intercessors, she said, involves words. Obviously, there are times when we are commanded to intercede through prophetic acts and specific types of fasts or by simply showing up at a strategic location and waiting for God. Yet the most potent weapon we typically use for warring against the enemy in the spirit is what comes out of our mouths. Proverbs 10:20–21 says, "The tongue of the righteous is as choice silver, the heart of the wicked is worth little. The lips of the righteous feed many, but fools die for lack of understanding." To fellow believers, our words can be wonderful weapons that inspire, uplift, motivate, and challenge. This is especially true if you lead an intercessory group. I have been in charge of countless prayer sessions in which my words sparked a unique battle cry from within each fellow prayer warrior, and the result was a powerful dismantling of the enemy's plans in the heavenly realm. It was as if I handed each intercessor a five-foot sword like the legendary Scottish patriot William Wallace used in battle and gave them the same rousing speech Mel Gibson offered when playing Wallace in *Braveheart*. By the power of my spoken, Spirit-inspired words connecting with the Holy Spirit inside each of them, these intercessors were brought to life and invigorated to overrun any demonic activity. In the spirit, I imagine the enemy saw them approaching as wild-eyed, blue-streaked warriors running down the hillside with swords swinging, ready for serious destruction.

But there is a flip side to the power of words, even in the context of intercession. Words can have the opposite effect: they can be deflating, disheartening, and demeaning. Without knowing what we are doing, we can pronounce defeat over a spiritual conquest before it ever begins— simply by uttering a few careless words. We all know what it feels like when someone tosses reckless words our way. It stings. It cuts to the heart. And it leaves a mark that heals over time but causes a lasting effect of trust betrayed. The next time we are around the person who spoke foolishly, we're less likely to be completely open or vulnerable. At the very least, we are a little more hesitant to share certain things.

God does not hold such grudges against us. Yet the same principle exists in our relationship with Him: the more God can trust us with His secrets, the more He will share His secrets with us. For some, this may be a new concept. When I speak at conferences about God trusting us with secrets, I'll undoubtedly see a few puzzled faces and some raised hands: "You mean God has secrets that He actually shares with us?" Yes, He does—and Scripture is clear about this. Three times in the second chapter of Daniel, God is described as the God in heaven who reveals secrets (Dan. 2:28–29, 47, NKJV), while one of Job's friends also tells his buddy how he wishes God "might speak, and open His lips against you, and show you the secrets of wisdom" (Job 11:5–6).

If God isn't sharing any secrets with you, could it be that you have not proven yourself trustworthy with keeping a secret? Proverbs 11:13 says, "A gossip betrays a confidence, but a trustworthy man keeps a secret" (NIV). When someone tells us a secret, it gives us a sense of power because we know something that other people do not. The mature believer keeps this information confidential yet acts upon it in a responsible manner by continually taking it to the Lord in prayer. Immature intercessors, on the other hand, tend to use secrets as a cover for gossip. They try to uphold their oh-so-holy intercessor demeanor by presenting an "unspoken request" to their prayer group, yet before the prayer session is over they've shared most of the details via their public petitions to God. By the time a few concerned intercessors have approached them after prayer to get the real scoop on the situation, their request has become full-fledged gossip.

In cases like these, is it any wonder God isn't sharing those matters that are dear to His heart? We must prove ourselves worthy of keeping

His secrets by not betraying His trust with the words we use. We are to be careful with what we say, not careless. It is essential that we restore integrity to intercession as we keep confidentiality.

DISTORTED WORDS

Gossip is just one of the tools Satan uses to negate our most effective weapon of warring in the heavens with words. Remember, as the "prince of the power of the air," Satan was given rule over the airwaves. Since most of our communication travels through the airwaves, his primary means of rendering our words ineffective is to distort them as they are being communicated. He loves to create enough static that eventually we will tune out and turn off altogether.

Today Satan has loosed a new level of attack on those who are attempting to scale the cultural mountains. He is not only targeting foot soldiers on the ground; he is also trying desperately to distort intercessors' communication in the air. Because of this, he often uses our words against us—in dealing both with others and with ourselves. When we speak careless words to others, the enemy of our souls quickly swoops in to create distrust and confusion among those who should be rallying together in prayer. Instead of being one cohesive mouthpiece for God, we become fragmented by our jealousy, anger, bitterness, resentfulness, and offense. Satan may be the mastermind behind this scheme, but it is our careless words that serve as the ammunition he needs to separate and scatter us.

The devil also often uses our own words against us. Like looking in the mirror the morning after a fistfight, he loves to remind us of whatever words we've spoken throughout our lives that gave us a black eye. How many times have you heard the phrase, "Those words will come back to haunt you" or, "That'll come back to bite you someday" or, "What you say is what you get"? This is just as true in a spiritual sense. Satan wants to haunt us with words from our past filled with shame, guilt, curses, and defeat. One of the only tactics he has when it comes to words is to remind us of those we've carelessly uttered that have sown bad seeds in our own life. By concentrating on his reminder rather than God's redemptive forgiveness of our mistakes, we come into an unholy agreement with the very statements we may have made over others: "I can't believe you did that, you dummy. What were you thinking? How could you say that? How could you do that?"

Satan is also a legalist and holds us to our words. He takes us literally, measuring every word by its full weight, whether we want him to or not. This is why we must be cautious with the words we choose—even those that most of us consider throwaways. Phrases such as *sort of* or *kind of* are the very tools the enemy uses to neuter our effectiveness as God's messengers of His power-filled Word. For example, you don't *sort of* know God's will or sense His presence—you either do or you don't. Likewise, I don't *kind of* believe the Holy Spirit will move on my behalf as I intercede—He either will or He won't. We cannot continue to short-change God's empowering upon our words by removing that power with wishy-washy, doubt-filled, weak utterances. We must realize that our poorly chosen words fall right into the destructive plans of our enemy.

Rightly chosen words, on the other hand, carry great worth and weight. As Proverbs 25:11 says, "A word aptly spoken is like apples of gold in settings of silver" (NIV). To speak such accurate, timely, and precise words, we must make a conscious effort to be clear about what we say and what we pray. When we do this, we leave less of a margin for error and more room for understanding and agreement with others. Satan hates this kind of unity, of course, and he despises our faith even more. He wants nothing better than to disrupt both of those elements by distorting and perverting the words we use.

This is why it is essential to say what God says when we pray, not what we feel like saying or whatever comes to mind. When we declare the Word of God, we make way to establish God's will in the earth. Of course there are times the Holy Spirit will prompt each of us in unusual, sporadic ways. You may suddenly feel the urge to speak out in a group prayer setting, even though you're unsure what you will say. Or you may have a sudden message from the Lord for someone on the street that isn't a typical "prophetic word" you'd give in a church setting. These are instances we must allow for when we come together with a group in prayer and lean on the Holy Spirit's guidance. I am not referring to these, but to those times when we casually offer up our prayers—when instead of taking a warrior-like stance to interceding, our spiritual position becomes slouched and our prayers lax. That is precisely what Satan wants and exactly the point at which he can enter in and distort our words.

There is power to destroy the works of the evil one, and there is power to keep us in bondage with our tongue. It is up to us which power we will wield, yet we often make our choice by the words we use. Words are power; they are life. As intercessors, they are also our main weapons of warfare. We must respect and understand their power and learn to use them wisely. And the best, foundational way to do that is to speak God's words rather than ours. Learn how to declare the Word of God into any situation, on any mountain.

A Lesson in Lingo

My husband, Ralph, and I are passionate people. Whatever we do, we give 110 percent. So before we came to Christ, we sinned with everything we had. We lived wild, crazy, fighter-pilot lives—about as far removed from the usual churchgoing lifestyle as possible. Because of that, I remember vividly how it felt when I first walked into church. It seemed as if I was in another country—not necessarily because of the way people looked or acted, but more because of what they said. *"I'm so blessed today by God's grace on my life. He's set me on fire again and called me into a new ministry to reach the lost."* It was as if some of them were speaking a different language!

Even my salvation experience proved this stark contrast. I had been invited to a Full Gospel Businessmen's Fellowship military prayer breakfast at the Hilton Hotel in Washington, DC. During the speaker's message, God spoke to me in an undeniable way. Though still an unbeliever, I heard Him say, "Tommi, I want you—I want you to walk with Me." I didn't know what that meant or what I needed to do. In fact, as I think about it today, I don't even know if the gospel was being preached that morning when I showed up at the meeting. But since I knew God was talking to me about walking, I responded the best way I knew—by walking up to the front of the platform when the speaker invited people.

I will never forget the man who led me in what I later learned was the "sinner's prayer." He didn't try to heap guilt on me, nor did he once say I was a sinner—I probably would have punched him out if he had said that! Since in my mind I had never broken any of "the ten big ones," I'm sure I would have at least had some choice words for him. After meeting him up at the front of the platform, he asked me the same question the speaker had: Did I want to walk closer to God? I said yes, prayed "the prayer" with him, declared that "I believe Jesus is Lord"...and seconds later ended up on the floor speaking in tongues. Even though I knew several languages at the time, I certainly didn't know that one!

Later that evening, Ralph and I went to a fighter pilot's party.

(Remember, I had been a Christian for all of seven hours.) When I walked in, everyone looked at me as if I was an alien.

"What happened to you?" my friends asked. I had no idea what they were talking about. "Your face—it's glowing," they pointed out.

"Um, I don't know...this morning I went forward to walk closer to God, and the next thing I knew, this language starting coming out of my mouth, and then I was lying on the floor."

"You're charismatic!" they said, as if giving me a doctor's diagnosis.

"Well, what does that mean?" I asked.

"It means you've been born again."

"Uh, no, I'm pretty sure I didn't get born all over again," I said with a chuckle. I had no idea what they were referring to and actually figured the alcohol was doing most of their talking. But as our conversation went on, my friends continued to mention several other "Christianese" terms I had never heard. I was left utterly confused.

Looking back, the situation (and my naïveté) makes me laugh. But it also reminds me of how foreign our language as Christians can be to the rest of the world—even to the point of sounding like gibberish. If we hope to invade the cultural mountains with any degree of success, that must change. We are of no good to unbelievers on the mountains if we can't speak their language. In fact, most of the time, our Christianese does more harm than good.

I recently read a story from a Christian journalist who worked in the secular media. A friend of his was a newspaper editor and called him one night to ask a question about a story he was working on. "I'm copyediting a news brief," the editor said, "and it's about a concert at a church, and it says there will be a 'love offering.' Does that mean what I think it means? Thought I'd check before we promote an orgy."

The man wasn't joking. He had heard of one too many cults that blend sex with a loose interpretation of "evangelism," and he thought he had stumbled upon one of their undercover promotions. The Christian journalist assured him there would not be an orgy at the church and that a love offering was in fact a collection taken up for a visiting musical group or speaker.

"Well, why don't they just say that?" the editor asked in an embarrassed tone.[2]

He has a point. Often it is as if believers have forgotten what it means to speak plain English, or at least the English that's spoken in our "B.C." (before Christ) days. We must shift our mind-set and learn to speak

whatever dialect is used on the mountain we are assigned to pray for—
or risk losing any hope of influencing the millions of souls in that territory. Each mountain has its own language, and I would venture to say
none of them is the Christianese we tend to use in our tight-knit church
circles.

Think about it. When you talk to a five-year-old, you do not speak in
the same way you would with someone who has a doctorate. When my
grandson was five years old, trust me, I didn't talk to him the same way
I did to my friends; I talked "five-year-old talk" so that I could communicate with him. Likewise, the way professionals relate to each other on
the Business Mountain is different from how those on the Government
Mountain or Education Mountain interact. As intercessors, we must recognize these differences and train ourselves to speak the language of
whichever group God has called us to. We have to communicate with
words others will receive and understand. When these people can comprehend what we are saying, they will be more eager to hear what we
have to say, especially when God speaks to them through us. But if they
cannot understand, they won't be excited about what God has to say. In
fact, more than likely they will be turned off by our religiosity.

USING THE WORD WITHOUT THE WORD

As we learn the language of each mountain, we begin to earn the
right to speak into people's lives. Often what we *do not* say is just as
important as what we end up saying. Don't expect a group of college
professors to hear you, for example, if you spout out Bible verses while
they discuss the merits of Darwin's evolutionary theories. Often the
Word is best received when it's not presented verbatim with chapter,
verse, and translation.

Not long ago, I was at a conference teaching on the Seven Mountains
when a former pastor shared the following story with the group:

> After serving as a pastor for several years, I went from full-
> time ministry to full-time business. I'd come from a pastoral
> background—went to Bible college, then worked as a pastor,
> administrative pastor, and eventually senior pastor—so I was
> well-versed in "Christianese." God led me to start a business,
> however, and as it quickly became successful, I began to get
> invitations to speak to businesses and investment groups. These
> people wanted to know how I conducted my business and what

principles I lived by so they could implement them into their own organizations and find similar success.

The first time I was invited, I was worried that I'd revert into pastor mode and launch into, "Praise God! Hallelujah! Amen!" As time went by, I began to understand that I couldn't teach these biblical principles by going into a seminar and telling business people to open up to the Book of Isaiah—I'd lose them right then. Instead, what I tried to do was apply the Word of God using principles and a lingo that they could understand. As I did this, I'd notice that the soil of people's hearts softened. God was setting them up!

One time, the CEO of an internationally known company attended an event where I was speaking. At the end of the last session, while God was moving powerfully (even though most of the people didn't recognize it), the CEO's operations manager approached me and asked if he could speak to me for a few minutes. I never had to use the "Roman Road" or present the ABCs of salvation or any of that. This manager came to me and told me about how he had been weeping the previous night over the stirring in his heart. For some reason, he Googled me and discovered that I had preached a sermon on Easter years earlier at his mother's church. He called his mother and, as a prodigal, surrendered his life again to the Lord. A month later, he texted me and said, "I now know that the only one I need to put all of my trust in and really fear is God." He and his wife both gave their lives to the Lord—simply because I was talking about the principles of God in a language they could understand.

If we hope to have the same kind of results, we must know how to use the Word without even quoting the Word. As intercessors and residents of the cultural mountains, this is part of our strategic preparation for invasion. To take the mountains, we must be able to relate to the people we come in contact with. The enemy may currently possess the Seven Mountains, but as we learn to communicate more effectively—with a language that can be understood by all—we will take them back.

This is not a foreign concept. Jesus did the same thing when He communicated with parables. His primary way of teaching people about kingdom principles was through stories and verbal illustrations that relied heavily upon language, visuals, and tangible things His audience came in contact with on a daily basis in their own sphere of life. For example, in Mark 4, when Jesus spoke of sowing seeds (vv. 1–20), growing seeds (vv. 26–29), and mustard seeds (30–32) all in the same setting, you can be sure there were farmers in the crowd He was addressing. Mark even adds an aside following these passages: "With many such parables He was *speaking the word* to them, so far as they were able to hear it; and He did not speak to them without a parable; but He was explaining everything privately to His disciples" (vv. 33–34, emphasis added). I can imagine those private sessions were filled with exegesis of Old Testament passages and more detailed illustrations of what the kingdom of God looked like. But to the general public, He knew His most effective way to portray this heavenly dimension was to speak their language—while still "speaking the Word."

We must do what Jesus did, relying on God's Spirit to move among unbelievers on whatever mountain we're called to while we speak His Word in a language they can understand. Our responsibility is to trust and believe in the power of God that resides in His Word, not in our own power to use "persuasive words of wisdom" (1 Cor. 2:4). We must change our words to change our world.

Lance Wallnau, whom I mentioned in the first chapter, provides a great example of this with a system he now has trademarked and teaches around the world. To market the Lance Learning 7M™ Consulting Process, he describes it using the following words:

> Lance Learning's unique 7M^{tm} process transforms organizations! Our process zeroes in on the specific organizational constraint that is keeping your company from maximum effectiveness at the Individual, Team and Business level. Each project and client is different, but the outcome is always the same: significantly increased business and customer results, new levels of organizational and team effectiveness, and remarkable levels of individual change; people change from the inside out.[3]

Do you notice the language shift? Wallnau isn't speaking to believers, though he certainly offers the same process to them in other forms (with different verbiage). He speaks specifically to the general, non-Christian business community, using general, non-Christian business community language. When he says his process hones in on "specific organizational constraint," for instance, he is referring to deliverance. Throughout his resources, he uses phrases such as *emotional intelligence* and *intuition*—these are wisdom, favor, and prophetic guidance. When he promises that people will "actualize and find the zone," he's simply speaking of the victory and abundant life Christ offers. So far, Wallnau has had incredible results with his process, all while He communicates kingdom principles!

WARRIORS WITH WORD WEAPONS

Language is a powerful force, and words are a potent weapon. But we must not forget that God did not empower words to defeat the enemy; He enlisted us, His people. Wars are not won purely with weapons but with warriors who know how to wield those weapons most effectively and with power. Likewise, the war for the Seven Mountains—which begins upon the spiritual battleground of intercession—will not be won simply by words but by prayer warriors who know how to use those words to declare God's sovereign power. No longer do we have to believe the religious teaching that intercessors must spend countless hours alone in our personal prayer closets, crying out to God on behalf of others. That approach caused many of us to become discouraged by the costliness of our calling. But we believed a lie! The truth is, apostolic intercessors are the ones who open the pathway between heaven and earth. Our value as apostolic intercessors is far greater than we can ever imagine.

Second Chronicles 16:9 says, "For the eyes of the Lord move to and fro throughout the earth that He may strongly support those whose heart is completely His." When we intercede by the Holy Spirit, we offer our hearts, minds, and tongues to God. By yielding ourselves to be vessels of prayer, it is as if we posted a huge banner outside our front door that read in big, bold letters, "Use me!" and was sure to capture God's attention as He scanned the earth for those He could use. All He is looking for are warriors—He has already supplied the weapons and the strategy, and He has (ultimately) even secured the victory.

We are His intercessory warriors, called to pick up these word weapons and use them as Jesus did. Our Savior will "draw all men to Himself," often by using the common denominator of language (John 12:32). With those who reside on the mountains—teachers, elected officials, soccer moms, business owners—we can bear weapons of peace in a hostile land, creating bridges of communication by the Holy Spirit–inspired vernacular we use. By speaking the language of those around us, it is possible for us to open doors that otherwise would remain shut.

Christ also used His words to declare war on the enemy. He claimed every territory in which He walked by the power of His Word. In the next chapter, we will begin to follow His lead with greater understanding as we enter a higher realm of intercession in which proclamations, declarations, and decrees are the language of the land.

Chapter 7 Notes

1. Dutch Sheets, *Authority in Prayer* (Bloomington, MN: Bethany House, 2006), 91.

2. Mike Wendland, "Let's Watch Our Christianese," Oct. 1, 2009, http://mikewendland.com/2009/10/01/let%E2%80%99s-watch-our-christianese/ (site no longer active).

3. From website: http://www.lancelearning.com (accessed August 11, 2011).

Chapter 8

PROCLAMATIONS, DECLARATIONS, AND DECREES

O N SEPTEMBER 22, 1862, President Abraham Lincoln issued the most famous proclamation in American history, the Emancipation Proclamation. With a mere 721 words on five pages tied together with red and blue ribbons, he changed the shape of a nation by declaring the freedom of every slave within the Confederate states. Eventually, this would become the legal declaration that emancipated more than 4 million slaves throughout the Union.[1]

Less than a century earlier, on July 4, 1776, the fifty-six delegates of the Continental Congress signed the Declaration of Independence and affirmed the autonomy of thirteen American colonies from British rule. Written on a single piece of parchment, the Thomas Jefferson–drafted document formed a new nation founded upon the principles of its famous preamble: "We hold these truths to be self-evident, that all men are created equal, that they are endowed by their Creator with certain unalienable Rights, that among these are Life, Liberty and the pursuit of Happiness."[2]

Across the Atlantic, on November 21, 1806, Napoleon Bonaparte issued the Berlin Decree to restructure Europe by establishing the Continental System. An attempt to defeat the British Empire via economic sanctions, this legal pronouncement barred any European country from trading with the United Kingdom and was followed a year later with the Milan Decree, which authorized France to capture any ships caught dealing with the British.[3, 4]

Words have power, yet words backed by the authority of those in rule have even greater power—enough to reshape cities, countries, continents, the entire world, and history itself. Lincoln, the Founding Fathers, and Napoleon all understood the profound impact made by issuing a proclamation, declaration, or decree. In each case, they were not merely pronouncing a governmental change. They recognized the far-reaching cultural shift their words enforced.

God has given us the power to change entire cultures and to seize and conquer territory stolen by the enemy. When we are aligned with His Holy Spirit through intercession, our words have His official authority behind them. Like the officials and representatives sent out to enforce the Emancipation Proclamation, the Declaration of Independence, or the Berlin and Milan decrees, we confront the powers of darkness with an official Word from the ruling powers of heaven. In fact, what we bring is, as the famous Stevie Wonder song says, "signed, sealed, and delivered."

Yet when we pray only from a position of petitioning God, as we discussed in chapter 6, we limit this authority that the Lord has passed on to us. We act like a poor orphan who is adopted into a royal family and appointed heir to the throne, yet who continues to live as if he were a beggar. The Bible tells us we have been grafted into a royal lineage by way of Jesus Christ. (See Romans 11:17–24.) Throughout His Word, God calls us His sons, even declaring, "For all who are being led by the Spirit of God, these are sons of God" (Rom. 8:14). Only a few verses later, we find more evidence of our royal inheritance: "The Spirit Himself testifies with our spirit that we are children of God, and if children, heirs also, heirs of God and fellow heirs with Christ, if indeed we suffer with Him so that we may also be glorified with Him" (vv. 16–17). Whether we act like princes or paupers, the truth is the same: we *are* sons of God and have been given the authority to match such a high position.

Why, then, do so many of us continue to approach the Seven Mountains as if we were illegal immigrants? I believe it is because we fail to understand the function of proclamations, declarations, and decrees.

TO PROCLAIM AND DECLARE

A man stands up in the middle of a crowded restaurant and announces with a beaming smile, "I just asked the most wonderful woman in the world to marry me, and she said 'Yes!'"

A young married couple invites both sets of their parents for a casual dinner to inform them they'll soon be grandparents for the first time.

An employee nearing retirement gathers his co-workers in the break room to tell them the company is downsizing, he's just been given the option to take a severance package, and tomorrow will be his last day.

These are all proclamations by the mere fact that they officially announce something. We hear or read proclamations on a weekly basis, whether via a television news network or from our friends. Even a simple advertisement for a "going out of business" sale is a proclamation, as is someone standing at the front of theater box office and informing the rest of those waiting in line that tickets have just sold out.

Only slightly different from a proclamation, a declaration is in the same vein in that it also serves as an official announcement. The difference, however, is that a declaration pronounces something with authority by *someone* in authority. It is one thing, for example, to stand outside a company's headquarters and proclaim to anyone within shouting distance that the business should be closed down because you believe it is involved in unethical practices. Yet the situation would take on extra weight if an FBI agent stood in front of the facility and pronounced the business closed immediately until further notice. Likewise, there is a different sense if you are warned about defaulting on a mortgage loan by your spouse compared to receiving an official notification in the mail from your lender—or, worse still, your lender's attorney. Declarations are made from those in authority, while proclamations can come from anyone.

Many intercessors often use these two terms interchangeably without understanding what distinguishes one from the other. There is a difference. But because God has already given us His authority when it comes to interceding on His behalf—because we have all been made His official representatives as "ambassadors for Christ" (2 Cor. 5:20)—then splitting hairs over whether something is a proclamation or declaration can be futile. In fact, throughout this chapter, I refer more often to proclamations for the sake of clarity and consistency, yet in almost every case the same principles can be applied to making declarations, as long as the context is a person of authority making the announcement.

The important thing to understand is that proclamations and declarations are not just words spoken into thin air or written on a piece of paper; they are weapons of warfare. Whenever we pray, we come in the name of Jesus to face off against the forces of darkness, and some of the most powerful weapons we can wield are proclamations and declarations.

In Jeremiah 1:9, the prophet recalls, "Then the LORD stretched out His hand and touched my mouth, and the LORD said to me, 'Behold, I have put My words in your mouth.'" Speaking forth God's intended will for the earth carries great power to perform His intended purpose. It is not about our own words but those that God has placed in our mouths—words that, in the context of intercession, can feel like burning coals on our tongues: "'Is not My word like fire?' declares the LORD, 'and like a hammer which shatters a rock?'" (Jer. 23:29). Whether with a mighty sledgehammer or a piercing arrow, the Lord empowers us with His words to strike down every plan of the enemy. Isaiah spoke of the precision these word weapons carry: "He has made My mouth like a sharp sword, in the shadow of His hand He has concealed Me; and He has also made Me a select arrow, He has hidden Me in His quiver" (Isa. 49:2).

Proclamations, declarations, and (as we will discover later in this chapter) decrees are weapons of warfare designed by the Lord to destroy every onslaught of wicked spirits. But these power-filled words are also used to release the blessings of God. Believers have the authority to create God's will on earth through kingdom "announcements" that cause God's preexisting will to be fully released. As we speak out in faith and boldness, we release things that are on the Father's heart but have not yet manifested on earth. We usher in His kingdom through our words and literally change the face of the planet.

To do this in the fullness of His power and authority, however, requires discerning God's will through both the Word and the Spirit. God's Holy Spirit, which He has placed within each of us who calls Him Master, will always testify with His Word—and vice versa. These two elements are intricately connected throughout Scripture. Too often, I find intercessors who neglect one or the other. Some will downplay the Word and claim that all they need is the Spirit's leading: "We have the Holy Spirit guiding us from within. The Bible is great and all, but since God dwells within us, we just need to trust our feelings and know that He'll lead us." Others will disregard the Holy Spirit's life within them and rely solely on the written pages of the Bible. This typically leads to a life of legalism—and a mechanical, lifeless one at that!

We cannot have only the Word or the Spirit if we hope to walk in the fullness of God's truth. Both are not only necessary, they will always align with each other. The key, then, is discerning God's will through both as we make proclamations and declarations to enact His kingdom on earth.

STEPS FOR SPEAKING GOD'S WORDS

Often when we intercede with God's words, using His authority to rend the heavens, we make a prophetic proclamation or declaration. We already know that to proclaim something is to announce it. According to *Webster's Dictionary*, to prophesy means "to declare or predict by or as by the influence of divine guidance."[5] To make a *prophetic* proclamation, then, means we announce the coming of what has yet to be in the natural realm of earth. It is important to point out that we do not make this announcement by our own power or authority, but by the One who empowered us to make such a proclamation. At its core, intercession allows us to proclaim into being what has yet to be, as we represent God's will on earth. I don't know about you, but having this awesome responsibility gets me fired up!

It also fired up several of the Old Testament prophets to the point that they stuck out like sore thumbs amid a people who repeatedly turned their backs on God. Prayer-warriors-cum-prophetic-megaphones such as Isaiah, Ezekiel, Jeremiah, Amos, and Hosea were not afraid to speak out against the cultural norm. As they swam upstream by proclaiming God's sovereignty, righteousness, and holiness, these prophets also displayed the steps in making a prophetic proclamation.

In Isaiah 40:9, God spoke to the prophet Isaiah on behalf of the entire nation of Israel: "Get yourself up on a high mountain, O Zion, bearer of good news. Lift up your voice mightily, O Jerusalem, bearer of good news; lift it up, do not fear. Say to the cities of Judah, 'Here is your God!'" There is rarely an easy, four-step process when it comes to intercession— or anything spiritual, for that matter. Yet it is hard to deny God's clear instructions in this passage for making prophetic proclamations that are filled with His power.

1. *Get in a high place.* Obviously, this book is all about high places since we have continually addressed the issue of invading the Seven Mountains with intercession. As we approach each cultural mountain, it is important to set a single goal before us of ascending higher and higher. The enemy has already reached the summit; our task is now to play a spiritual game of "King of the Hill." If you ever played that childhood game, you will remember how uncomplicated it was. The lone purpose was to knock off whoever was on top of the hill—the "king." Intercession is our most potent weapon for dethroning Satan from his perch atop the mountains of religion, family, education, government, media, arts and entertainment, and business. As we load the powerful ammunition of proclamation into this weapon, we would do well to follow God's first step for making a direct hit on the enemy.

Think of it this way: the higher you climb on a cultural mountain, the greater influence your proclamations have on those below. Any mountain climber knows that words shouted from the top of a mountain reverberate more than those screamed at the bottom. Our prophetic proclamations carry increasing power as we gain altitude on the mountains of society.

2. *Lift up your voice.* God didn't just tell Isaiah—or Israel, for that matter—to speak out a few words. His instructions were to "lift up your voice *mightily*" (emphasis mine). Don't whimper or murmur or mumble or mutter. Whispering is not an option in the realm of prophetic proclamation. God wants us to be heard loud and clear!

Shouting has been a part of my lifestyle ever since I was a child. When I was growing up, it seemed the best way to make my needs known. After all, the one who shouted the loudest got my parents' attention—and so my brothers and I perfected the art of shouting. We could shout with the best of them and never lose our voice.

But shouting on behalf of God takes on a different meaning. It is not just about being loud or getting His attention (which you already have fully at all times, by the way). I have come to understand that the religious spirit hates it when we shout on behalf of the Lord. Recently I was in my prayer room interceding for a breakthrough for GateKeepers International. I raised up a war cry against the enemy with my shout. Immediately God came and broke through in the situation. And what followed was more shouting—shouts of joy, praise, exaltation, celebration, and victory!

Shouting releases something powerful into the atmosphere. As you intercede, the God of the universe joins with you in your proclamation. And when the Lord lifts up His voice, it shakes the heavens and the earth. Now *that's* power!

In 1997, I traveled to Uzbekistan to train pastors with a Youth With a Mission team. Despite the Central Asian country's recent fall of communism and a widespread acceptance of orthodox Christianity in past generations, Muslims now dominate the area, and persecution of believers is common. The pastors I met with risked their lives on a daily basis, but they were filled with an unquenchable fire to tell others about Jesus. Some had been leading underground churches for a few years, yet because Protestant Christianity had begun to spread on a larger scale only three years prior, most of the pastors were extremely young. In fact, the average age of the group I taught was only nineteen, and the youngest pastor was fifteen years old! If you were saved, you automatically became a pastor, and those with whom you shared the gospel became your congregation.

During one of our sessions, I instructed the pastors on the basics of prophetic proclamation, including this point of lifting up your voice. I had the group stand on their chairs (to "get up on a high place") and pray over the people groups and cities they represented using Isaiah 60. Several of the pastors were from Tashkent, the capital of Uzbekistan, so I led them to pray God's words specifically for their influential city: "Listen, Tashkent, hear the Word of the Lord; Arise, Tashkent, and shine; for your light has come, and the glory of the LORD has risen upon you, Tashkent. For behold, darkness will cover the earth and deep darkness the peoples; but the LORD will rise upon you, Tashkent, and His glory will appear upon you. Rise up, Tashkent! Rise up!"

One young man, however, refused to stand up and join the group. I interrupted our praying and asked him why he didn't want to pray with us. He shrugged his shoulders, looked away, and apathetically said, "Oh, I'll do that when I get back to my town."

After he responded similarly to a couple of other questions I asked, something rose up in my spirit. I pointed my finger at him, leaned over close to his face, and sternly asked, "People are dying and going to hell in the city of Tashkent, and you refuse to proclaim the Word of God over them?"

I wasn't the only one who felt this way. Others urged him to pray with the fervor they felt burning inside. The young man stood on his chair and began to softly repeat our prayer, but his fellow pastors would not let him get away with a feeble attempt. These leaders had a passion to save their city, and they were not about to let their brother slack on such an important task. By the time we had finished praying, the young man had joined us in proclaiming God's Word with all the force he could muster. And I am convinced it made a difference in the spirit realm.

When we raise our voices in declarative intercession, we are not just shouting for the sake of being loud or dramatic. We are sternly—*mightily*—making a prophetic proclamation with the authority of God Himself. His words, spoken through us, are not to be treated lightly. They have power, and, when delivered in the face of the enemy, they will effect change in the landscape.

3. *Do not be afraid.* How many times is this phrase repeated throughout Scripture? I once heard a preacher refer to it as the most common greeting whenever heavenly representatives come face-to-face

with earthly beings. Fear is the natural response of the flesh, yet the Bible clearly points out that "God has not given us a spirit of timidity" (2 Tim. 1:7). In the context of making a prophetic proclamation, the Lord intentionally reminds us to go against our natural tendency to recoil when we encounter opposing forces. As we position ourselves to stand on high places and lift up our voices, Satan will undoubtedly try to confront us with a spirit of fear. Yet we have no reason to fear because:

❖ *We know who we are and who God is.* It is pointless to entertain thoughts of fear when the Master of the Universe has your back. As Paul says with enemy-mocking words, "If God is for us, who is against us?" (Rom. 8:31). When we truly know who God is and understand His character, we can be fearless in every situation and encounter.

❖ *We know our authority in Christ.* The religious spirit keeps us from knowing the true authority God has given us. Even when believers have knowledge of their authority, this spirit can prevent them from fully embracing it. Regardless of our level of acceptance, God has already empowered us through His Son, which means there is no justification for us to remain fearful.

❖ *We speak from the kingdom of light into the kingdom of darkness.* We are "children of Light" (Eph. 5:8) and belong to a kingdom that by its very nature casts out every shadow and hint of darkness. As John 1:5 so eloquently puts it, "The Light shines on in the darkness, for the darkness has never overpowered it [put it out or absorbed it or appropriated it, and is unreceptive to it]" (AMP). Notice it is not the reverse; the darkness does not, nor cannot "shine" in the light. That is reason alone to not fear. When we ascend high places and mightily proclaim God's words, *we* are the force to be reckoned with—not the other way around.

4. *Speak the truth.* God instructed Isaiah, "Say to the cities of Judah, 'Here is your God!'" (Isa. 40:9). The prophet was to offer a succinct proclamation of God's presence—a grand "Everyone, may I have your attention? I'd like to introduce..." But notice that God provided Isaiah with exactly the words he was supposed to say. Not only did God give

him the authority to speak out, He also supplied him with the means to enact that authority.

It is no different with our prophetic proclamations that will ring out through the valleys of every cultural mountain. God will provide the words—in fact, in most cases, He already has through His written Word. Jesus taught and modeled to us that God's Word *is* truth (John 17:17). Our task, therefore, is simple: we are to tell the truth. Just as the prophet was instructed, we must get in a high place, lift up our voices, stand fearless, and speak out God's power-filled words.

In Some Places, They'd Lock You Up for This

Do you ever talk to your car? Your television? Your microwave? Most of us have to admit that, at one point or another, we have spoken to an inanimate object with no thought of it responding (or so I'd hope). In the movie *Night at the Museum*, a down-on-his-luck security guard named Larry experiences something completely different when he discovers that the artifacts of the American Museum of Natural History suddenly come to life during the night. With wax statues engaging the night watchman in conversation and a fossilized dinosaur running around like a puppy, Larry finds himself surrounded by a world of liveliness in the very facility built to celebrate dead history.

Unlike Larry, I doubt the prophet Ezekiel played catch with any skeletons among his raised-from-the-dead army. But I suspect he and the security officer might have a few similar conversation starters given their shared experience with inanimate objects coming to life. Ezekiel was given a prophetic proclamation straight from God, and the results of him following orders rival the products of any Hollywood screenwriter's imagination. In Ezekiel 37, we find the prophet's version of what occurred:

> The hand of the LORD was upon me, and he brought me out by the Spirit of the LORD and set me in the middle of a valley; it was full of bones. He led me back and forth among them, and I saw a great many bones on the floor of the valley, bones that were very dry. He asked me, "Son of man, can these bones live?"
>
> I said, "O Sovereign LORD, you alone know."

Then he said to me, "Prophesy to these bones and say to them, 'Dry bones, hear the word of the LORD! This is what the Sovereign LORD says to these bones: I will make breath enter you, and you will come to life. I will attach tendons to you and make flesh come upon you and cover you with skin; I will put breath in you, and you will come to life. Then you will know that I am the LORD.'"

So I prophesied as I was commanded. And as I was prophesying, there was a noise, a rattling sound, and the bones came together, bone to bone. I looked, and tendons and flesh appeared on them and skin covered them, but there was no breath in them.

Then he said to me, "Prophesy to the breath; prophesy, son of man, and say to it, 'This is what the Sovereign LORD says: Come from the four winds, O breath, and breathe into these slain, that they may live.'" So I prophesied as he commanded me, and breath entered them; they came to life and stood up on their feet—a vast army.

—EZEKIEL 37:1–10, NIV

Ezekiel was human like any of us. He could have easily laughed at the thought of God taking him into a virtual ghost town and telling him to talk to a pile of bones. This certainly was not the setting for a glamorized, heart-warming, crowd-pleasing prophecy that would make Ezekiel the talk of all Israel. No, this was a test of faith and obedience. Ezekiel was doing the unthinkable, speaking directly to the dried-up bones of people who had died decades before. Yet notice that he did not question his directives by saying, "Um, excuse me, God...You do realize those are *bones*, right? It's not like they can hear me!" Nor did the prophet hedge on what he was supposed to do. He followed God's promptings with every step.

Could it be that Ezekiel's willingness to obey God's "crazy" commands had something to do with his prior experience in making prophetic proclamations? Is it possible that he actually didn't think speaking to bones was so far-fetched after all, given his earlier testing from God? Only a chapter earlier, in Ezekiel 36, the Lord instructed this obedient servant to prophesy to the mountains of Israel and the surrounding landscape: "Therefore, O mountains of Israel, hear the word of the Lord GOD. Thus says the Lord GOD to the mountains and to the hills, to the ravines and to the valleys, to the desolate wastes and to the forsaken cities which have become a prey and a derision to the rest of the nations which are round about" (v. 4).

Which is crazier: talking to mountains or dry bones? Maybe the better, albeit deeper, question is this: Do mountains or dry bones have ears? Can valleys or forsaken cities actually hear our words? Our natural minds would say, "Of course not!" Yet how else can we explain the response Ezekiel actually saw with his own eyes after prophesying to these seemingly inanimate objects? Ezekiel's prophetic proclamations would be considered crazy by anyone not tuned in to the Spirit or anyone viewing the situation with purely natural eyes. Likewise, any intercessor who hopes to see dry bones, homes, cities, businesses, leaders, or nations come to life again can expect to be ridiculed for losing his natural mind. If you have already endured a fair share of these insults, take them as compliments—indeed, you are out of your *natural* mind—and becoming more in tune with the spiritual mind of Christ.

God will often test intercessors in valleys where it appears we are surrounded by nothing more than dry bones and lifeless terrain. As He did with Ezekiel, He wants to bring us to a place where we see with spiritual eyes and where our response in making a prophetic proclamation is immediate obedience, no matter how "crazy" our words sound to the natural mind.

SPEAKING AS GOD

Throughout history, ambassadors have played a key role in worldwide diplomacy. While premiers, presidents, prime ministers, and kings and queens may garner more public attention, ambassadors serve as the "foot soldiers" most involved in improving the relationship between two or more countries. Yet as crucial as these representatives are, they would be useless if they did not have the authority to speak on behalf of their governments or territories. An ambassador's effectiveness is solely linked to his power to represent.

As we intercede for one of the Seven Mountains, we must never forget that we have already been appointed as ambassadors for Christ. God has selected us as stand-ins for His presence throughout the earth. We are God's heart in this world. We are His hands and feet, walking where Jesus would walk and touching those whom He would touch. We represent every aspect of the character of God. And within the realm of intercession, that means we also represent the voice of the Lord.

Some believers have a difficult time with this. They find it hard to believe that their words could ever be considered on the same plane as God's. Obviously, none of us is God. When we speak, we are not God—there is a difference. But we are His representatives and have the authority to speak on His behalf. That means our voice, as a "stand-in" for God's, carries as much clout as His spoken words would. As Psalm 103:20 indicates, angels are assigned to "perform His word, obeying the voice of His word." Because we are God's voice on earth, then, we have the power to initiate heavenly activity.

This is true for both angels and demons, for powers of light and darkness. Through declarations, we, as the official representatives of God, remind the enemy of his defeat and the angelic armies of their victory. We also remind the Lord of His promises that ring true for eternity. As Isaiah 55:10–11 attests, God's words do not return void but stand forever: "For as the rain and the snow come down from heaven, and do not return there without watering the earth and making it bear and sprout, and furnishing seed to the sower and bread to the eater; so will My word be which goes forth from My mouth; it will not return to Me empty, without accomplishing what I desire, and without succeeding in the matter for which I sent it."

If God's words will always come to pass, and if He has appointed us to speak on His behalf, is it any wonder why Satan does all he can to silence us? He is unremitting in his attempts to suppress our voices. Years ago I remember a teaching circulating among prayer groups that said believers should pray in our minds so the devil will not hear us. Instead of praying out loud and drawing attention to ourselves, it stated, the most effective approach is to keep our prayers silent and within our heads. Hogwash! Where is our greatest battlefield, according to the Bible? And where does Satan love to torment us most with false beliefs, lies, and self-degrading thoughts? In our minds!

Another teaching said we should pray in tongues because then the devil cannot understand us. I was taught this, passed it on to others, and believed it wholeheartedly until one day a Scripture verse came to mind as I was pondering the logic of this concept. First Corinthians 13 famously opens with the words, "If I speak with the tongues of men and of angels…" We know Satan was an angel before he was cast out of heaven. If that is the case, then don't you think he would understand the same language angels speak?

Though seemingly minor, these are examples of ideas Satan uses to gradually mute voices and silence strong declarations that pronounce the kingdom of God. Satan hates it when we say what God says. He loathes every minute we spend declaring God's perfect will on earth. And he abhors the sound of our voices because they remind him of the One who dominates him with a single thought. Our enemy is fully aware that with one empowered word, we, like Christ, can call upon legions of angels. Remember, the primary purpose of these angels is to perform the word of God, to put into action the fulfillment of all His promises—His perfect will on earth. Because we have been given the authority to unleash such divine power, Satan will do all he can to silence us. *This* is why a war wages over our voices.

It is also why our enemy has done everything in his power to close the ears of those within his domain—in this case, the Seven Mountains. Until he is displaced from every territory he has been given reign over, he will continue to distort our words and muffle the sound of our voices enough so that those dwelling on the mountains cannot clearly hear the truth of our words. To overcome this, we must thwart his plans and break the strongholds he creates. One way we do this is by officially announcing the Word of the Lord over each of the Seven Mountains. By calling things not as they are, but as they *should be* (see Romans 4:17)— which is the disposition of God's ever-creative Word—we establish both the perfect will of God and the dominion of all His angels. Furthermore, we lay the groundwork for what follows next: making decrees.

DECREE THIS!

In her book *The Cyrus Decree*, Jane Hamon offers this insight to explain what decrees do in both the spiritual and natural realms:

> When God releases a decree it causes a shift to happen in the heavens and sets events in motion in the earth. An unseen force begins to move things in a certain direction to fulfill the divine decree. Sometimes the fulfillment comes instantaneously. When God spoke and decreed the worlds and the universe to be formed, instantly, out of nothing, creation took place. When Jesus declared forgiveness of sin, healing, and deliverance to many people He came in contact with, His decree of the King had an immediate result.
>
> Not all decrees are fulfilled instantaneously. God decreed that Abraham would bring forth nations out of his loins and that they would rise up and take the land from the Nile to the Euphrates

[see Genesis 22:17–18]....Obviously all these descendants would not spring forth overnight. In fact, it was years before Sarah even conceived their first child. This decree set a course for generations to follow to fulfill the decree of God.[6]

Whether we see their impact immediately or generations later, decrees are long-lasting and have a more permanent nature than proclamations or declarations. Up to this point, we have established proclamations and declarations as two potent weapons in the arsenal of intercession. When spoken by those in authority, these announcements carry even greater weight—which is what occurs every time we open our mouths and release the Word of God. As a third weapon in the trio, decrees are comparable to a president signing a law into action. Proclamations and declarations may be *spoken* by someone in authority, but decrees are *written* and officially establish the law.

By definition, a decree is "an official order, edict or decision, as of a church, government, court, etc."[7] As a formal charge, it is authoritative direction or instruction. Whereas a proclamation is an announcement and a declaration is a pronouncement, a decree trumps them both as an official command. Every decree comes with the force of law behind it.

Many people think of decrees as an older extension of government, but they are still just as relevant in today's world. In 2007, Venezuelan President Hugo Chavez made history when his country's lawmakers granted him the authority to rule by decree for an eighteen-month period. Amid shouts of "Long live socialism!" Chavez received the right to effect immediate change by remaking laws and transitioning his economically fragile South American country into what he called "socialism for the twenty-first century."[8] With a single vote, Chavez's words took on unprecedented power—what he said went. In fact, his words could immediately become written law. If he decided to make Wednesday "Red Hat Day," then by golly, Wednesdays became Red Hat Days for everyone in Venezuela.

As silly as that example might be, the power wielded with a decree is anything but. In the same way Chavez could suddenly rule by decree, believers have been given the ultimate authority to enact God's laws by decree. God wants us to rule and reign over the earth as we establish His kingdom. Yet how many of us actually treat our words in intercession as law? One of Webster's insightful definitions of the word *law* is "a divinely appointed order or system."[9] Just as an apostle's role is to bring order, every intercessor's role is to establish order in the heavenly realm. By our words of decree, we establish order to a situation, person, city, or even an entire cultural mountain.

A decree is also a judicial decision or order. Whenever a judge slams down his gavel at the end of a court session, he sets in motion a decree that establishes judgment upon a case. His ruling is sanctioned and enforced by the court of law. How many of us are aware that God's gavel has already fallen on our behalf? The courts of heaven have already declared a ruling; we simply enforce it with our authoritative words. What we decree on earth is backed by the law of heaven—the law of God's kingdom. By its very definition, to decree something is to render a concluding decision, settle a dispute, and award victory to one side.[10] That means when we confront the powers of darkness with decrees, we remind them of the gavel that has already been sounded, declaring God's kingdom as the winning side. I certainly like the sound of that gavel!

DECREES IN ACTION

In the Book of Esther, we find several perfect illustrations of decrees in action. The ruling king of the time, King Xerxes, held a seven-day feast for all his nobles and officials. As the elaborate festivities wound down, he summoned his queen to present herself before his guests. Queen Vashti refused, however, causing the king to become enraged. As he consulted with his lawyers on what legal options he had (OK, that's my paraphrase), one of his experts offered the following advice: "Therefore, if it pleases the king, let him issue a royal decree and let it be written in the laws of Persia and Media, which cannot be repealed, that Vashti is never again to enter the presence of King Xerxes. Also let the king give her royal position to someone else who is better than she" (Esther 1:19, NIV).

It is debatable whether Xerxes' lawyers were trigger-happy in suggesting a decree. They undoubtedly understood the severity of the matter—that once this decree was made and written into law, Vashti would be stripped of her crown and effectively ruined for life. Yet later in the account, we see that at least one of these advisors, Haman, was fully aware of the power decrees held. In fact, power-hungry and manipulative Haman managed to garner enough authority from the king to set in motion his personal vendetta to exterminate the Jewish people:

Then Haman said to King Xerxes, "There is a certain people dispersed and scattered among the peoples in all the provinces of your kingdom whose customs are different from those of all other people and who do not obey the king's laws; it is not in the king's best interest to tolerate them. If it pleases the king, let a decree be issued to destroy them, and I will put ten thousand talents of silver into the royal treasury for the men who carry out this business." So the king took his signet ring from his finger and gave it to Haman son of Hammedatha, the Agagite, the enemy of the Jews. "Keep the money," the king said to Haman, "and do with the people as you please." Then on the thirteenth day of the first month the royal secretaries were summoned. They wrote out in the script of each province and in the language of each people all Haman's orders to the king's satraps, the governors of the various provinces and the nobles of the various peoples. These were written in the name of King Xerxes himself and sealed with his own ring.
—ESTHER 3:8–12, NIV

Besides recognizing King Xerxes' foolishness in carelessly sharing his power, we can also learn a few things about decrees through this passage. Decrees were not only written in the language of those they concerned to ensure clear communication, they were penned in the name of the king so that none would mistake the authority behind their words. To finalize this even further, decrees in ancient times were sealed with the king's signet ring. In fact, this is part of the history behind our modern-day phrase of getting someone's "stamp of approval."

Yet there is another vital characteristic of decrees that the Book of Esther displays. Later in the story, after Haman's plot to destroy the Jews is exposed, King Xerxes grants Esther and her cousin, Mordecai, the authority to make another decree in his name—this time to return to the people of Israel their rights "to defend their lives, to destroy, to kill and to annihilate the entire army of any people or province which might attack them" (Esther 8:11). But notice that King Xerxes tells them to make another decree, not rewrite the one Haman penned. He offers a clear explanation: "For a decree which is written in the name of the king and sealed with the king's signet ring may not be revoked" (v. 8).

You cannot use Wite-Out® on a decree, nor can you erase part of it and update the rest to better match the times. Once a decree has been issued, it is permanent and irrevocable. Therein lies the power we inherently wield as intercessors who can enact laws in the spiritual realm by our words. We must consider our words carefully and use them wisely. My friends and family know I am a stickler for not using certain words flippantly, but there is a reason. As I pointed out in the last chapter, words and phrases such as *just* ("I'm just an intercessor"), *only* ("I was only asking for healing"), *kind of* or *sort of* ("I kind of did some warfare in the spirit and sort of got a breakthrough") are common yet incredibly destructive. They dilute and neuter language that is meant to be powerful and forceful.

Imagine a judge announcing his final decision to the court before giving a serial killer the death sentence. Right before hammering his gavel, he suddenly announces, "Well, I'm sort of unsure of my decision. It seems I kind of overslept this morning and now I'm a little bit tired and feeling sluggish, so to be honest, I'm just not certain if I'm making the right decision. But, oh well, here goes nothing." Not a person in the room would have confidence in a judge like that. Furthermore, if every sentencing he made came in such a wishy-washy manner, you can be sure he would not hold court for long. His words would lack certainty and therefore eventually have little power.

When we dilute our language with doubt, ambiguity, and hesitation, we not only invite the spirit of fear to creep into whatever situation we are praying for, we also prove to the forces of darkness that we are not coming with much authority after all, regardless of what we want them to think. We must be sure of the things we offer in intercession and convey them with certainty. That is yet another reason the most powerful words we can speak are ones that have come straight from God—both from the Word and from His Spirit speaking from within us.

Decrees are, by nature, forceful. Our language should follow suit.

CHOOSE YOUR WEAPON—AND AMMUNITION—WISELY

Not every situation calls for a decree. Whenever I teach this lesson regarding proclamations, declarations, and decrees, I inevitably find intercessors who tell me how they decree this or that from the time they wake up to when their head hits the pillow. "That's a lot of unnecessary law enforcement," I often think. Other people will offer proclamation after proclamation in prayer—to the point that I wonder how many more things can be announced in the heavens without the angels covering their ears.

It is the challenge for every prayer warrior to discern which form of intercession is appropriate for a given circumstance. To proclaim healing over a generational curse of cancer, for instance, may not be enough; the spirits that have been allowed to establish roots within an entire family for years will likely need to be struck down with more law-enforcing decrees. Remember, when you proclaim something, you make an official announcement—the demonic spirits hear this, as do the angels who will always agree with what God says. To announce to a generational curse that it has to stop does not carry the necessary weight. Though a believer's declaration announces something with authority, a decree sets into law that which cannot be revoked. Decrees carry the weight of heaven. So as in the case of praying against generational curses, you have to look at the battle or war that needs to be fought and determine the size of the sphere of influence.

Peter Wagner offers a great example of the power of decrees in his book *Wrestling With Alligators, Prophets, and Theologians*. He writes:

> Doris and I are beefsteak eaters. When time permits on our domestic and international trips, we like to try out the finest prime steak houses. We found some excellent steak houses in Hannover, Germany, where we convened our first international meeting for our 40/70 Window prayer initiative in 2001....As we dined at some of the restaurants, I began to notice that the menus all indicated that they were serving "Argentine beef" or "American beef." It suddenly dawned on me that the reason the German steakhouses couldn't serve German beef was because of a devastating epidemic of mad cow disease that had been reported in the media! Because Doris and I are farmers, we became incensed that innocent German farmers could be victimized by this terrible plague.
>
> I hadn't given much more thought to it, however, until I was enjoying one of our plenary sessions in which the presence of God had obviously fallen. Much to my surprise, a word from the Lord came to me quite clearly: "Take authority over mad cow disease!" Such a thing had never occurred to me, so I began to pray over it and when I did it came even more strongly. Because I was in charge of the meeting I needed to ask no one's permission, so I made my way forward. By the time I got on the platform I could sense a strong divine anointing. When I began to describe the scenario to the crowd, I broke down into an embarrassing fit of weeping and sobbing. By then I knew

that God wanted me to take the apostolic authority He had given me and decree once and for all that mad cow disease would come to an end in Europe and the U.K., which I did. The whole assembly noisily agreed with me with sustained cheers and applause.

That was October 1, 2001. A month later, a friend of mine sent me a newspaper article from England saying that the epidemic had broken and that the last reported case of mad cow disease had been on September 30, 2001, the day before the apostolic decree!

Up until then I had been reasonably aware of the potential power of apostolic decrees. The one I had known best was the decree that Apostle James made in the Council of Jerusalem, which opened the door of the kingdom of God to Gentiles as well as Jews. Since Hannover, I have been cautiously moving toward using apostolic decrees a bit more, although I have yet to experience again as dramatic an effect as the eradication of a plague like mad cow disease.[11]

Deciding whether situations call for proclamations, declarations, or decrees is not a natural gift for every intercessor. This may take time. As you learn through trial and error, give yourself grace—God does. His kingdom does not hinge upon whether you correctly pray something as a declaration or a decree. At the same time, He is eager to see His children step into a higher realm of authority in prayer. As we seek to invade the Seven Mountains with intercession, we will soon discover that proclamations, declarations, and decrees must become a native tongue to us. No matter which mountain we pray for, it is certain we will face long-established strongholds and spiritual structures that control those mountains and need to be reminded with words of authority and power. Church, let's rise up and wise up to the authority He's given us via the words we choose in interceding for those mountains!

CHAPTER 8 NOTES

1. Wikipedia.org, "Emancipation Proclamation," http://en.wikipedia.org/wiki/Emancipation_proclamation (accessed July 31, 2011).

2. Wikipedia.org, "United States Declaration of Independence," http://en.wikipedia.org/wiki/United_States_Declaration_of_Independence (accessed July 31, 2011).

3. Wikipedia.org, "Berlin Decree," http://en.wikipedia.org/wiki/Berlin_Decree (accessed July 31, 2011).

4. Wikipedia.org, "Milan Decree," http://en.wikipedia.org/wiki/Milan_decree (accessed July 31, 2011).

5. *Webster's New World College Dictionary*, 4th ed., s.v. "prophesy."

6. Jane Hamon, *The Cyrus Decree* (Santa Rosa Beach, FL: Christian International Ministries Network, 2001), 89–90.

7. *Webster's New World College Dictionary*, 4th ed., s.v. "decree."

8. *BBCNews.com*, "Chavez Gets Sweeping New Powers," January 31, 2007, http://news.bbc.co.uk/2/hi/americas/6315819.stm (accessed July 31, 2011).

9. *Webster's New World College Dictionary*, 4th ed., s.v. "law."

10. Ibid., s.v. "decree."

11. C. Peter Wagner, *Wrestling With Alligators, Prophets, and Theologians* (Ventura, CA: Regal Books, 2010), 242–243.

Chapter 9

DIVINE STRATEGY: HOW TO PRAY FOR EACH MOUNTAIN

PROVERBS 24:5–6 SAYS, "A wise man is strong, and a man of knowledge increases power. For by wise guidance you will wage war, and in abundance of counselors there is victory." I love the way *The Message* paraphrases these verses: "It's better to be wise than strong; intelligence outranks muscle any day. *Strategic planning is the key to warfare*; to win, you need a lot of good counsel" (emphasis added).

Ask an experienced sports coach, business leader, or army general which is more valuable—strength or strategy—and he will likely agree that strategy wins out any day of the week. A professional football team can have the greatest athletes in history and yet never win if it does not have a strategy. Likewise, an army is destined for defeat if its leaders send soldiers to war without a plan. Strategy is essential.

One of the reasons prayer warriors can feel tired, drained, or even defeated after times of intercession is because they fail to ask God for a plan beforehand. Instead of being tactical in their approach, they subconsciously believe that just showing up is good enough. The result is a "wing it in the spirit," anything-goes time of prayer. Though the Holy Spirit may lead us to pray this way on occasion, that is rarely the case when confronting the powers of darkness that rule the Seven Mountains. Satan has already declared war, and whether we believe this and approach our prayer life accordingly does not matter to him—he will remain in an attack mode regardless. If our prayer times often feel like we have gone twelve rounds with a heavyweight, it's because the enemy of our soul does not stop swinging. And when we enter the ring without a strategy, we might as well be standing with a "Hit me" sign on our forehead, waiting for yet another knockout punch.

Rather than allowing ourselves to be routinely beaten, we must understand the importance of receiving God's strategy as we intercede for kingdom advancement on each of the cultural mountains. It is no wonder why demonic forces attack us so heavily when we pray for a specific mountain. If we are praying with the Holy Spirit's *dunamis* power (forceful, miracle-working, dynamite power), then we are, after all, announcing Satan's defeat and reclaiming the territory. He will not go down without a fight, and that is precisely why we must have a plan of attack that is heaven-sent.

CONSULTING WITH GOD

Every mountain is unique and therefore must be approached differently. As Peter Wagner teaches, each mountain has a distinct culture, language, and rule book. Just as we have learned the importance of speaking the unique language of each mountain, we need to recognize that every mountain requires a unique strategy. King David discovered this almost immediately after he was anointed king over Israel. In 1 Chronicles 14 we find the Philistines trying to spoil David's inauguration party. As soon as they heard about the new king on the block, they attempted a raid at the Valley of Rephaim. Given their previous success against Saul, Saul's family, and a segment of the Israeli troops, the Philistines likely believed this would be a walk in the park. There was one major difference, however: unlike Saul, David sought the Lord.

Going to God in wartime was not an uncommon thing for Israel. Throughout the Old Testament we find God's people consulting with Him before a particular battle (see 2 Chronicles 11:1–4; 18:1–34; 20:1–30; 25:5–13; 32:1–22; 1 Kings 20:13–34; 22:2–38; 2 Kings 3:4–27; 18:17–19:37). Prior to David, however, this had always been done through the prophets, and Saul had repeatedly (and foolishly) acted without considering God's direction. Now we find David showcasing his unique calling as prophet, priest, and warrior-king, yet with all the humility that made him "a man after [God's] own heart" (1 Sam. 13:14). David was not about to presume certain victory and asked the Lord if he should face off against Israel's notorious adversary.

"Go up," the Lord said, "for I will give them into your hand" (1 Chron. 14:10).

Don't you wish every battle with the enemy were that easy? Believe it or not, some contests *are* that simple, and yet most of the time we fail to seek God's instructions—or even approval to engage in battle—prior to a showdown with the enemy of our souls.

Israel's victory could have easily given David a big head. He was a newly appointed king, and already in his first official battle he had topped Saul's efforts to defeat his nation's primary foe. Yet David learned his lesson well and took the same approach the second time, coming to God on his knees *first* before running into battle with swords swinging. He had spent enough intimate time with God on the back-side of a mountain, worshiping His Creator and learning the sound of His whispers—and had not forgotten this as he ascended through the ranks—that he knew any move without God's guidance was pointless. He was unwilling to risk the lives of his men in battle if the Lord had not first instructed him to fight.

I imagine David was not surprised, then, when God gave him a completely different strategy the second time he asked about fighting the Philistines, who were once again on the attack: "David inquired again of God, and God said to him, 'You shall not go up after them; circle around behind them and come at them in front of the balsam trees. It shall be when you hear the sound of marching in the tops of the balsam trees, then you shall go out to battle, for God will have gone out before you to strike the army of the Philistines'" (vv. 14–15).

Talk about a crazy battle plan! It made no sense in the natural to "circle around" the Philistine army in what was a potentially dangerous move to avoid engagement. Yet the reason is apparent with God's instructions to wait for a specific supernatural sound. The Lord's strategy, as unique as it was in this case, highlighted a common theme throughout Israel's warfare that proved their God went before them in every fight. *He* would war on their behalf; it would not be by their strength that battles were won.

We fight the same battles in intercession against an enemy that is even more ruthless and relentless in pursuing us. Yet God is our sword and shield, our offense and defense. *He* fights for *us*, not the other way around. Too many prayer warriors forget this as they launch into solo attacks against the enemy. I am not suggesting intercessors are never to take an offensive position; we most definitely must! (We have played defense far too long.) However, we can never forget it is "not by might nor by power," nor is it by our proclamations, our declarations, our decrees, our words, or our *anything* that victory comes (Zech. 4:6). God not only fights for us, He secures the victory.

CONFRONTING THE ENEMY WITH GOD'S WORDS

The key, then, is to model David's actions. We must press into God before every encounter with the enemy, seeking His counsel, guidance, and strategy for warfare. Hundreds of years after David, Jesus replicated this in His showdown in the desert with Satan. Rather than giving the devil a piece of His mind after Satan attempted to entice Him, Christ relied on His Father's already mapped-out strategy found in the Word.

When "the tempter came and said to Him, 'If You are the Son of God, command that these stones become bread,'" Jesus spoke the Word (Matt. 4:3). When the enemy asked Christ to throw Himself off a cliff—even using Scripture to justify calling down angels to rescue Him—Jesus spoke the Word. And when Satan promised Him the world in exchange for one weak moment of adulation, Jesus spoke the Word.

Often the Word *is* our strategy; sometimes it is a combination of Scripture and other words the Holy Spirit gives us. Other times it is a specific prayer language that sends a dagger to the enemy's heart. Whatever the case, in every instance, our task is to do just as Jesus did and consult with the Father first. I have no doubt that as Satan mustered up his best shot at the imminent Savior, Jesus was conferring with His Father about each answer He was to offer in defense. Each temptation required a unique response delivered straight from heaven. Stated another way, each attack from the enemy required a different weapon. It is important to use the appropriate weapon for the battle at hand, the weapon that will get the task done without destroying other things. For example, you would not use an M-16 to kill a mouse or a hammer to kill a fly. Likewise, we must listen carefully to the Father's instructions for what weapon we should use so that we inflict damage only on our target.

As we encounter the enemies upon each of the Seven Mountains, we must remain in a posture of having our spiritual ears tuned into heaven's channel. In Genesis 1:28, we see that the Lord has given us the "Seven Mountain Mandate" to take dominion; this is our authoritative order from God. Yet we must not only have strategy to follow through with this order, we must also recognize that our ultimate Commander is ready and willing to provide us with this strategy.

In my years of personally interceding for these cultural spheres and leading others in a similar prayer journey, I have discovered a few recurring elements of strategy that the Lord continues to provide for each mountain. The prayer points that follow in this chapter have come through years of experience, including specific points gleaned from a key prayer gathering with Aglow International at the Capitol building in 2008. More importantly, these points target specific areas upon the ascending landscape where the kingdom can advance through the strategic words of God's chosen warriors—us!

RELIGION MOUNTAIN

Presently, the religious spirit dominates the Religion Mountain. I believe 2 Chronicles 20:6–12 is an anthem of prayer for those called to invade the mountain of religion with intercession. Jehoshaphat's entire prayer is remarkable and inspiring, yet verse 9 is worthy of highlighting in this context: "Should evil come upon us, the sword, or judgment, or pestilence, or famine, we will stand before this house and before You (for Your name is in this house) and cry to You in our distress, and *You will hear and deliver us*" (emphasis added).

The "house" Jehoshaphat referred to then was a physical temple, and we know through Christ we have become the living temple of God. Yet when we pray for the Religion Mountain, we are praying for the specific community that assembles to worship—which is essentially the gathering at the temple. The Religion Mountain is more than the temple or building; it is any gathering of people who worship God, Allah, Buddha, Satan, or Shiva. The war in the heavens has always been over *who* will be worshiped. Almost three thousand years after the king of Judah lived, we stand in a similar place as he did when he uttered those words: on the brink of war with a fast-approaching enemy, declaring with assurance the faithfulness of God. With that stance in mind, here are the specific points we can pray:

❖ *Pray believers upon the Religion Mountain will reflect Christ.* Christians are not the only ones on this mountain; there is an assortment of religions and spiritual views represented. This wide spectrum includes everything from Wiccan covens to Satanists, Pantheists, or those who practice the occult. We can pray in a spirit of love for all. Christians who model their Savior will reveal the one true God above every other religious idol.

❖ *Pray those upon the mountain—believers and non-believers—will worship the one true God in spirit and truth, and with passion.* Many upon the mountain of religion know from an intellectual standpoint how to go through the motions of worship, but they are devoid of passion. Their worship is full of routine and ritual, and they have completely divorced themselves from a heartfelt, genuine expression of adoration toward

God. Just as we spoke of Ezekiel prophetically proclaiming life over dry bones in the last chapter, here we have the opportunity to declare the same life over those worshipers on the mountain. We can call forth a renewed passion for God in these believers. Author Graham Cooke describes this passion as "the most intimidating thing to the enemy."[1] Indeed, it isn't our intercessory war cries that he fears most, but instead our intimate love relationship with Jesus. Because of this, we should also pray fervently for the following points.

❖ *Pray believers on the mountain will pray out of an intimate, living relationship with Jesus.* As Cooke also says, it is time "to stop praying like a widow and start to pray like a bride."[2] We must stop acting like our husband has left us alone to die a long, painful death. We can toss aside our black garments of mourning and instead embrace the reality that Jesus awaits a vibrant, beautiful bride—His church. Just as Ruth went from being a helpless widow to the adored bride of Boaz, we have been chosen by our Kinsman Redeemer. Yes, we are still in the preparation stage for when our Groom comes, but we are still His *bride.* Let's start talking to Him like we are!

❖ *Declare those upon the mountain will rise up in prayer and overcome the religious spirit.* In chapter 5 we identified one of Satan's most powerful tactics for keeping believers from ascending the cultural mountains. The religious spirit rules this mountain with tremendous power, and it will take a unified, praying people to overcome the strongholds already established by the enemy. These spiritual fortresses exist not only in general culture but also within the church, proving just how deeply the religious spirit has infiltrated the armies of God. By praying as one voice, we can expose this spirit with the truth and demolish the work of the enemy.

❖ *Pray God will eliminate religious rituals.* In Mark 11:15–19, Jesus cleansed the temple of God, driving out the moneymakers and moneychangers who were cheapening God's holy house. I believe intercessors must pursue a similar cleansing within the church—God's living temple— through their prayers. Only this time, the ones devaluing the house aren't businesspeople but those who insist on keeping a religious spirit alive through lifeless rituals. Most rituals started with good intentions and pure hearts. Within Christendom, we have wonderful rituals that were created for powerful worship but have become stale icons. While we pray against the overriding religious spirit, let us also pray that God cleanses His temple once again of those idols that have replaced Him.

❖ *Pray the Holy Spirit will stir up a passion for the Word within every person on the mountain.* Herrnhut, Germany, is known as the center of the worldwide Moravian Church founded by Count Nikolaus Ludwig von Zinzendorf. For more than a hundred years, the Moravian community at Herrnhut prayed twenty-four hours a day, seven days a week, and established a culture unlike any seen on earth since. The "Moravian Pentecost," as this longstanding renewal is often called, fostered a sense that God's Word was integrated into every facet of life.

I visited Herrnhut years ago and was amazed as I walked through the Moravians' famous burial grounds called God's Acre. Rather than the usual cemetery filled with tombstones memorializing people's lives and accomplishments, I saw row upon row of massive markers (still tombstones) engraved with the plan of salvation. There were no "Here lies Joseph Schmidt and this is what he did" epitaphs, but instead carvings of scriptures about healing, God's faithfulness, Christ's love, and other glorious proclamations. Every aisle featured another awe-inspiring aspect of God. The scene was so powerful, I wanted to get saved all over again after walking through it!

Several generations after the Moravian Pentecost, my spiritual grand-father, a German preacher named Werner Morgenstern, founded count-less underground churches during the communist rule of the former East Germany. He was a powerful minister who traveled the country teaching the Word. Yet amazingly, he rarely preached with a Bible present because the government did not allow Bibles. He had God's Word within him. I believe—and have heard similar cases that verify this—that the Word lived powerfully within my spiritual grandfather as a direct result of the spiritual seeds sown by Zinzendorf and the Moravian community.

When nonstop prayer, steeped in Scripture, is offered for more than a century from a single area of the world, I doubt there is much the enemy can do to suppress the spiritual harvest produced generation after generation from such fertile soil. Regardless of how much control Satan has over the Religion Mountain at this point, we can create rich soil in the land and, through intercession, plant seeds that cry out for a passion for God's Word in both this generation and those to come.

❖ *Pray believers on the Religion Mountain will have a strong presence upon the other six mountains.* Those who rule the Religion Mountain have profound influence within the other cultural spheres. Pray that the key leaders upon these other mountains would be forced to give attention to the rising tide of empowered, Spirit-led believers.

FAMILY MOUNTAIN

In an era of soccer moms, little-league dads, and tiara-queen toddlers, many people believe American culture has become more child-centric than ever. If this shift is legitimate, however, it is failing to yield good fruit for nourishing the family structure. Families have never been as fragmented as they are today, and our modern cultural progression— or digression, in most cases—continues to wear away at the core unit of society. Focus on the Family recently identified at least five major threats every family faces in our current culture:

1. Changing definitions of family

2. Increasing child vulnerability

3. Diminishing parental influence and authority

4. Growing financial pressures

5. Diminishing family intimacy[3]

These are five specific shifts intercessors can pray against as they use their words to shield families from the enemy's continuous onslaught. Yet there are other prayer points we must hold up in the spirit.

❖ *Declare marriage will remain the foundation of the family unit.* This seems basic enough, yet it is no secret that the enemy has released a full-fledged, multifrontal assault against the institution of marriage.

❖ *Pray marriages are restored.* This involves praying for healing in marriages fractured by affairs, alcoholism, pornography, drug addictions, and other vices the enemy uses to tear husbands and wives apart. We must intercede against the spirit of abuse and violence that has established such a stronghold in enough households that it affects a quarter of all women in the United States.[4] As intercessors, we can stand in the gap for those who have no hope of mending the breaches in their marriage. God is certainly powerful enough to overcome whatever damage and destruction Satan has managed to cause. But in addition to the relational attacks the enemy brings, we must also be on the offensive against the demonic shift in legal courtrooms that are attempting to change the very meaning of the word *marriage*. Whoever controls the language controls the culture. And today, more than ever, it is crucial that we pray for the term to be restored to its original intent: the union of a man and a woman.

❖ *Declare the Family Mountain will stand for life.* It is not just believers who need to be pro-life. Our entire culture's future depends on how well we defend the unborn. If we continue on our current path of not only allowing abortion but actually having a governmental system that supports it, we will end up as other nations have when the next generation is killed off before ever having a voice. Most Americans know about China's population control policy that resulted in families killing or abandoning millions of baby girls. In that culture, it was a case of families wanting a son for honor; in our culture, it has become a matter of convenience. The spirit of abortion is an immense demonic force, rooted in the practice of child sacrifice to Molech (see Leviticus 18:21), which intercessors must wage war against and destroy.

Prior to the 2008 national elections, I discovered a statement on a Catholic website that I found particularly prophetic in its call for those on the Family Mountain: "The family must be strengthened, not redefined. Human life is paramount from conception to natural death. Now, more than any time in history, a new generation must stand for truth. The strength of our nation is not only in its military or economic power, but in our commitment to moral values for the good of the world. We can protect the values that this great nation was built on: life, faith and family."[5]

❖ *Pray parents would step up as the authority in the home and would model godly behavior.* If there has been a cultural shift with the family structure now revolving around children, it can be pinpointed to this aspect. When parents are passive, they fail to establish the boundaries necessary for healthy growth in their children. The result is a child-centric, child-dominated household where parents rarely reflect God's model of family leadership. Sadly, many parents today have abdicated their authority to the Education Mountain and the Religion Mountain, expecting those upon these mountains to raise their children for them. We must pray for fathers to be proactive in leading their families not only in words, but also in actions such as scheduling family times together. And we must pray for mothers to understand how to partner with their husbands in establishing a healthy, nurturing environment. Parents are often the most prominent mirrors of God in their children's lives; they need our intercession to not only reflect an image of Christlikeness, but to train their children to succeed in life by embracing godly values. Remember, parents are usually the main encouragement children receive to pursue their destiny upon any of the Seven Mountains.

❖ *Renounce family curses from previous generations and release blessings upon the next generation.* Generational curses and blessings are not magic spells found in fairy tales; they are real and more common than most people realize. I am living proof of this. I was not raised as a born-again Christian. In fact, I was the first person in one hundred fifty years on my father's side of the family to accept Jesus as my Lord and Savior. But my great-great-great grandmother, a circuit-riding Quaker preacher during the Civil War, laid a prophetic foundation of prayer for our family line, and I believe I am the direct fruit of her labor in the spirit.

I am blessed today to have her handwritten prayer journal, where page after page is filled with evidence of the same calling I have on my life. Penned on one page in particular is the following: "It hath been much on my mind for several years past to leave some memorandums of my life particular to my children and grandchildren, and now in the forty-ninth year of my age the impression seems so strong that I believe it not safe to put it off much longer. Although feeling unable to preserve much of a diary as my education is very limited, but He who has promised to be a present help in the needful time (Ps. 46:1) will fulfill His promise to all those who obey Him."[6]

I am a living answer to this woman's faithful prayers. Yet I recently saw a different side to generational blessings and curses as I watched a spirit of rebellion try to reemerge within my family. My coming to Christ pushed back this spirit that had reigned in our family for more than one hundred fifty years. But while in her early twenties, my own daughter began to walk away from the Lord, and in her teenage years my granddaughter entered into even further rebellion. In both situations, I prayed and prayed, but it wasn't until recently that I fully understood what was occurring. One day, while listening to John Eckhardt speak at a conference, I suddenly heard these words: "There is such a thing as an anniversary demon, and this is a demon that shows up in generations or in times."

I immediately walked out of the meeting, called my granddaughter, and began proclaiming the truth. I wasn't just speaking to her but to the demons and angels warring over her future—and I told her so. I reminded the opposition that, unlike my great-great-great grandmother, I knew how to engage in war for my own granddaughter—and that she *would* preach, she *would* pray, she *would* prophecy, and she *would* go to the nations. After my intense words, she offered a short response and we hung up.

Her rebellion did not immediately end there. Six months later, on the brink of graduating from high school, she still had not decided what to do once she finished school. As I continued to pray against the rebellious spirit that remained, God instructed me to "offer her the nations." I called her and offered her a paying job to travel around the world with me—and to sweeten the deal, reminded her that my first trip was to Paris. For the next year and a half, my granddaughter didn't just travel the world, she preached, prayed, prophesied, and was used by God to bring healing to people everywhere. Today she is a different person, and I believe that is partly because I knew how to war against a generational curse that attempted to rear its ugly head.

❖ *Pray Christian families will recognize how to engage in spiritual warfare.* It is time for us to take up the same call that Nehemiah gave almost 2,500 years ago: "When I saw their fear, I rose and spoke to the nobles, the officials and the rest of the people: 'Do not be afraid of them; remember the Lord who is great and awesome, and *fight for your brothers, your sons, your daughters, your wives and your houses*'" (Neh. 4:14, emphasis added). Make no mistake: Satan is out to destroy as many families as he can—yours and mine included. We must recognize how to combat his assault in the spirit and natural realms with intercession.

EDUCATION MOUNTAIN

The first textbook published in America was called *The New England Primer.* Originally printed in Boston around 1690, this first-grade-level textbook served for more than two hundred years as the introductory guidebook for students learning to read. Its pages were divided into three main sections: the "Rhyming Alphabet," the "Alphabet of Lessons for Youth," and the "Shorter Catechism." In the first two, each letter was matched to either a Bible-based memory marker (A—In Adam's fall, we sinned all; B—Heaven to find, the Bible mind) or direct scripture (C—"Come unto me, all ye that labor and are heavy laden, and I will give you rest"—Matthew 11:28). The final section, intended to improve students' vocabulary, could have passed for a Bible quiz: "What is *required* in the fifth commandment?" "What is *forbidden* in the fifth commandment?" "What is the reason *annexed* to the fifth commandment?"[7]

Imagine a politician even *attempting* to place such a textbook in today's public schools! Clearly, we are light years away from the Bible-based education system our nation originally used. Given that sober fact, here are some key prayer points to use as we intercede for the Education Mountain:

❖ *Pray educators will teach knowledge and truth that is applied with wisdom.* We have more information in this day than any time in history, and yet our own knowledge has incrementally given rise to more problems. Feeding students more information is not necessarily the answer; they must have the tools to process that information correctly and discern right from wrong. Today *truth* is taught as a relative term; yet through warring in prayer, intercessors can push back the enemy's attempts to deceive. We must call upon God for His solution. God often gives us words of knowledge, which is information we would have no way of knowing in the natural. Yet it is wisdom that decides what we should do with the knowledge we have. To thwart the enemy's schemes, we must pray for a spirit of wisdom for those who teach.

❖ *Pray educators will teach the truth about God.* As Christians, we believe all truth derives from God, who is truth Himself. Yet as our education system now proves, it is possible to teach facts without ever revealing the ultimate source of those facts. To take this a step further, we now make it illegal to actually reveal God as that ultimate source. Although it seems our country has digressed to irreversible proportions, we must pray for the Light to be revealed even in the darkness of our current education system. As our nation spirals out of control in its political correctness and moral relativity, more students will search for something they can hold on to—a truth that lasts. We must pray for open doors to reveal God as the ultimate truth and for opportunities to display Him as who He says He is rather than what the general public thinks of Him.

❖ *Pray educators will teach the full view of creation.* The evolutionary battle has been raging for more than eight decades, yet it is as fierce today as it was twenty years ago. Changing the term to "intelligent design" does not solve the problem of teachers being prohibited from stating biblical truth. We must pray for the veil to be removed from the eyes of those who govern the education system.

❖ *Pray educators will impart destiny and purpose.* About 70 percent of high school students in the United States graduate on time, while a whopping 1.2 million drop out each year. In seventeen of the nation's fifty largest cities, the graduation rate dips below 50 percent—including Detroit, where a mere one out of four students in the public school system graduates.[8] Even among those who earn a diploma and go on to college, most enter their higher education clueless as to what major to pick or what field to enter. Obviously, not everyone knows what career path he wants to choose by the time he is eighteen years old. Yet the fact that this is the norm reflects an overall lack of destiny and purpose among students.

Teachers can change that, but they need our help in fighting the spiritual battle. Countless students already hear enough doubt, criticism, and negativity from disbelieving parents and friends; the classroom can be the lone environment in which these children and young adults can be encouraged, challenged for good, and shaped for a bright future. We must pray for an atmosphere of receptivity and openness among students and for educators to have the wisdom and discernment to speak into students' hearts rather than just their heads.

❖ *Pray parents will take authority over what their children are taught.* Our nation's education system is not a babysitting service, yet many parents treat it as if it were and stay uninvolved with what their children learn. Others take a more active role yet throw up the white flag when it comes to challenging the hidden agendas of school and city educational boards. Neither is the right solution.

In our local public elementary school, for example, my grandchildren are being taught moral ethics in the classroom, while their parents are expected to teach them ABCs and math at home. When my daughter confronted the school's teachers and administrators, she was told that the education system's first priority was to teach morals and values and that parents were responsible for making sure their children learned the curriculum at home. It is time for parents to resist abdicating their responsibilities and to stand up and confront the lies being taught in the classroom. Yet for their objections to make a difference, they must first win the battle in the heavens.

GOVERNMENT MOUNTAIN

The call to prayer for the Government Mountain is the continual responsibility for all Christians, not only intercessors. Paul, the apostle, challenges us:

> First of all, then, I urge that entreaties and prayers, petitions and thanksgivings, be made on behalf of all men, for kings and all who are in authority, in order that we may lead a tranquil and quiet life in all godliness and dignity. This is good and acceptable in the sight of God our Savior, who desires all men to be saved and to come to the knowledge of the truth.
> —1 TIMOTHY 2:1–4, NAS

There is a clear connection between praying for those in authority, praying for their salvation and coming to the knowledge of truth. This is an important key to governmental intercession. Truth in government often seems very difficult to discern among elected leaders *inside* the government and even more difficult to discern from the *outside*, especially when the media is added to the mix. Every major political issue at its root is about discerning truth and having the character to make a righteous decision. When the body of Christ gets unified in this, it will have a very significant impact on the civil governments of nations.

The government of the United States has three branches: legislative, judicial, and executive. We are in a season in which the division within and among those three branches runs deep. Despite a Democratic majority, a Democratic president, and the usual political rhetoric of working "across partisan lines," unity and truth are severely lacking. With that in mind, intercessors can focus on the following key points of prayer.

❖ *Declare a holy alignment of the nation's civil laws to God's laws.* Despite today's dangerous reinterpretations of history taught in classrooms nationwide, our country *was* founded upon biblical principles. Our laws originated from scriptural standards fleshed out through human vessels. We are currently seeing a government bent on leaning further away from these standards, and that alone is reason for concern. Can believers stem the tide? I believe so, as Scripture proves repeatedly that God always preserves a remnant. (See Romans 9:27.) Yet 2 Kings 19:4 prophetically calls us to a specific task for the day: "Offer a prayer for the remnant that is left."

In chapter 3, I mentioned the profound impact William Wilberforce had on history simply by being a "remnant" intercessor. Elected to the British Parliament at age twenty-one, Wilberforce had a divine destiny to end the slave trade that ran rampant in the British Empire. He had such a profound encounter with God that he considered a life of ministry, but a mentor convinced him that he could do far greater works in Parliament than in the pulpit. Wilberforce returned to politics and gathered a remnant who sought God on how to take up the fight to outlaw slavery. Over the next twenty years, he persistently took on the English government and, after decades of fighting, eventually persuaded those in power to end the inhumane trade of slavery.

Intercessors, like Wilberforce, let's *be* the remnant that stands on behalf of God's truth and prays that there is perfect alignment with the laws of heaven and those of our country.

❖ *Pray government officials will tremble at God's Word and walk in the fear of the Lord.* To have such an alignment between heaven and earth requires an alignment of hearts between God and His creation. Many politicians today offer lip service to God because crediting the Creator still remains a patriotic stance (thank God this is still the case). Yet few truly know Him as He is—and their lack of holy fear shows with every self-serving political maneuver. We must press in through prayer to contend for the souls of our elected officials, recognizing their need to honor God's Word as truth and the Lord as our country's ultimate King. Jesus spoke of our posture toward the rulers of the day, and Paul echoed His sentiment in 1 Timothy 2:1–4.

❖ *Pray God will raise governmental apostolic prayer teams.* It takes a government to displace a government. Apostolic intercessory teams have a vital role in forming the kingdom government structures. The objective of displacing government structures cannot be accomplished without the combined anointings of apostles, prophets, and intercessors, among other spiritual gifts, working together on apostolic teams. These teams are now forming to help propel those who have been called by God to occupy the seats of government, and to govern righteously after they are elected or in some cases appointed. Too often, the church has been tripped up by the "divide and conquer" strategy of the religious spirit, aided by the media. Apostles are called to set things in order. Many times they can help unify intercessors to pray God's will in situations. It is important to remember those who serve on the local school board and city council are often future members of the state legislature, governors, and congress.

❖ *Pray our political leaders will guide with wisdom, revelation, and truth.* This is particularly apt for the judges who preside in courts throughout our country. We have seen a dramatic rise within the judicial ranks of activist judges who legislate from the bench and impose their own will rather than ruling with justice. This is not a Republican or Democrat issue, nor is it about liberals or conservatives; it is about leaders—judges, politicians, city council representatives, state officials—listening to the Holy Spirit for divine wisdom, revelation, and truth. Receiving direction from any other source eventually leads to chaos, which is why we must specifically pray for wisdom at the gates (see Proverbs 8). Indeed, God's spirit of wisdom stands "beside the gates, at the opening to the city, at the entrance of the doors" (v. 3). It is available to all, yet we must pray that the hearts of our political leaders will be soft enough to welcome such divine input. Prayer for the government should almost always be focused on praying for the person and against the spiritual forces which oppose God's kingdom. This is a major key of governmental intercession. As the Holy Spirit continues to unfold the full revelation of 1 Timothy 2 to the body of Christ, we will get beyond the blurred line between praying against ungodly policy and for the governmental official.

❖ *Release a spirit of justice in the land as the armies of heaven restrain evil.* As we learned in the last chapter, our proclamations, declarations, and decrees enact heavenly principles. God is a God of justice, and as His earthly representatives we have been empowered to enforce His justice. Because of the fallen nature of our surrounding world, we must take command over the demonic spirits that cause decay and deterioration where God would desire revival and restoration. By aligning with God's Word over the territories of this earth, we can intercede with power and release justice wherever we go. Though this will not be an overnight victory, we must know that with every prayer we offer, we are sending armies of angels to take action against the hordes of hell.

MEDIA MOUNTAIN

If you think your local television news coverage is saturated with reports of murders, kidnappings, shootings, traffic accidents, domestic disputes, and other negative news, you are not alone. A nationwide study of audiences' responses to local coverage found the majority of people believe local newscasts are too negative. "You get slammed every day with all the bad stuff," said one survey respondent. "Everything is negative, negative, negative....We don't want to spend an hour just listening to everything that's bad."[9]

The problem is not necessarily stations reporting negative news—obviously, bad things happen that are worth reporting—but instead the media's general failure to present the *entire* truth. As a result, the average American carries a sense that he is being inundated with negativity whenever he turns on the television or picks up a newspaper. And this tide of coverage is not going unnoticed. "If you project a presence of doom and gloom on a constant daily basis, then it's going to have a profound effect on people's psyches," remarked one keen participant in the study. "The negativity is impacting our children and how they're growing up."[10]

Sadly, the media's lack of holistic reporting has already made a mark on generations who are now conditioned to distrust any news report. As intercessors, we can pray for a restoration of truth in the Media Mountain as we lift up the following key points.

❖ *Pray those on the Media Mountain will report the truth with integrity and without exaggerating the facts.* A mere 29 percent of Americans believe that news organizations get their facts straight, while almost two-thirds believe these media outlets frequently offer inaccurate reports. This lack of confidence in the media—which, according to a recent Pew Research study, marks a twenty-five-year low—translates to an increase in relativistic thinking: *If I didn't see or hear it happen, then it didn't happen, because it seems I can't trust anyone to give me the truth these days.*[11] As the lines of what is presented as truth continue to be blurred, so do the morals and values of the land. Unfortunately, rather than being concerned about upholding the truth in every situation, news outlets today often fall into the temptation of reporting what generates buzz and increases ratings. Thus, we get a steady stream of titillation and sensationalism—yellow journalism—instead of truth. When truth is not reported accurately, it releases confusion among listeners, readers, and viewers. We must therefore pray against the spirits of deception, confusion, and manipulation, while declaring in the spirit that God's eternal truth will not only reign, but that it will be trumpeted by the media throughout the land.

❖ *Pray those shaping media coverage will report both the good news and the Good News.* Since the economic recession began in late 2007, I have seen an unusual number of news reports highlighting churches and ministries that have helped those in need. From offering seminars on financial planning to job placement to food pantries, these churches stood out because they signified hope in a time dominated by fear. And because their light shone in such direct contrast with today's prevailing darkness and uncertainty, members of these churches were given free reign to boldly declare the gospel within these secular reports. I believe we as intercessors can decide whether this is just a fleeting trend or a shift in how the media views believers. As we stand in the gap on behalf of those who lead and shape the media, let's press in for the Good News to be declared more frequently and in even bolder terms.

❖ *Denounce information that is reported through the lens of evil.* The primary tactic Satan, as the "prince of the power of the air" (Eph. 2:2), uses to create fear, disunity, and dissension is to distort the airwaves of communication. He thrives on using his tools of miscommunication and misunderstanding, and in recent generations he has increasingly used the media to accomplish his purposes. We must denounce every hidden agenda within the industry that has opened doors for demonic activity to propagate lies and deceit. Truth will always be distorted when told through the lens of evil. Those who have been called by God to stand on the Media Mountain battle this every day. As we clear the atmosphere through our intercession, let's proclaim that media outlets will no longer spread Satan's deceptive viewpoint, but instead that God's truth will be the only lens through which reporters view their stories.

❖ *Call for the voices of righteousness and truth that have not been heard.* Just as Ezekiel called forth life from a dead environment, we must call out those whom God has appointed to declare His character upon a mountain that has been ruled by the forces of evil. These believers are strategically positioned and awaiting their appointed time to raise their voices and be heard, yet it is our role as intercessors to clear the path in the spirit and declare this as their *kairos* (perfect opportune) moment. There are reporters, news anchors, radio and television announcers, columnists, editors, and bloggers who have the Spirit of God residing within them and are prepared to declare the truth, yet their voices have been silenced until now. We need to call them forth! Remember, whoever controls the language controls the culture.

Arts and Entertainment Mountain

In 2004, Hollywood discovered evangelical Christians. When Mel Gibson's *The Passion of the Christ* surprised the entire movie industry by earning a staggering $370 million stateside (the fifteenth-highest domestic earnings in history), suddenly Hollywood found out that born-again believers actually *like* going to the theater and will show up in droves when a movie's values and content don't contradict or compromise our beliefs.[12] Obviously, moviemakers have known about godly values since the beginning of film, which explains the dozens of epics based on Bible stories. But as Western culture has entered into postmodern thought, biblical values have been completely ignored, replaced by "edgier" (read: seedier) and "more artistic" (read: gratuitously graphic) depictions of everyday life not only onscreen, but throughout the arts. Only in recent years has the Christian entertainment industry (movies, music, publishing, etc.) come even remotely close to matching the production standards of the secular entertainment arena—and we still have far to go.

Christians have been working in Hollywood for decades trying to make a difference. I believe it has taken this long for those believers not on the Arts and Entertainment Mountain to wake up and realize the significance of this cultural sphere. Culture is not only *reflected* by its arts and entertainment, it is *shaped* by them. Today, sports dominate our society; the sports industry is worth *$422 billion* in 2011.[13] And although statistics blend media and entertainment earnings together, Americans spent a whopping $1.092 trillion on the combined forms in 2010.[14]

Diane Wigstone, Director of YWAM Hollywood, and author of the book *Hope for Hollywood: Reclaiming the Soul of Film & TV,* shared with me, "The main battle in Hollywood is worship. Who will you worship? Will you worship the latest star or Director/Producer who can 'make your career'? Will you worship yourself? Or, will you worship Jesus? Worship in Hollywood is often about how people make decisions about their time. Do they spend their time in ways that will advance the kingdom of God, or to advance their career and *their* kingdom?"

Diane continues, "What it takes to be 'successful' in Hollywood often causes those hoping to make a difference for God to feel they have no option but to compromise. The evil spiritual forces in Hollywood are overwhelming. Spirits of seduction, greed, and fame—what I often refer to as the 3G's: Guys/Girls, Gold, and Glory—are all front and center in Hollywood. Not to mention the 'independent spirit' of "I will make my career happen for me"—instead of relying on God to 'make something happen.'"

It is impossible to say that arts and entertainment are not setting the standards for our culture—the proof is in the numbers. This is a key mountain that the Lord desires to reclaim through His kingdom ambassadors. Given that, those called to intercede for this mountain should pray specifically for the following.

❖ *Pray believers called to this mountain will overcome darkness with the Light.* Second Corinthians 4:6 says, "For God, who said, 'Light shall shine out of darkness,' is the One who has shone in our hearts to give the Light of the knowledge of the glory of God in the face of Christ." Through prayer we can empower those in the entertainment industry to shine the Light of the Holy Spirit within them and reflect the glory of God that casts out every hint of darkness.

"Many Christians come to Hollywood to make a difference," Diane Wigstone shared. "At first they are focused on trying to be excellent, and do well. Which is great! We want to be the best we can be! Yet, soon many are seduced by all that is here, and they are trying to become famous or wealthy so that *then* they can make a stand for the Kingdom of God. However, the compromises made as they 'climb the ladder' actually disqualify them from their original goal. Many become so much like the culture around them, they no longer have a platform of godliness, holiness and purity to stand on. It is the age old battle for popularity and to 'fit in.' Incorrectly thinking that you must be popular (fame) and successful for others to listen to what you have to say. It's hard to stay holy when you feel that you must attend all the industry 'parties' and be seen with 'all the right people.' That would be my biggest prayer request for Christians in the entertainment industry, that they would have the strength, courage and resilience to stand firm in their faith, and to pray that they would not be seduced by the spirits that attack them in the entertainment industry."

"The enemy often wins the battle one small compromise at a time," Diane continued. "It takes great courage to maintain holiness, purity, humility and simplicity when surrounded by sensuality, pride, great wealth and greed and the independent spirit that says "I'll make this happen for me.""

❖ *Pray this mountain will produce entertainment that displays godly lifestyles, behaviors, and values.* On this prayer point, we are not just warring in the Spirit for a holier mountain; we are fighting for the souls of entire generations. Children develop their worldview, learn social behaviors, and establish thought patterns and moral values based on what influences them most. Yet sadly, most parents are allowing the entertainment culture to shape their children rather than bearing the responsibility themselves. What MTV has done to mold teenagers' minds for the last twenty-nine years, Disney is now doing for the tween-and-younger crowd. Both of their influences are on display daily at schools around the country, and yet how much are God's values being projected by these global entertainment-media enterprises? Intercessors must certainly cover the overall market in prayer, yet it is *key* that we press in on behalf of the younger generations who are being influenced every day by the powerful forces on this mountain. As Diane mentioned, the spirits of seduction are strong in Hollywood. Pray for the Christians in Hollywood to stand strong and set the example for holiness, purity and righteousness.

❖ *Renounce corruption within this mountain.* This is not just financial corruption on the business side, though it exists and must be cast down in the heavenly realm. The moral decay within this mountain over the past two decades is possibly unmatched by any of the other cultural spheres during that time. What else can explain an "adult entertainment" industry that now earns more in one month than most professional sports do in an entire year? Or major television networks now allowing twice as many expletives during prime-time "family" hours as they did in 1998—with the f-word alone appearing in various forms almost 1,150 times in 2007 (compared to *once* in 1998)?[15] Obviously, we have already reached a slippery slope in the corruption of morality within secular arts and entertainment. It is essential that intercessors expose and overcome this corruption in the Spirit as we call out for redemption.

❖ *Pray believers will actively support Christ-honoring entertainment.* As in any battle, you cannot fully possess a territory until you have actually replaced those areas the enemy once inhabited. Combating Satan on the mountain of arts and entertainment begins with exposing his deceptive ways and ultimately declaring his defeat. But the battle is not finished then; we must move in and possess the territory with entertainment that lifts up the name of Jesus. Within the movie industry we have seen this in recent years with such God-honoring films as *The Passion of the Christ, Amazing Grace, End of the Spear, Facing the Giants, Fireproof,* and the *Chronicles of Narnia* series. For Christian filmmaking to improve in both production quality and overall exposure, however, requires believers' support—which in movie terms translates to theater ticket sales. Diane commented, "It also means that Christian investors must be willing to make the big investments in films that tell the truth of God. It is unrealistic to expect Christian films that have a $1 million budget to look like Hollywood films that have a $200 million budget. Until we are willing to make the investments in content that will disciple the nations, we cannot expect the production value will be able to compete with the Hollywood Studios." Other forms of entertainment need similar active reinforcement—from attending Christian events to supporting professional athletes, actors, or artists who proclaim Jesus as their Savior. It is no longer good enough for believers to talk about the need for godlier entertainment; if we want to see change, we must do something about it. That starts with supporting those who are already pioneering as foot soldiers on the mountain. On this front, we can truly intercede with our actions.

❖ *War against the outright celebration of ungodly values and the distortion of godly virtues.* The attack on God and His people is clear within the secular-run entertainment industry. Christians are either a punch line or a commodity, while God is regularly mocked or portrayed as irrelevant. When Focus on the Family sponsored a 2010 Super Bowl commercial with football star Tim Tebow and his mother, for example, those with ungodly values were up in arms. Critics distorted the Tebows' godly values, mocked them, and portrayed the family as "Jesus freaks"—all because they celebrate life.

As intercessors, we must discern the spirits and the times—choosing to love those who oppose us, while fighting in the spiritual realm. Paul's oft-quoted statement is particularly applicable for the Arts and Entertainment Mountain: "For our struggle is not against flesh and blood, but against the rulers, against the powers, against the world forces of this darkness, against the spiritual forces of wickedness in the heavenly places" (Eph. 6:12). Rather than falling prey to hating those who curse us, we can love them as Jesus called us to do, while renouncing the demonic spirit that has blinded them to the truth. When the enemy celebrates his perversion of morality and values, we must raise up the *kingdom standard* even higher and declare our Lord's righteousness over this highly contested cultural territory.

❖ *Pray for relationships and unity in the body of Christ.* "Sometimes it seems that everyone in Hollywood is trying to sell themselves," Diane shared with me. "Many are often 'pitching' their project to get their movie made, or spending time trying to convince agents and others they are the right actor/actress for the part. One of Satan's prime strategies is to wear down the saints of God. The enemy constantly applies pressure to conform that causes actors and actresses to compromise their values. Some of my acting friends have said that their whole life feels like an audition. They believe they always have to look their best, dress 'just right' and trendy, even when they are just going to the grocery store. Satan constantly assaults their spirit with this kind of pressure to conform as a way to wear out the saints of God (Dan. 7:25). It is tough to not focus on 'selling yourself' when your job is dependent on 'auditions.' Unfortunately, relationships are often formed because of 'what you can do for me.' And when you can no longer help my career, you are no longer in my life. For Christians to have success in Hollywood, we must work together, and lay aside our own projects and agenda for the kingdom's agenda." You will find this on all of the Seven Mountains, but it is especially critical in Hollywood.

BUSINESS MOUNTAIN

God knew about the stock market crash of 2008. He was not surprised by the dot-com bubble bursting or Black Monday in 1987 or the Wall

Street Crash of 1929 or even the Great Panic in 1873. Regardless of whether it is a bull market or a bear market, our God remains in control.

Too often as believers, however, we lose sight of this and succumb to the prevailing spirits of fear and panic. Worse still, we ignore the all-conquering, all-redeeming power of the Holy Spirit that allows us to soar above every economic storm. Depending on God's strength does not mean Christians in the business world will be immune to life in the red, but it provides us opportunities to shine a light of eternal hope regardless of the current financial climate. In our modern world, the language of money is universal; if your company "miraculously" thrives amid a recession, you not only stand out, but your business model undoubtedly becomes the new template for success. As sons and daughters of a God who desires to bless His children, we must recognize and seize the opportunity during such times to proclaim the goodness, faithfulness, and sovereignty of our Lord.

Satan, obviously, would like nothing better than to see every Christian upon the Business Mountain fall on his face. He does not want us to flourish amid a drought (he's well aware of the spotlight believers get when theirs is the only store on the block prospering) and will do all he can to prevent our success. This does not only apply to believers' work within the entrepreneurial world, but also in the arenas of science, medicine, and technology. Because of this clash of wills, the spiritual war we fight upon the Business Mountain is both intense and integral to every other mountain's success. Without finances, none of the other mountains can effectively grow, given today's world structure. Keep this in mind as we intercede using the following prayer points.

❖ *Call forth companies, leaders, and workers who build for the glory of God.* Kingdom construction is the only type that lasts. Although most worldly business leaders aim for the biggest short-term gains possible while hoping for long-term success, those working for God's kingdom understand they are building for eternity. As God's walking mouthpieces on this earth, we inherit the responsibility, then, to call out the laborers in the spirit so we can eventually see them rise in the natural realm. When Jesus told His disciples, "The harvest is plentiful, but the workers are few" (Matt. 9:37), I believe He was describing the condition on multiple mountains—one of which is the Business Mountain. We often interpret that verse strictly through an evangelistic lens, yet today the business field is white both for souls and finances. We need leaders who will step up to claim the earth's resources for God's purposes rather than their own selfish desires.

❖ *Declare an abundance of resources consecrated for the kingdom of God.* Whether your business requires you to invent, ship, supply, manufacture, send, serve, cook, fly, create, distribute, import, export, construct, mend… whatever the case, you need resources to build and expand that business. Those resources may be as tangible as a fleet of eighteen-wheelers or as fluid as intellectual rights, but either way, they are necessary and vital for growth. With intercession, we can stand in the gap for Christian businesses and declare an overflow of heaven-sent supplies and riches that will serve kingdom purposes.

❖ *Pray leaders on the Business Mountain will not only be concerned about the bottom line, but will also have compassion for those affected by their leadership.* The world loves to define success using terms of revenue shares, percentage growth, and other dollar-dominated measurements. While on earth, Jesus proved that our heavenly Father defines success using terms of internal transformation: love, forgiveness, mercy, grace, self-control, and other Holy Spirit fruit that characterizes the healthy branches we are supposed to be. (See, for example, Galatians 5:22–23 and John 15:5.) When leaders realize these markers of success can only be found in people—not money—their workplace becomes a mission field. This does not negate a holy calling to succeed in business (which, in our world, translates to financial prosperity), yet as intercessors we have the opportunity to undergird these leaders with prayer that points them to a higher calling of growing hearts, souls, and lives.

One of my friends is a hospital equipment manager. After this man spent years discontented with his job, the Lord gave him a new leadership position at a different facility where part of his initial responsibility was hiring additional staff. He loved what he did and developed a great reputation among his co-workers, but a few months into his new role, he still felt something was not right in the office. He spoke with me about this, and I prayed that God would give him discernment in the matter.

Not long after, my friend was walking among the rows of workstations on one floor and accidentally knocked against an employee's computer. As the monitor came on, he discovered a pornographic website onscreen. His heart sank, as this employee was an outstanding worker on the team. Though he knew he had to confront the man and, because of company policies, fire him, my friend wrestled with how to go about the process while truly caring for the employee's well-being. He again called me, not only for counsel about the situation but to ask that I intercede on his behalf.

When my friend met with the worker to inform him of his firing, he showed such compassion and sorrow that by the end of their conversation, the employee was actually relieved to receive a pink slip. Rather than engage in a power trip, as many bosses would have done, my friend saw into the heart of the matter—that this man's inner healing was more important than him collecting another paycheck or the company's bottom line. He did not back down from the truth that the employee had been viewing pornography on company equipment, but he showed such mercy that, despite receiving a "harsh word," the worker actually felt better after their encounter. Let's pray for more leaders in the Business Mountain who would show such a blend of Christlike mercy, kindness, righteousness, *and* justice.

❖ *Pray kingdom-minded leaders in this sphere will learn to receive—and integrate—intercessory prayer into their businesses.* As we discussed in chapter 2, there is a breach between workplace leaders and ministry leaders. Though I believe this division is eroding (in chapter 14, we will discuss one way this is happening), it still exists. Often past church wounds cause business leaders to discount the need for incorporating intercession into every part of their business. As a result, their companies are left unprotected in the spirit and Satan is given opportunity to attack any weak points within the corporate structure—including the leaders themselves.

A friend of my husband's was a highly successful real estate developer from the 1970s through the 1990s. Dwayne was a devoted believer, and everything he touched seemed to turn to gold as the Lord guided him into profitable venture after profitable venture. He and his wife lived debt-free in a paid-for house in the most prestigious part of Colorado Springs and were known by name at all the finest clubs and dining rooms in town. Along with their Mercedes Benzes, airplanes, motor home, and other expensive possessions, they traveled the world on mission trips whenever the opportunity arose without worrying about cost. Life was good.

Dwayne's wife began urging him to stop his real estate developments so they could go full time to the mission field, but Dwayne told her he would develop just one more property and then their financial future would be completely secure. To this thriving businessman, the large shopping center on a forty-acre lot and the downtown Colorado Springs property-cum-future high-rise seemed like just another project.

It was anything but that.

Dwayne once again prayed for the Lord to guide him and bless him so he could better serve Him. He communed regularly with God, waking up at two o'clock every morning to read his Bible and pray. But somewhere along the way, pride and arrogance crept in to the point that he ignored the Lord's warnings against embarking on the new project.

"Dwayne, don't do this. It will fail," he heard throughout the early stages of development. Yet the further Dwayne got into the project, the more he rationalized away this still, small voice: *I know what I'm doing. Plus, this development will allow my wife and me to serve You for the rest of our lives.* As his only intercessor, his wife pleaded for him to stop up to the day the financial papers were signed, yet he ignored both voices and argued that everything had worked well for so long—surely God was behind this.

Not long after he signed his name to millions of dollars of loans, the financial system crumbled and he was left with the entire debt. The project wiped out everything Dwayne and his wife owned—their house, cars, country club memberships, even their entire savings. Almost overnight they went from living large to occasionally having to depend on their church to pay rent.

"My problem was not in communing with the Lord, it was in my not listening to my only intercessor (my wife) and the Lord's quiet voice," Dwayne now says. "They warned me many times, but my pride and arrogance led to my financial destruction. I can look back now and see the mistakes, the sin of not listening. The Lord, in His grace, was trying to spare me what was coming."

The former picture of the American dream, Dwayne now realizes how God used a nightmare situation to get rid of the pride, arrogance, and other issues that he was unaware existed deep within. But although he is thankful for the lessons learned on the other side of the journey, he admits, "Going through it was brutal."

The enemy of our souls uses any opportunity he can to destroy us— even when, like Dwayne, we are seemingly close to God. This is especially true for leaders, who may feel like they're walking in complete faith and relying on the Lord, yet deep within they have gaping holes that Satan uses against them. This is why an intercessory covering is essential for every leader on every cultural mountain. As leaders ascend higher and become more influential on these mountains, they must rely on the prayers of supporting saints even more. Without that prayer shield, they are open targets, waiting to be picked off for the fall. Whether you are an intercessor or a leader, it is crucial that you not only recognize but also incorporate the power of intercession into every aspect of life upon the Seven Mountains.

CHAPTER 9 NOTES

1. Graham Cooke, Aglow Conference lecture, October 24, 2009.

2. Graham Cooke, "Stop Praying Like a Widow and Start to Pray Like a Bride," The Church in Transition Conference, Frederick, MD, April 25, 2002.

3. Focus on the Family, "Five Threats to Your Family...and What You Can Do to Protect Those You Care About," pamphlet (Colorado Springs, CO: Focus on the Family, 2008).

4. Patricia Tjaden and Nancy Thoennes, "Extent, Nature, and Consequences of Intimate Partner Violence: Findings from the National Violence Against Women Survey," National Institute of Justice and the Centers of Disease Control and Prevention, 2000.

5. Statement originally found at http://www.catholicvote.org.

6. Prayer journal of Ruth Bond, written 1851–1869.

7. Drive Thru History America with Dave Stotts, "History of American Education," http://dthamerica.com/about/history-of-american-education/ (accessed July 31, 2011).

8. Associated Press, "High School Graduation Rates Plummet Below 50 Percent in Some US Cities," FoxNews.com, http://www.foxnews.com/story/0,2933,344190,00.html (accessed July 31, 2011).

9. Insite Media Research, "The Right to a Better Balance of Positive and Negative News," Local News Viewers' Bill of Rights Survey, http://www.tvsurveys.com/billofrites/balance.htm (accessed July 31, 2011).

10. Ibid.

11. Pew Research Center, "Press Accuracy Rating Hits Two Decade Low: Public Evaluations of the News Media: 1985–2009," September 13, 2009, http://people-press.org/report/543/ (accessed July 31, 2011).

12. BoxOfficeMojo.com, "The Passion of the Christ," http://www.boxofficemojo.com/movies/?id=passionofthechrist.htm (accessed July 31, 2011).

13. Plunkett Research, Ltd., "Sports Industry Overview," http://www.plunkettresearch.com/Industries/Sports/SportsStatistics/tabid/273/Default.aspx (accessed July 31, 2011).

14. Plunkett Research, Ltd., "Entertainment and Media Industry Overview," http://www.plunkettresearch.com/entertainment%20media%20publishing%20market%20research/industry%20statistics (accessed July 31, 2011).

15. Parents Television Council, "PTC Finds Increase in Harsh Profanity on TV," October 29, 2008, http://www.parentstv.org/PTC/news/release/2008/1029.asp (accessed July 31, 2011).

Chapter 10

INTERCESSION @ WORK

A T LEAST FIVE of the seven cultural mountains can be categorized
as "the workplace." The mountains of government, business,
education, arts and entertainment, and media all fit the billing
of career-oriented, professional environments. Even the remaining
two—family and religion—though not purely work surroundings,
have definite vocational aspects to them. (I dare you to tell stay-at-
home moms or full-time pastors that what they are doing isn't work!)
Ultimately, that means every person on earth spends most of his
time in the workplace.

Why, then, do most people divorce the calling of intercession from
what they do all week? How is it that few of us feel the need to have
intercession integrated into our everyday work? Why are Sunday morn-
ings, Wednesday nights, and whatever other times we set aside for
official prayer meetings the only occasions in which intercession—or
general prayer, for that matter—is a primary focus? Something is askew.

Until He began His three-year ministry period, Jesus worked like
the rest of us to provide for Himself and His family. The son of a car-
penter, He undoubtedly learned a trade—probably woodwork, as it was
customary during His time to follow in your father's footsteps—and
labored to earn money and put food on the table. So for the first thirty
years of His life, Jesus felt the soil of the Business Mountain under His
sandals every day.

Scripture is not explicit in detailing what those thirty years
looked like. We have to read between the lines and guess at some
things. But as the Gospels recount the day-to-day events of Jesus'
ministry years, we see Him incorporating dialog with His heavenly
Father—prayer—into every aspect of what He did. Before daybreak,
He would regularly go away to a secluded place and pray (see Mark
1:35). As He performed miracles amid the masses of those who followed Him, He addressed the heavens as if in an ongoing conversation with God (see John 11:41–42). When He was tired and needed a

break from constantly ministering, He "sent the crowds away [and] went up on the mountain by Himself to pray" (Matt. 14:23). Even in the middle of a conversation with His disciples, Jesus would talk to God (see Luke 10:17–24).

Jesus did not develop this discipline overnight. This was not some act He learned as soon as He stepped into the sphere of "full-time ministry." No, I have no doubt Jesus established prayer as a lifestyle during the same years He was employed in the workplace. It was *while* He labored on sanding a table or whittling a chair that His verbal intercession became like breathing to Him. Prayer was not reserved for a Wednesday night function or a Saturday morning men's breakfast; it was just as integrated into His workplace as His constant posture of worship.

If we hope to walk in the same power as Jesus did and, as He promised, do even "greater works than these" (John 14:12), we must learn to embed intercession into every part of who we are and everything we do. It must permeate whatever workplace environment we call our home turf and on whichever mountain we hold the most influence.

Praying for Warriors in the Workplace

In the last chapter, we identified prayers specific to each mountain. Because each of us may be called to intercede for a different mountain, it is vital that we understand the key prayer points for those individual mountains. Yet in my years of praying with the Seven Mountain paradigm and then teaching these principles to others around the world, I have discovered there is far more common ground than most people think. Just as we have established intercession as the force that connects each of the Seven Mountains (chapter 3), there are connective prayer points that apply to the entire mountain range.

These items for prayer originally came as I interceded for those on the Business Mountain, simply because that has been the sphere I have been most connected with in recent years. It did not take long, however, to recognize that what the Lord was leading me to pray was just as relevant on any of the other mountains that constituted a workplace environment. What follows, then, is a list of fifteen prayer points, some of which have been gleaned from Ann Bandini, one of the pioneers of prayer in the workplace. We can offer these prayers up as we intercede for the foot soldiers whose battlefield is the workplace, regardless of which mountain they technically work on.

1. *Pray they will know their calling and walk in it with a sense of the Lord's full confidence and affirmation.* We all want to know what we are called to do. Yet the term *calling* is one of the most misunderstood and abused words in Christendom. I have met sixty-year-olds who have walked with the Lord most of their lives yet were still clueless about their calling. How much easier would it have been if they had just asked an intercessor to come alongside them and pray that they would discover their calling? It does not take much to ask for such prayer support, yet I am amazed at how few of us do this.

Obviously, Satan would love to minimize believers' effectiveness by keeping them in the dark about what God has called them to do. That is why intercessors are so crucial for those who still do not know their calling; we fight in the spirit and clear the path for those foot soldiers who need to advance. It is also why I have listed this prayer point first. Every person needs to know his specific assignment on earth! When people are affirmed in their calling, they walk in confidence. And when they walk in confidence, not only can the enemy not push them around, they also sense a greater power in accomplishing the kingdom purposes for which God has equipped them.

Notice, however, that confidence—a holy, godly confidence—is closely linked with affirmation. Everyone in the world needs to be affirmed. No matter how remarkable we may be, we all need to be told that what we are doing and who we are becoming is of value. When we pray for those in the workplace, something happens internally that helps them realize the affirming words of God. Often our prayers open emotional doors inside of them for God to validate who they are. They discover His love for them does not come and go depending on what they do. They find His presence will never leave them, regardless of how they feel or how badly they think they have sinned. And as they sense God's pleasure for them through His Word, spoken directly to them, they establish new confidence.

This confidence is not the same thing as pride, though many equate the two. Pride is thinking we are either higher or lower than God says we are, whereas humility is agreeing with what God says about us. Godly confidence, then, is knowing who we are in Christ. As God affirms us with who He has *already* made us to be through His Son, we find a renewed reason to be assured and sure-footed. Then we can stand against anything the enemy throws our way.

2. *Pray they will walk in clarity.* Just as we need confidence to accomplish the work set before us, we also need clear vision to see the obstacles or potential hazards that surround us. Whether you are a businessman, teacher, soccer mom, or politician, you need more than instructions to do your job; you need the ability to discern good from bad. By interceding for those in the workplace, we can clear the distractions and distortion the enemy sends their way. Instead of walking in a fog that prevents them from seeing what lies around them, they can venture out with solid ground underneath their feet and a clear path laid ahead to reach the goal set before them. (See Philippians 3:14.)

3. *Pray they will receive divine strategies that apply on multiple fronts.* Confidence in their calling? Check. Clear vision? Check. Intricately connected to these prayer points is a third element those in the workplace must have to be effective: strategy. In the last chapter, we addressed how successfully invading each mountain requires a unique strategy. This need is undeniably necessary for us to win the battles for each mountain. Yet just as an army general must think beyond a single battle to win the overall war, often God additionally equips leaders on these mountains with more universal strategies for the bigger picture. Intercessors have the important task of opening the heavens and securing clear communication for God to download these multifaceted plans to His key people.

4. *Pray they will walk in integrity and not compromise their values.* Though this prayer may sound overly generic, there is a reason: the need for integrity is crucial on every part of every mountain today. In business, even Christian companies justify unethical deals by saying their owners haven't received direct kickbacks. In education, Christian teachers fail to take action against cheating student-athletes because they fear being reprimanded for hindering their school's moneymaking athletic department. In government, born-again city councilmen and councilwomen turn a blind eye to corrupt officials because failing to do so affects their own chances of future promotion. The examples from each mountain are endless yet underscore the common need for a return to integrity. We must pray that those in

the workplace, regardless of whatever temptation they face, can stand before God with a pure heart.

5. *Pray they will stand against the lure of power, sex, and money.* Satan uses each of these weapons in his arsenal to reduce even the greatest leader to a lowly sinner. Think of any high-profile moral failure witnessed in the last five years—from Spirit-filled pastors to Fortune 500 CEOs to talk-show hosts to superstar athletes—and the person's fall can be traced to power, money, or sex (or a mix of the three). Even those who understand the importance of intercessory covering are not immune to being lured by these temptations.

Years ago, I prayed regularly for a couple who owned a hotel in Europe. They were godly people, known all over their country and loved by everyone in their tiny village community, which had seen the business passed down in the family for hundreds of years. Every time I traveled there, the couple would bless me far beyond the norm. This was typical of them, as they often invited missionaries, pastors, and ministry workers to stay as guests, with no charge, for months of sabbatical rest.

These believers understood the power of prayer. In the past, they had regularly made sure intercessors were praying for their business, but shortly after I met them this began to wane. Their laxness opened a door for the enemy, and eventually the husband fell into sexual sin.

Fortunately, their story did not end there. I gathered a team of prayer warriors to once again push back the darkness on their behalf, and eventually the man was restored to his wife, his community, and the Lord. He is living proof, however, that Satan frequently resorts to his triple-threat weapon of power, money, and sex—and is effective much of the time even among veteran believers. As intercessors, our job is to continually occupy territory in the spirit on behalf of workplace warriors, so that when these attacks occur, the battle is as brief as exposing Satan's tools and declaring the Lord's strength.

6. *Pray they will be able to resolve issues without taking drastic measures.* Jesus offered explicit instructions for how His followers should handle conflict with fellow believers: "If your brother sins, go and show him his fault in private; if he listens to you, you have won your brother. But if he does not listen to you, take one or two more with you, so that by the mouth of two or three witnesses every fact may be confirmed. If he refuses to listen to them, tell it to the church; and if he refuses to listen

even to the church, let him be to you as a Gentile and a tax collector" (Matt. 18:15–17). As we intercede for Christians in the workplace, pray that they will resolve conflict before it becomes a public ordeal.

Most believers work in a secular environment, however, which begs the question: how are we to pray when these professionals have a conflict with a non-believer? Scripture frequently mentions taking the higher path of examining your own faults first (see Matthew 7:5), being a peacemaker (see Matthew 5:9), and considering everything through the filter of love (see 1 Corinthians 13:4–7). In countering the "eye for an eye" approach the world takes, Jesus even mentioned what to do if a conflict escalates to taking legal action: "If someone wants to sue you and take your tunic, let him have your cloak as well" (Matt. 5:40, NIV). This does not mean workplace Christians are to be pushovers—and that is not what we should be praying. Instead, we are to stand in the gap and declare that in every situation, God's kingdom principles would reign and that His ambassadors would showcase those heavenly values.

Conflict is a perfect opportunity to show kingdom principles amid a naturally selfish world. We are forgiven people; let's pray that those we pray for will extend the same forgiveness they have been shown by the Father. As Paul writes, "So, as those who have been chosen of God, holy and beloved, put on a heart of compassion, kindness, humility, gentleness and patience; bearing with one another, and forgiving each other, whoever has a complaint against anyone; just as the Lord forgave you, so also should you" (Col. 3:12–13).

7. *Pray they will walk in accordance with God's Word and not be hypocritical.* One of the biggest complaints against Christianity has nothing to do with Jesus and everything to do with His followers' two-faced living. We need authentic believers who will remain true to the same values in every circumstance. Pray against the religious spirit that says it is acceptable to act one way at church but another way in the corporate structure. God is looking for those who will remain consistent on the Family Mountain, the Education Mountain, the Arts and Entertainment Mountain, and every other mountain. Declare that those in the workplace will shine as examples of truthful, biblical living.

8. *Pray they will walk in peace, not anxiety.* Not long ago, a friend of mine was diagnosed with breast cancer. Her immediate reaction was fear, anxiety, despair, and hopelessness. The manager of a large corporation,

she didn't want anyone to know of her diagnosis and was afraid to talk about her condition or even consider the treatment options available to her. All she wanted to do was lock herself in her home and disappear. Fear and anxiety paralyzed her.

She eventually asked an intercessor to pray for her, who then called a group of intercessors to war on her behalf. There was a huge battle in the spiritual realm for her peace, yet amid this, God miraculously reconnected her with a previous acquaintance who was a breast cancer survivor. I believe prayer brought this woman back into my friend's life, and she was able to speak truth into her. It was as though my friend was instantly blanketed in peace. She walked through the treatments with tremendous peace; fear no longer had a hold on her. Today she is a cancer survivor who believes in the power of intercession!

9. *Pray they will walk in favor.* Lance Wallnau defines favor as "the affection of God toward you that releases an influence through you so that other people are inclined to like, trust, and cooperate with you." In an article he wrote about favor, Wallnau describes a lesson taken straight from Job:

> The oldest book of the Old Testament is Job. As such, it is the first real insight into favor and how it operates. In the very first chapter we read about the phenomenal blessing that is on Job's life: "This man was the greatest of all the men of the east" (v. 3, KJV).

> What is not fully understood is how the blessing of God came upon this righteous man. We find a hint in the following verse: "Thou hast granted me life and favor and thy visitation has refreshed my spirit" (10:1, KJV). Job was a man who walked under the supernatural blessing of God's favor because God visited him when he prayed. What was the effect of that favor? He opened his mouth and his "words were like butter" to those who heard him. The elders at the gates sought wisdom from his mouth. Talk about the power of persuasion!

> To guard the blessing of God, Job was very careful to build a hedge of prayer around his life—a point that Satan made a complaint about before the throne of God. The force of favor attracts not only God's blessings, but Satan's envy. Thus when Job came out of his troubles, God restored Job's fortunes in a double portion! Job shows us how God restores to His embattled

saints a double portion of blessing and power at the end of the conflict!

Favor makes ordinary students shine in an extraordinary way. It makes lonely singles attractive, married people desirable to their spouse, employees receive recognition, employers gain influence, entrepreneurs attract contacts. Favor is a magnet to the blessing and promotion of God.[1]

In fact, our cry for favor for those in the workplace can be as simple as this: "Open the floodgates of heaven, Lord!" Through intercession, we can foil every attempt of the enemy to create a blockade for the blessings God desires to pour on His workplace ambassadors.

10. *Pray they will use their career to promote Christ instead of using Christ to promote their career.* A few years ago my husband and I were asked to visit the home of an award-winning architect. He was a proud man who had all the markers of worldly success—money, fame, influence. In fact, he had received awards for his work. Although he accepted Jesus as his Savior (believing Christ died for his sins) in 1983, there were areas of his life that needed to be surrendered to Christ by making Him Lord (Master and Ruler) of his life.

His purpose for inviting my husband and me over was that he wanted us to pray throughout a house he had designed because he thought that might help his work influence grow even more. Essentially, he wanted Jesus to help his career expand.

The Lord had other plans. When I arrived, I looked at him and felt a boldness rising in me. My heart was filled with compassion for this remarkable man.

"You know God wants you," I said, staring straight into his eyes. I then began to speak his destiny in the Lord over him. I am always amazed what the Word of the Lord will do to people, and in this case it was no different. I watched before me—and before a faithful wife who had prayed two decades for this moment—a man whose defenses could not stand against the all-pursuing, unrelenting love of his heavenly Father. Tears began to stream down his face as I declared God's plans over his life, and through his sobs he eventually asked: "What must I do?"

That day Jesus also became Lord of his life. He has since become an extremely humble, powerful kingdom warrior in the workplace. Instead of building for himself, he now asks God for His blueprints, His designs, and His plans for kingdom construction. He remains a major influence in the international architectural industry and uses his career to promote Christ.

11. *Pray they will have a sense of mission and ministry.* Every mountain is a wide-open mission field, as is every office, classroom, operating room, concert hall, living room, movie theater, courtroom, press room... the list is endless. Too often those in the workplace delegate the work of sharing the gospel to those in "full-time ministry." The truth is, we are all called to be full-time ministers just as Christ was, bringing the Good News to the world every Spirit-appointed opportunity we get, no matter where we are. As we stand in the gap for those in the workplace, pray for a revelation within them of this missionary spirit.

12. *Pray they will have the wisdom of God.* During my trip to Rwanda following the horrific genocide of 1994, the group I traveled with decided to visit parliament as part of our prayer journey. While walking through the government building with us, our host, who was a prominent local pastor, asked if we wanted to meet with the president of parliament. (We took it as a rhetorical question—of course we did!) Within minutes, we were ushered into the office of the president, who turned out to be a gracious, humble, thirty-three-year-old man. He was desperate for encouragement and direction and asked us if we would spend time praying with him. In a move that stunned us all, he then knelt before us and softly said, "Pray for me for wisdom. I need to know how God wants me to lead my country. I need to know how to bring reconciliation back to the land. Pray for me—I'm just a young man."

We prayed for this servant-leader, and the Lord actually gave me a prophetic word for him. But that was not all. In the following months, we sent emails and faxes with specific prayers and prayer strategies from the Lord. We continued to invest in him because he desired God's wisdom, and through prayer we knew the Lord would supply it.

13. *Pray the gifts of the Spirit will operate through them.* In 1 Corinthians 12:8–10 we find a picture of how the Holy Spirit's gifts can function through us in any workplace setting: "For to one is given the word of wisdom through the Spirit, and to another the word of knowledge according to the same Spirit; to another faith by the same Spirit, and to another gifts of healing by the one Spirit, and to another the effecting of miracles, and to another prophecy, and to another the distinguishing

of spirits, to another various kinds of tongues, and to another the interpretation of tongues."

Often when Christians refer to this verse, they use it in the context of a typical church service setting. Those who think slightly more outside the box may see it appropriate within the context of a house church or a small-group meeting. But we must not forget that Paul was not limiting his words to a Sunday morning, church-building setting. Instead, he understood what we so often forget: that we *are* the church wherever we go. That means the church is just as powerful in the workplace as it is in an official church sanctuary. (In fact, I would argue it is *more* powerful, though we rarely realize this.) Let's bolster those in the workplace by praying for a fruition of the Holy Spirit's gifts already contained within them. Let the church arise!

14. *Pray they will receive and respond to the word of the Lord.* This does not mean they will only hear the word or that they will just pass along the word. We must declare into the heavens that those in the workplace will receive with open hearts God's *kairos* word that comes at just the right time, for just the right situation.

Years ago I was asked to attend a German organization's annual board meeting. The company had asked for there to be intercessors praying throughout the meeting, which included interviewing a man for a potential high-ranking position within the business. We watched, prayed, and listened for what the Lord had to say as they asked the man a series of questions. When they finished and the man left the room, the board leaders turned to us and asked for our input.

"The word I keep getting is *sleazy*," I said. By the puzzled look on their faces, it was obvious it did not translate well into German.

"What is sleazy?" they asked. I tried to explain the meaning the best I could but soon realized I did not have a decent grasp of the word, so I searched for a dictionary. When I looked up the word, I read the meaning aloud: "Contemptibly low, disreputable, disrespectful of rules and orders, repulsive, filthy, dishonorable, and discreditable."

They did not hire the man. Several months later, several of the board members discovered he was working for a direct competitor. They had not only sought out the Lord's input (through us), they had received it and responded to it—and I believe it saved their business from a major headache.

15. *Pray they will succeed in every endeavor.* This seems like a no-brainer prayer along the lines of, "God, help me do well" or, "Lord, keep me healthy." Yet this remains a key prayer throughout the Seven Mountains for two main reasons. First, it is a given that Satan and the powers of darkness will try to do whatever they can to enforce failure for those in the workplace. The enemy does not want Christians walking in the fullness of God's plan for them—which, as the oft-quoted verse says, involve "plans to prosper you and not to harm you, plans to give you hope and a future" (Jer. 29:11, NIV). Our words turn back the plans of the enemy. Second, success looks different on every mountain, and it is important to pronounce into each cultural atmosphere the overriding goal of blessing rather than curse. There are enough demons already launching whispered curses into believers' territory; we must counter these with the voice of God that cancels out every negative word against those in the workplace.

PRAYING IN CIRCLES

One of the most frequent criticisms I hear of intercessory meetings and, for that matter, intercessors in general is how we pray. Non-intercessors often perceive our approach to prayer as chaotic and unorganized. Although I certainly know plenty of shoot-from-the-hip prayer warriors, I can attest that some of the most effective, Spirit-led intercessors I know are also the most systematic when it comes to standing in the gap for people, companies, nations, and situations. By military standards, the greatest armies are almost always the most structured. As the number of troops increases, this organization is paramount to the overall success of an operation.

So it is with intercession. Guerrilla warfare may suffice in confronting a demonic force for a season or two, but if we hope to be a unified army of prayer warriors with a single goal of destroying Satan's reign, we must learn to recognize the importance of organization. One of the many tools that can be used to do this in both personal and corporate intercession is praying in concentric circles.

Concentric circles are multiple circles that share a common center. In intercession, our center is Jesus Christ, and our central goal is establishing His kingdom here on earth. Everything we pray—from demonic deliverance to workplace success to a cry for righteousness—should always revolve around those elements. But as you pray through the various prayer points contained in this chapter and the last, it is possible you will feel somewhat scattered or disoriented (particularly if you have never prayed some of these items before). To create a consistent structure, try applying the idea of concentric circles as you stand in the gap for those in the workplace.

THREE CONCENTRIC CIRCLES OF PRAYER

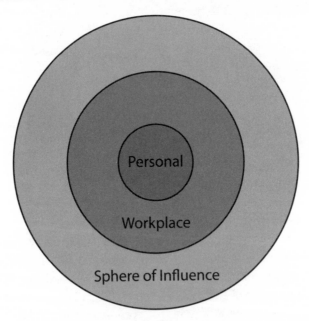

The first or innermost circle represents an individual's personal life—everything that involves family, health (spiritual, physical, emotional, mental, financial), life goals, spiritual calling, guidance for future, etc. Examples of praying in this sphere include interceding for someone's struggle with alcoholism, for victory in a battle with breast cancer, or for the Holy Spirit's direction on a major relationship decision. Often the most specific personalized prayers are found in this circle.

The second circle stands for the workplace environment—a person's business, organization, employees, contracts, vendors, investors, customers, etc. Within this sphere, intercessors pray for all those who come in contact with the specific person for whom we are standing in the gap. For example, if that person is in a legal business battle, an intercessor would pray for every judge involved, as well as an overall atmosphere of justice. This concentric circle can extend beyond people, however, to include workplace situations and future expansion. It also entails renouncing the demonic spirits that restrict such growth or are preventing further forms of success.

The third and outermost circle corresponds with a person's broader sphere of influence. In most cases, this will be the industry or general field in which the person works—whichever of the Seven Mountains could be considered home base. For example, if you were standing in the gap for a third-grade teacher, you would pray for the city, state, and national education systems in which that teacher has to abide by. Then pray the teaching curriculum would glorify God by revealing complete truth rather than spreading lies from the enemy.

FROM CHAOS TO ORGANIZED PRAYER

In thermodynamics, the term *entropy* describes the steady, inevitable process of deterioration within a system from order to disorder. A natural progression of maturation in intercession moves in the exact *opposite* manner, going from chaos to order. Most intercessors start out as freewheeling, "watch out, my prayers could go anywhere" prayer warriors. But the more battles we fight in the spirit, the more we recognize the need for underlying structure and discipline. This in no way is meant to squelch or limit the Holy Spirit's movement and leading in our prayer lives. In fact, it serves the opposite purpose of establishing a solid, structured groundwork from which we can venture out into new territory as the Spirit leads us.

Think of such tools as the three concentric prayer circles as home base for a battle. When a troop engaged in battle pursues their enemy beyond the normal boundaries, it is crucial for them to know where they can return. In prayer, our home base is the structure we develop to keep us in line with the ultimate vision of progressing God's kingdom on earth. There are days when I will begin my prayer time for someone in the inner concentric circle and work my way out. When the Spirit prompts me to veer from this "linear" approach, I follow, and undoubtedly I will end up in a more powerful place of prayer that could have only been directed by God. Yet as I have the impression that the time is right to return from that place, I have a sense of direction in my prayers and can return again to that inner concentric circle. And if I feel the Spirit telling me to move on to the second circle, I do so.

Though I am not consciously aware of this process, I am staying in tune with the Holy Spirit and His guidance. It's like cooking. The first time you make a dish, you follow the directions exactly. But as you practice making the dish over and over again, you intuitively know what ingredients to add, when to stir, how long to cook, and so on. As you become more experienced, the dish becomes more personalized and delicious each time you prepare it.

Likewise, the result of learning how to stay attuned with the Holy Spirit is a beautiful demonstration of following the Leader, as every time of prayer should be. God has given us His Spirit to "teach [us] all things" (John 14:26, emphasis added) and "guide [us] into all truth" (16:13, emphasis added). As we pray for those in the workplace across the cultural mountains, we can establish a solid framework on which we can stand faithfully in the gap and from which we can follow the Spirit's every move, knowing He will not fail us.

CHAPTER 10 NOTES

1. Lance Wallnau, "The Force of Favor," http://www.lancelearning.com. Reprinted with permission.

Chapter 11

COVER ME! (LEADERSHIP AND INTERCESSORY SUPPORT)

THE CARGO SHIP *Maersk Alabama* may not be remembered for any daring ventures, but its crew most definitely will. On the morning of April 8, 2009, the container vessel was en route to Mombasa, Kenya, carrying 17,000 metric tons of food aid for Rwanda, Somalia, and Uganda when four Somali pirates wielding AK-47s and pistols hijacked the ship. As the raiders climbed aboard, Captain Richard Phillips ordered his crew of twenty to quickly make their way to the ship's bridge and hide in designated safe rooms. Although one of the crewmen was captured, most of the others locked themselves in the engine room down below.

Phillips' directions proved key to the outcome. The captain surrendered himself and spent the next several hours trying to placate the restless teenage pirates in the control room. The rest of the crew, meanwhile, managed to transfer control of the vessel's steering and propulsion to the engine room, rendering the pirates powerless over the sailing course. By barricading themselves in, however, the Americans now faced the risk of dehydration, as the room's temperature soared to above 120 degrees with no water in sight.

The tide turned within a couple of hours when, in yet another heroic move, captured crewman ATM "Zahid" Reza volunteered to escort the pirate's ringleader to the engine room. As the two made their way through the darkness below, the awaiting Americans overpowered the leader. With each side now possessing a key hostage, the crew set up an exchange. But things went awry when, after the crew gave up the ringleader, the remaining three pirates failed to release Phillips and boarded a lifeboat.

For the next four days—with the world now tuned in to the high seas standoff—US Navy officials aboard three trailing warships attempted to negotiate with the pirates. At one point, Phillips even jumped overboard during the night, but his escape was foiled when his kidnappers shot at him and quickly captured him in the water. By Easter Sunday, the chances of Phillips returning safely appeared bleak as the pirates became even more agitated from lack of sleep. As darkness fell that night, Navy SEAL members saw one of the kidnappers point an AK-47 at Phillips' back. In a matter of seconds, an order was given, and snipers took out the three pirates.[1, 2]

Phillips reached land a few days later in good condition and was immediately surrounded by a blitz of media coverage labeling him a hero. But the Vermont native was quick to deflect any praise for his own bravery. "I'm not a hero, the military is," he said. "They're the superheroes. They're the titans. They're impossible men doing an impossible job, and they did the impossible with me....They're at the point of the sword every day, doing an impossible job every day. I would not be here without them."[3] Even when the ship's crew thanked and commended their captain for his heroism in separate media interviews, Phillips remained firm on who deserved the credit: "It was the crew who was working united together as a team to save myself, for no other reason than it was your duty, your job, your role."[4]

Phillips understood a key principle: we all need help. Even the greatest among us—even the most heroic in the spirit—needs the support of others. We need to know we are surrounded by those who will have our back when we are at risk, those who will come to our rescue when we are under attack.

I asked a question in the last chapter that remains unanswered to this point: why do so many in the workplace feel it is unnecessary to have intercessors praying for them? How is it that we can recognize the importance of prayer when making a major life decision, yet we refuse to safeguard our everyday activities against the enemy's attacks by stationing prayer warriors in key positions of our lives?

Why Leaders Do Not Have Intercessors

Unfortunately, this lack of prayer covering is particularly true among leaders throughout the Seven Mountains. By leaders, I do not necessarily mean an exclusive club of VIPs, VPs, and MVPs. Leadership in today's world looks different than it did in years past. Marketing expert Seth Godin, in his book *Tribes*, asserts that everyone is a leader—of *something*, at least—but not everyone leads. He expounded on this idea with prophetic insight in a recent interview: "Everyone isn't going to be a leader. But everyone isn't going to be successful, either. Success is now the domain of people who lead. That doesn't mean they're in charge, it doesn't mean they are the CEO, it merely means that for a group, even a small group, they show the way, they spread ideas, they make change. Those people are the only successful people we've got. So the challenge is: your choice."[5]

Leaders are influencers. And we all have influence over *something*— family decisions, work tasks, others' perception of us, the spiritual climate around us. If each of us influences others, then, as Godin says, it is our choice whether we take that role to heart and aim for success. Because our definition of success is based on elevating God's kingdom rather than our personal kingdom, this brings us back to square one: why would we dare not have people interceding for us? Anyone who influences others for good and aims to progress the kingdom of God becomes an automatic target of Satan. He is after believers who make a difference—leaders.

Why, then, do so many leaders not have intercessors? Peter Wagner has identified five main reasons for this in his book *Prayer Shield:*[6]

1. *Ignorance.* The devil has done a masterful job of convincing the average believer that the only people who need intercessors are those who spend all of their time on the Religion Mountain. It makes sense to us why a pastor, missionary, or ministry leader might need prayer covering for day-to-day work. Yet it is as if we have blinders on when it comes to recognizing our own need for this. We fail to connect such "coincidences" as regular mishaps or never-ending obstacles with the amount of prayer support we have.

2. *Rugged individualism.* The "I can do it myself" attitude runs rampant among headstrong leaders. It does not help that in American culture we are conditioned to think individualistically. Even humble servants will refuse prayer using a common excuse: "I can hear God for myself." Self-reliance is not listed among the fruit of the Holy Spirit. Let's realize that we all need each other, *especially* when it comes to prayer.

3. *Fear.* This operates like a domino effect. A leader may be afraid of intercessors because he knows they hear from

God. If God reveals hidden things about him to these prayer warriors, that makes him vulnerable (supposedly another leader no-no)—which, in turn, means he will have to be accountable to God or to another person. Few leaders enjoy such a call to transparency, and even fewer take it up.

4. *Spiritual arrogance.* Closely connected with rugged individualism, this trait puts a leader's sheer pride on display. *Why would I need an intercessor? After all, God appointed me as the leader; I'm sure He will speak to me about whatever it is I need to know.* Pastors are a classic example of this, as they are often the last to request personal intercessors for fear they might appear spiritually "lower" than those they are supposed to shepherd. Some even refuse prayer support because they see it as an indication that they lack discernment or wisdom. *If I need others to tell me what God is saying, then why am I leading a church?* The truth is, Scripture says that in the multitude of counselors there is wisdom (Prov. 11:14; 15:22; 24:6). In addition, God stands in direct opposition to the proud (James 4:6)—so rejecting prayer assistance because of your own ego does not sit well with Him.

5. *Undue timidity or humility.* I have heard major leaders of the Seven Mountains make pitiful statements such as, "Oh, I'm no better than anyone else. I'm not a leader in the church. I just work." I have even heard comments such as these from CEOs of major companies or principals of high schools—people who, like it or not, have significant influence over others. Regardless of a leader's level of self-confidence (or in most cases, false humility), he has influence—period. That means he also needs a network of prayer warriors surrounding him.

WHY LEADERS NEED INTERCESSORS

Cover me!

Those two words are universally understood, particularly on the battlefield. When a soldier attempts to make a daring run into the open—whether to recover a wounded soldier or to advance his troop's position—he uses the phrase before rushing into dangerous territory.

Leaders do the same thing every day, whether our daring maneuvers are on the business front or the mission field. Whatever mountain we lead on is already a war zone; therefore, we need the same kind of protection soldiers receive in real life. We must be covered.

In *Prayer Shield*, Wagner also identifies reasons why pastors need intercessors.[7] I believe these same reasons apply to leaders on each of the Seven Mountains, not just the Religion Mountain. Leaders bear more responsibility. It is the nature of our role. As the well-known quote from the *Spider-Man* movies says, "With great power comes great responsibility." The power that accompanies a promotion—whether in the corporate world or the spiritual realm—is simply an indication of bearing a greater responsibility for others. If I am promoted to director over my department at work, for instance, I now not only have to be concerned with my own job, I am responsible for all those who work under me.

I would add another element to the *Spider-Man* principle, however: with great power comes great responsibility, and with great responsibility comes the need for great *accountability*. We have seen in recent years a widespread, astounding lack of accountability in the business world. When former Merrill Lynch CEO John Thain can spend $130,000 on area rugs, $87,000 on a pair of "guest chairs," $68,000 for an antique credenza, and $1,400 on a trash can—all part of his now infamous $1.2 million office renovation on the shareholders' dime—something is wrong.[8] Likewise, something is askew when other "Wall Street fat cats" can purchase $100 million paintings and beachfront mansions on a weekend whim simply because they have manipulated the corporate structure to the tune of an eight-figure salary.[9] With no accountability comes quick ruin.

As corrupt as some of these larger-than-life CEOs have been, we should not be so quick to point the finger. Any leader knows that as you rise in rank, you also rise in visibility. The higher up believers ascend on the Seven Mountains, the more they can be seen by enemy forces and the higher they move on Satan's hit list. When stationed at the bottom of a mountain, they do not pose a severe threat to overtaking that mountain. Sure, they may get hit with the occasional enemy attack, but it pales in comparison to the assault waged when they are atop the mountain. This is why Christian leaders desperately need an intercessory prayer shield comprised of faithful prayer warriors who will "cover them" as they move up in rank.

Satan knows that if he can take out a leader—especially one who is influential and rising—he can maintain control of a mountain. The higher leaders get, the easier they are to pick off. In fact, the devil often waits for them to ascend closer to the top before he uses his most effective tactic: temptation. Scripture makes it clear that everyone—leader or not—faces temptation (James 1:14). Charles Spurgeon once wrote, "Your occupation may be as humble as log splitting, and yet the devil can tempt you in it."[10] Yet headline after headline proves that when leaders take the bait of Satan, as John Bevere aptly termed it, they also take the hardest fall. And our enemy is well aware that a great fall translates to great damage not only over the entire landscape of a certain mountain, but also in an entire movement spanning multiple mountains.

For example, when my former pastor was exposed for sexual immorality and illegal drug use a few years ago, the news devastated our local body. Those in our church were not only stunned by what unfolded but felt betrayed and blindsided. The pastor was a prominent leader in our city, so the impact was also felt on multiple communities, both Christian and secular, throughout our area. Yet because this man's sphere of influence extended beyond our city to the entire nation and world, the ramifications of his actions were severe enough that to this day they are still talked about in the major secular media outlets. Among non-believers, he remains a symbol of, in their words, "typical Christian hypocrisy." Indeed, when the story originally broke, virtually every believer I knew had the same response: they grieved for the damage this would have on the larger body of Christ. My former pastor's failure obviously did not help further the kingdom's movement.

Don't think for a second that Satan did not plan that fall. He laid the groundwork one temptation at a time, carefully spacing out his traps with enough distance between them to make this man think he could handle things on his own. And like most leaders who experience a moral failure, my former pastor gradually drifted into a mind-set in which he believed he did not need intercessors around him—especially prophetic intercessors. Eventually, he did not want them around, for obvious reasons. (After all, who wants to be surrounded by people to whom God has revealed your hidden sins?)

Satan lobs the grenades of fleshly temptations—carnal trappings such as sex, gluttony, alcohol, pornography, drugs—at every leader. But he also uses more accurate weapons via his dedicated followers. Satan-worshipers are assigned to take down leaders by releasing specific spells, curses, and incantations. Just as a sniper waits in the shadows for the perfect hit on his target, a Satanist's hexes, chants, and blood sacrifices are aimed to hit a leader's weakest and most vulnerable spots. For instance, many witches and members of the occult actually fast one day a week for the destruction of Christian marriages. When I was in high school, the divorce rate among Christians was significantly lower than in general society; today, those in the church are just as likely to get a divorce as unbelievers. Is this because of curses specifically targeting the destruction of Christian marriages? While they may not have been the only factor, I believe these curses played a major role, just as Satan planned.

In releasing a targeted curse, often the enemy will aim at three specific areas of a leader's life: his root (foundational calling), his fruit (business, marriage, health, etc.), and his seed (children). Tragically, the targeted curses released often go undetected because the leader remains spiritually isolated, uncovered, and undiscerning with no prayer shield. And as long as a curse remains hidden, it has the opportunity to develop into an infectious disease that produces bad fruit in every aspect of a leader's life.

Proverbs 26:2 says, "Like a sparrow in its flitting, like a swallow in its flying, so a curse without cause does not alight." We can be certain every curse launched by the enemy has a cause behind it. Make no mistake: the enemy is always purposeful in his attacks. He understands that to have maximum effect, his curses must be given an open door—and so he waits for the exact opportune time. Sometimes these doors have been opened years prior and the curse has been passed down through generations. Other times, they are less subtle and bear immediate fruit. Whichever the case, once a door is opened, no matter how slightly, a curse can take root.*

Because leaders are in the spotlight and more vulnerable to such spiritual attack, they must be surrounded by a prayer shield—or risk ongoing exposure to the enemy's overt and covert attacks. Until we understand his schemes and recognize the importance of this type of prayer covering, we will continue to see great men and women achieving tremendous deeds for the kingdom and ascending closer to the peaks of the Seven Mountains, only to be knocked off by Satan.

---

* Deuteronomy 28:15–68 serves as an extensive list of the things that can open a door for curses. For a more detailed explanation on dealing with curses, I encourage you to read my book *Conquering the Religious Spirit*.

Three Shields for Every Leader

Everyone wants a sword. In movies such as *Braveheart, Gladiator, The Mask of Zorro*, or *The Count of Monte Cristo*, for example, sword fights are played up for all their glory. Some of these films highlight the dramatic, albeit familiar scene when the hero raises his sword before battle and we see a ray of light reflecting from the mighty blade. In the *Lord of the Rings* series, the swords of every hero even had their own names. Indeed, a sword is heroic, valiant, and powerful.

A shield, on the other hand, is completely unglamorous and, dare I say, boring. It is to a sword what an offensive lineman is to a quarterback in football. One gets all the glory; the other takes all the hits. Great offensive tackles are not household names, yet most professional football teams recognize just how important they are by often making them the second-highest paid players on a team (after the quarterback). An offensive tackle—usually a left tackle—protects the quarterback's blind side. Yet just as a quarterback is defenseless—and therefore manhandled—without his offensive line seeing what he cannot see coming, leaders are open targets for the takedown hit without a line of defense shielding them. We have already touched on some of the results when leaders fail to have intercessors coming to their defense. Now let's see what it looks like when a leader is actually protected in prayer.

Again in his book *Prayer Shield*, Peter Wagner lays out a strategy I believe every leader should adapt. It involves three levels of prayer protection, which I refer to as shields.[11] The first shield, which he calls I-1 intercessors, is the innermost guard and is comprised of prayer warriors with whom the leader has a close relationship. These are people committed to praying for the leader faithfully and dutifully, who will most likely know personal, even confidential information about the leader. Obviously, the leader must have a great sense of trust with these inner-circle intercessors, as he must remain vulnerable with them in relaying prayer items and daily life situations.

Some of these intercessors may pray every day, while others intercede at irregular times when the Lord prompts them. I recommend leaders have at least three of these close intercessors, and in some cases more are required. The important thing is that each prayer warrior is a different type of intercessor with a unique prayer anointing. (We will cover this in the next chapter.) If you were the leader of a financial business, for example, you would want a workplace intercessor, along with a financial intercessor or someone with an anointing to pray for money (this could actually be the same person).

I-1 intercessors are in regular contact with the leader and have direct access to him at any time. If they call him on his cell phone at two o'clock in the morning, he will still pick up because he knows they are not just calling to chat. If he is seconds away from signing a business deal and an I-1 intercessor calls with a word from the Lord, he stops and listens before putting pen to paper. (This again underscores the necessity of a high level of trust between the leader and these intercessors, who would know better than to ever abuse their full-access privileges.) I have thirteen intercessors that make up my inner shield. Each has my ministry itinerary and has permission to call me anytime, anywhere. In fact, there have been a few times when I took a call while ministering on the platform—that's how much I value my I-1 intercessors.

The second level of prayer shield (I-2 intercessors) is larger than the first and made up of intercessors who have a more casual relationship with the leader. These people still are in contact with him, though not as frequently as I-1 intercessors. They also have general knowledge of the leader's life events and situations but are rarely involved on a day-to-day extent and don't have as direct access as inner-circle intercessors. The leader keeps these second-level prayer warriors informed on a regular basis, but if they have a word to offer him, they must go through a less direct channel of communication, such as an email or a letter through the leader's assistant.

The third level of prayer shield (I-3 intercessors), which forms the outermost layer of protection, is comprised of people who have only a distant relationship with the leader, have little or no contact with him, and share no intimate exchange of information. In many cases, the leader has never even met these people, but the intercessor feels a nudge from God to pray on the leader's behalf. For major leaders, particularly ones in the national or global spotlight, this third level could possibly consist of thousands upon thousands of unseen I-3 intercessors. When Aunt Susie reads a report about you in the news and starts to pray for you, for example, she has just joined the ranks of your third-level prayer shield.

The beauty of this three-tiered prayer structure is the chain-link-like barrier it creates around a leader. Without a leader having prayer protection, the devil has a free shot to take him out and can use even the most basic of tactics to do so. But when a leader's multifaceted team of I-1 intercessors is working in tandem, it makes it extremely difficult for the enemy to get to him with the same weapons. When a second level of protection is added, it becomes even harder; and with a third, it is a feat for the enemy to ever get through at all.

WHAT TO LOOK FOR IN AN INTERCESSOR

Because we are all leaders in some capacity, each of us needs such fortified protection, regardless of whether you are in charge of a global company worth billions of dollars or the afternoon school bus route. Everyone needs to be covered.

The key, then, is finding people who will cover us in prayer. When soldiers enroll in the army, they don't get to choose who is assigned to their troop. But as that troop grows closer through experiences both in preparing for war and on the battlefield itself, it becomes a given that those soldiers will cover each other, back each other up, and even risk their lives for each other. Those in a leader's I-1 prayer shield should have the same willingness to take a bullet for him.

It may be difficult to find such trustworthy, dependable intercessors to cover you on your trek up a cultural mountain, but they are key to your success. Cindy Jacobs, in her book *Possessing the Gates of the Enemy*, identifies at least four qualifications to look for in an effective intercessor:[12]

❖ *They are committed to pray.* True intercessors will stick to the task they have promised to take on, which is to undergird you in the spiritual realm. Often leaders will endure such heavy attacks from the enemy that the option of giving up grows increasingly attractive. In those moments, their fight up the mountain can seem futile, yet that is exactly when they need to hear encouraging words from those who will stand by them through thick and thin. Committed intercessors will remind leaders of their calling and inspire them with words that evoke God's promises to them. These prayer warriors will not only catch a leader before he loses his footing and falls down the mountain, they will also strengthen him enough to keep him moving forward— all because of their commitment to be there in his times of weakness.

❖ *They uphold confidentiality.* Personal intercessors in your I-1 prayer shield will undoubtedly know details of your life that others do not. As a leader, you entrust them with valuable information that deserves to be handled with care and complete confidentiality. For business leaders, this can often include product information, processes, or systems that, if leaked to competition, could drastically harm them. It is essential that you have full confidence that those in your intercessory circle will not share your private matters with others.

❖ *They are able to listen to God and share in an unintimidating way.* I have encountered too many intercessors who use their gift, as great as it might be, to belittle those they pray for while emphasizing their "tremendous" ability to communicate with God: "John, I sense that you're struggling to get direction from God right now. You know I'm highly prophetic and can hear His voice, so it's a good thing you asked me to pray for you. Here is what God would say to you…" Not only are such statements filled with pride, they make it difficult for a leader to want to seek out intercessors who will undergird him. Regardless of how or where your intercessors hear from God—whether in heaven or in dreams and visions— they must be humble enough to deliver the word in an encouraging fashion that uplifts you rather than puts you down.

❖ *They are called by God to pray for you.* Flakey intercessors will tell you one day that God has sent them to pray for you, only to disappear the next week. The most valuable intercessors, however, will back up this unique calling with commitment and action not because they want to impress you, but in response to God's assignment for them. When you are headed to war on the Seven Mountains, the best intercessors to cover you are those responding not to your request but to a higher commissioning.

In addition to these four elements, an effective intercessor will possess the right prayer anointing to fit with others in your intercessory circle. It is crucial that leaders' prayer shields contain the right mix of intercessory gifts. For example, the owner of a media company *does not* need five intercessors who are each anointed to pray about issues of injustice. What he *does* need are intercessors who will intercede prophetically for his company's voice, with a gift mix to cover the financial side of his business, his personal well being, and family (just to name a few). The important thing is to create a team of prayer warriors who will pave the way for breakthrough.

Let's examine this further in the following chapter as we break down the types of intercessors. If you haven't already gathered, intercessors come in all shapes, sizes, and with unique anointings. The key for you, the leader, is to surround yourself with the right kinds of intercessory gifts so that your prayer shield is fortified, your enemy is thwarted, and you are truly covered.

Chapter 11 Notes

1. Chip Cummins and Sarah Childress, "On the Maersk: 'I Hope if I Die, I Die a Brave Person,'" April 16, 2009, http://online.wsj.com/article/SB123984674935223605.html (accessed July 31, 2011).

2. CNN.com, "Hostage Captain Rescued; Navy Snipers Kill Three Pirates," April 12, 2009, http://www.cnn.com/2009/WORLD/africa/04/12/somalia.pirates/ (accessed July 31, 2011).

3. Associated Press, "Hostage Captain: 'I'm Not a Hero, the Military Is,'" April 17, 2009, http://www.msnbc.msn.com/id/30259052/ (accessed July 31, 2011).

4. WTKR-TV, "Capt. Richard Phillips Reunites with USS Bainbridge Crew That Rescued Him From Pirates," http://www.wtkr.com/news/wtkr-bainbridge-reunion,0,3579312.story (accessed July 31, 2011).

5. Hugh MacLeod, "'Tribes': Ten Questions for Seth Godin," October 8, 2008, http://gapingvoid.com/2008/10/08/tribes-ten-questions-for-seth-godin/ (accessed July 31, 2011).

6. C. Peter Wagner, *Prayer Shield* (Ventura, CA: Regal Books, 1992), 104–115.

7. Ibid., 66–73.

8. CNBC.com, "Merrill Lynch CEO Thain Spent $1.22 Million on Office," January 22, 2009, http://www.cnbc.com/id/28793892 (accessed July 31, 2011).

9. Abbie Boudreau, David Fitzpatrick, and Scott Zamost, "Wall Street: Fall of the Fat Cats," October 17, 2008, http://www.cnn.com/2008/US/10/17/siu.wall.street/index.html (accessed July 31, 2011).

10. Charles Spurgeon, *Morning and Evening* (Peabody, MA: Hendrickson Publishers, 1997), November 17 evening entry, available at http://bible.christianity.com/devotionals/morningandevening/550758/ (accessed July 31, 2011).

11. C. Peter Wagner, *Prayer Shield*, 119–138.

12. Cindy Jacobs, *Possessing the Gates of the Enemy* (Grand Rapids, MI: Chosen Books, 1991), 164.

Chapter 12

RECRUITING AN ARMY

Y OU DID NOT have to be a basketball genius in 1984 to recognize that Michael Jordan was special. After being named Player of the Year and opting to turn professional following his junior year in college, Jordan took the National Basketball Association by storm. As a rookie, he ranked third in the league in scoring, while also leading his team in rebounding, assists, and steals. Despite a season-ending injury only three games into his second year, he came back to pour in a record sixty-three points during a memorable playoff game against the Boston Celtics. And for the next seven consecutive years, he led the league in points per game.

Yet for all his statistical achievements, All-Star appearances, and jaw-dropping highlight-reel plays, Jordan remained a one-man show. Throughout the remainder of the 1980s, Chicago Bulls fans knew the routine: their star would dominate games while seemingly dragging a cast of average players into the playoffs, only to be roughhoused by well-rounded teams who had the luxury of focusing solely on keeping Jordan in check. (Division rivals Detroit Pistons even created the "Jordan Rules," by which all five players would do whatever it took and expend as many hard fouls as necessary to limit No. 23's effectiveness.)

In the 1990–1991 season, everything changed. After years of giving their leader the ball and getting out of his way, the supporting cast around Jordan matured to the point where he could trust them to produce during pivotal moments of a game. Young players such as Scottie Pippen, Horace Grant, and B. J. Armstrong blended their raw talent with veteran center Bill Cartwright, three-point specialist Craig Hodges, and a host of role players. Although Jordan still dominated games, for the first time since he entered the league, his team had enough essential elements to roll through the playoffs and finally win a championship.

The celebration did not end there. The Bulls became the most dominant sports team of the 1990s, winning six titles during the decade. Jordan was obviously the prime reason for Chicago's championship era, yet upper management deserved credit as well. Beginning in 1987, several behind-the-scene leaders in the franchise worked hard to surround Jordan with complementary players—those who had the skills that would best suit the star's otherworldly talents. These franchise leaders (and a Hall of Fame coach) realized that by surrounding Jordan with players he could trust, the team would go much further than he could ever take it on his own strength. Jordan needed the sharpshooting of Armstrong, Hodges, and backcourt mate John Paxson. He could not make it through the physical playoff battles without the presence of big bruisers Grant, Cartwright, Will Perdue, Stacey King, and Scott Williams. And he certainly had to rely on the versatility of fellow All-Star Pippen to bring elements that he could not alone.

Were it not for the specific *type* of support he received during those years, Jordan might be just another great basketball player without a championship ring. True, he would likely still be acknowledged as *one of* the best players ever. Yet because of those around him, he is now widely accepted as *the* greatest. For Jordan, the teammates who supported, undergirded, encouraged, and sacrificed for him made all the difference in whether he reached the pinnacle of NBA greatness.

It is no different with those attempting to scale the Seven Mountains of society. Despite all the individual God-given talents you may possess, you still need the support of prayer warriors who will undergird you in the spirit and push you further than you could venture alone. As we learned in the last chapter, every leader needs help. Every leader needs to be covered.

But every leader also needs to be covered specifically according to his needs. Just as Jordan would not have succeeded with only outside shooters or only rebounders on the court with him, so will leaders fail to scale their specific mountains with only the support of one type of intercessor. A businesswoman doesn't just need an intercessor gifted in praying for finances; she needs a mix of intercessors anointed to pray for her family's safety, for personal integrity, for removing spiritual and natural obstacles, for God's kingdom to reign throughout her business decisions, and on and on. Every leader requires a unique mix of intercessors, according to which mountain he is climbing and what his unique circumstance is.

WHO'S IN YOUR CIRCLE?

In the last chapter, we probed into why leaders often remain uncovered as they scale the cultural mountains. Now that we have identified these reasons and proven the necessity of covering, the next logical question to ask, then, is this: Who should be covering you? What types of intercessors are necessary for you as a leader? In 1 Corinthians 12:4–6, Paul says there are "varieties of gifts, but the same Spirit. And there are varieties of ministries, and the same Lord. There are varieties of effects, but the same God who works all things in all persons." Within every prayer circle should be a variety of intercessory types and anointings. The word *anointing* has taken a bad rap in recent generations because of its misuse, but it simply refers to the release of God's power through us to passionately sustain what we cannot do in our human strength. Put in laymen's terms, anointing is God's *umph!* arriving precisely when we reach the end of ourselves.

When it comes to prayer, each of us has an anointing—a point at which the Holy Spirit arises from within us to take over our intercession and bring power to our words. When we pray in this unique anointing, a supernatural power sustains the passion in us and leads us into spiritual dimensions we otherwise could not venture. Yet as Paul indicates in his letter to the Corinthians, we are not limited to a single anointing; there are a "variety" of gifts that create a powerful mix of anointings in each person. We don't earn this or work up these anointings; they are in our DNA. But using our own unique combination, we can carry out the assignments for which God has set us apart.

After years of working with intercessors, I now recognize at least twelve different types of intercessors. These can also be described as twelve different prayer anointings. Either way, it is crucial for leaders to involve a strategic blend of these gift mixes to make up their prayer shield. It is equally critical for these leaders to recognize the pitfalls that can occur with each of these intercessory giftings. Without fail, Satan will try to use these God-given gifts against us. When you excel in public speaking and carry a natural charisma about you, for example, the enemy will naturally yet subtly use these positive aspects as fertile soil for pride to grow in your life. The same goes for intercessors who are gifted in a specific type of prayer. For this reason, I have included a few pitfalls of each type of intercessor.*

1. *List Intercessors.* The Bible depicts Ezra as someone who would qualify as a list intercessor. An orderly man, Ezra made a list for everything. (If you don't believe me, try reading Ezra 1–2 and 6–10.) Obviously, he was inclined to keep track of things in bullet-point fashion. List intercessors not only pray from a list, they believe a list translates to power, direction, and strategy.

List intercessors are the most faithful type of intercessors, with a designated time (and often place) of prayer. They pray for items on their list until they are answered or until they have the assurance from the Lord that it is accomplished.

Unfortunately, most intercessors begin their prayer life forced into list-based praying. For whatever reason, it is ingrained in us that true prayer warriors, being the spiritually disciplined kind, always use lists— like the little, old, gray-haired ladies who wake up at four or five o'clock every morning, sit in their rocking chairs, and dutifully go through their prayer lists.

In all honesty, praying from a list is sheer misery for me. I worked for Intercessors International for eleven years, and for more than six of those years I trained intercessors to pray with lists as if this were the only way true prayer was done. Praying through a list of items was tremendously boring for me, yet I persevered and even instructed others to follow my lead. I later discovered the error of my ways and changed my outlook on praying. My husband, on the other hand, thrives on praying from a list. When we come together to pray, he wants to know what the specific prayer points are and exactly what we will be praying about.

List intercessors, as is the case with each of the twelve intercessory types, are necessary and provide an aspect to praying that others cannot. Yet they can be prone to believing their way is the only way to pray—to the extent of being judgmental toward those who deviate from "The List." The sheer volume of their prayer "coverage" can create a sense of pride that they are doing magnificent deeds in the heavenly realm simply because they are following their detailed list. Is it any wonder, then, that Satan turns this positive aspect—covering much spiritual territory through organization—into an element that can bog

---

* For more details, I encourage you to read *Intercessors: Discover Your Prayer Power*, which I co-authored.

down and discourage these bullet-point warriors? The reality is that prayer lists can often get lengthy. And when a list intercessor is unable to get through all his prayer points in the time he has designated to pray, Satan swoops in with thoughts of guilt, inferiority, insecurity, and resignation. If an intercessor continues to hammer away at his list yet never feels as if he can get through it, he can be prone to eventually giving up.

I once taught at a women's Bible school in India where the president made all the students wake up at four o'clock every morning and pray from *his* prayer list for at least two hours. After prayer time, he would ask the students if they had finished their praying, and if they did not, he publicly chastised and disciplined them. When I spoke to this group about the different types of intercessory anointings, several of the students who were not natural list intercessors began to weep. For the first time in their lives, they began to understand why they would often get "stuck" on one item, crying and wailing for an hour or more as the Spirit moved upon them to intercede, despite the imminent shame they would face from the school's president.

If you are a list intercessor, do not let your anointing to pray in an organized fashion get in the way of what the Spirit wants to do during your prayer time. Order is good and often necessary, but so is flexibility. As you begin to pray, hold your list before the Lord and say, "God, I bring all of these prayer points before Your throne today; show me which one is on Your heart for right now." Then be willing to start with that one, whether it is number one or number twenty-seven. Let God order your list.

2. *Crisis Intercessors.* The most well-known crisis intercessor in history is King David. His psalms prove that if David did not have enough crises in his life, he created his own. And that is what crisis intercessors do: these paramedics of prayer often turn a serene situation into one that needs urgent care—flashing ambulance lights and all. In fact, some of the greatest scenes that prove who is anointed as a crisis intercessor and who isn't are stalled cars along the side of a busy interstate road. If you are a crisis intercessor and spot a car on the side of the highway, you immediately launch into praying for the people in the car, for any problems, accidents, or injuries that could have occurred, for the possible response team, for the families involved, and on and on. Within minutes, crisis intercessors will have covered every potential angle of that situation with prayer. Those who are not crisis intercessors,

however, are likely to drive by the scene and simply utter a "Dear God, be with those people"—five minutes down the road!

Crisis intercessors can often ward off a crisis with prayer. They are the first to respond to the Holy Spirit's call to pray. When a recent hurricane was clearly headed toward the Florida coastline, for example, a network of praying intercessors turned it back to the ocean!

Crisis intercessors are faithful to pray, even if they don't know why they are praying. They are more likely to get an uneasy "feeling" warning them about some situation, though they do not know the details of the impending crisis. They often cannot explain this feeling, but they sense something in their gut—and if they are attuned to the Holy Spirit, this is for good reason.

When our son Eric was in high school in San Antonio, he needed to drive to Houston to catch his flight to Virginia Beach where he would visit his grandparents. Because the air conditioner was not working in Eric's car, my husband Ralph, offered to let Eric drive his sports car to Houston.

After his visit with his grandparents, Eric arrived back in Houston. Before he drove home, he called to ask if it was OK for him to drive home. It was late and we expected him to spend the night, but he said he would rather come on home. I did not have a good feeling about the situation, so I said, "No."

"Come on, Mom. Why not?" he asked.

"I don't know—I just don't have a good feeling about it," I replied.

Like most children learn to do, Eric asked his dad, hoping for a different answer. He was honest enough to tell his dad that I did not want him to drive. Because I could not explain why I was feeling strange, Ralph allowed Eric to drive home that night.

By now you can guess what happened. While on his way home, Eric reached over to change the cassette in the tape deck when his car suddenly rolled over two-and-a-half times and landed upside-down. It was completely demolished, except for the one part over his head. Miraculously, our son was able to climb out with minimal injuries and run to safety.

Several months later, Eric once again asked if he could do something. This time, after hearing me say that I did not have a good feeling, he listened.

There are a few downsides to crisis intercessors, however. One is their tendency to interrupt corporate prayer situations with such urgency that they usher in a sense of panic and emergency, even if the Lord did not intend for them to send out an SOS signal. For this reason, it is crucial that crisis intercessors also possess a level of maturity from which they can discern when things are a red alert instead of an orange or yellow. Crisis intercessors can also form a habit of moving from one crisis to another and feeding off the adrenaline rush that comes with this. Unfortunately, this comes at the cost of completely abandoning a focused faith or even at the expense of spending quality time nurturing a loving, intimate relationship with the Lord.

3. *Issues Intercessors.* In Proverbs 31, we find traces of an issues intercessor in King Lemuel's mother. The king recounts her words: "Open your mouth for the dumb [those unable to speak for themselves], for the rights of all who are left desolate and defenseless; open your mouth, judge righteously, and administer justice for the poor and needy" (vv. 8–9, AMP). Lemuel's wise mother urged her son to stand against injustices, and that is exactly what issues intercessors do.

Those who pray over issues will find that the Holy Spirit puts an assignment on their souls. Sometimes issues flow out of personal experiences or their own hurts; other times the Lord simply drops a burden like a seed into their heart's soil and then pours out prayers to water it.

Issues intercessors are invaluable in bolstering those who ascend up the Seven Mountains of culture. Who else speaks for a child in the womb who has no voice? Who stands in the gap for the orphans? Who cries out to the Lord on behalf of homosexuals or drug addicts? Who fights in the heavenlies for single mothers, broken families, latchkey kids, and prisoners? The list goes on, yet these are all examples of the things issues intercessors have a unique anointing to pray for. Where few others are willing to put in the time to rend the heavens, issues intercessors continue to declare justice for those in need.

As noble as their anointing sounds, however, issues intercessors have a few potential pitfalls. Often those who do not share the same passion for specific issues can easily annoy them. They can sometimes fall into the trap of believing whatever issue they are praying for is the only important issue, and this can lead to pride as they wear the issue as a red badge of courage. Issues intercessors also have the potential to step outside the boundaries of what God has called them to intercede for, and the result is a soulish desire to rescue others rather than a pure call of God.

4. *Salvation Intercessors.* The apostle Paul was one of God's greatest intercessors for souls. As with any salvation intercessor, his heart beat for the lost. Virtually every Christian desires to see others come to know Jesus as their Lord, yet salvation intercessors have a unique anointing to pray these people into the kingdom. Their prayers expand the kingdom of God. This anointing is often combined with others to create a unique gift mix. Many salvation intercessors, for example, are also list intercessors and are disciplined in regularly praying for a roster of names that have yet to encounter Jesus. Other salvation intercessors are also gifted for crisis intercession—as was the case in the aftermath of the January 2010 earthquake in Haiti, when a network of intercessors saw more than 40,000 Haitians, including 101 voodoo priests, come to Christ.[1,2]

One of the biggest snares for salvation intercessors is discouragement. When they pray faithfully for weeks, months, or years on behalf of a lost person yet see no results, it is natural for them to be disheartened. The same reaction often meets those who are overwhelmed by the sheer number of lost people. At times, either path can lead to fatigue, depression, hopelessness, and even the decision to abandon a prayer post.

I thank God this did not happen when my mother-in-law, Esther, prayed for me. When my husband Ralph and I were married, she was convinced there was no way a marriage between a calm Norwegian (him) and a fiery Greek (me) would work without God. So she began to pray. As a list intercessor, she placed me atop her prayer points and faithfully interceded on my behalf every day—for ten years! In fact, the night before I accepted the Lord, she had grown angry with the Lord over the fact that I had yet to be saved. According to her, the Lord responded with these words: "Would you leave her alone? She is in My hands!"

I am grateful to have a mother-in-law who was so tenacious in praying for my salvation. Were it not for her prayers, I wonder if I would be writing this book.

5. *Personal Intercessors.* In the Book of Esther, we see that Mordecai was Esther's personal intercessor. He wanted to see his cousin fulfill her destiny more than she wanted to. When she felt like quitting, he stood in the gap and said, "Hold on—you have been born for such a time as this!" Like Esther, every leader needs a personal intercessor—and this is particularly true for leaders who are rising on a cultural mountain

and becoming easier targets for the enemy. They need prayer warriors who will lay their lives on the line for a single person for whom God has assigned them to pray.

Personal intercessors make up the prayer shields for individuals. They prevent the person they are praying for from being deceived. God used Esther's personal intercessor, Mordecai, to change history. God entrusts personal intercessors to carry confidential information in and out of His throne room on behalf of the person they are praying for. They partner with that person for provision, protection, and prayer priorities.

With such a calling, however, come potential negatives such as sharing private information about their prayer target under the guise of achieving "agreement in prayer." Personal intercessors can also become susceptible to using their own "words" in place of divine correction or delivering a true word from God at inappropriate times. At times, these intercessors can think so highly of the one they pray regularly for that they neglect to speak truth into that individual's life, instead offering "soft" prophecies birthed out of a fear of disapproval.

6. *Financial Intercessors.* Though Scripture does not explicitly state this, I believe Joseph was a financial intercessor who, in time, was catapulted by God into a position of governmental leadership so he could then stand in the gap for the riches God had in store. (See Genesis 37–48.) The Lord gave Joseph a plan for how to store up wealth—or, in his case, food—during a long, severe famine. God's word, through Joseph, positioned Egypt to not only feed its people, but to also come to the aid of other nations. Financial intercessors have the faith to believe for large amounts of money. They have faith to believe for funding and can often discern the blockage that holds finances back. God gives financial intercessors ideas to create wealth, including witty inventions.

The church desperately needs financial intercessors like Joseph who will stand in the gap to claim God's riches. Yet one of the most common pitfalls among these intercessory types—particularly when their prayers are not answered—is the notion that they must be rich to have the faith to believe for large amounts of money, either for themselves or for others. In God's economy, money is not a prerequisite for faith. Neither is it an inherent evil, as many Christians think. Praying for money is not evil. First Timothy 6:10 says, "The *love* of money is a root of all sorts of evil" (emphasis added). We need money—lots of it—to get the gospel out. We need money to transform the Seven Mountains. We need money to change cultures. Who will stand in the gap to call these riches in for the kingdom?

God anoints financial intercessors to do just this. When a ministry needs to raise $3 million in one week to help an earthquake-ravaged nation, financial intercessors are the ones who instantly respond with faith and believe that it can be done. When others say it is impossible, they speak it into being.

But let me offer a warning to those who are financial intercessors: be cautious of praying for finances alongside those who you know are doubters in this arena. Nothing squelches an intercessor's faith in God's ability to fulfill His word and provide millions (or whatever the amount is) like a group of naysayers. God owns "the cattle on a thousand hills" (Ps. 50:10), which is the Bible's way of saying all the wealth of the world is under His control. He has the power to provide any amount, even when it seems impossible. (This is why it's good to have financial intercessors praying over offerings.)

Years ago, I was teaching this principle in Switzerland to a relatively small crowd of 120 intercessors. The organization that brought me in, Campus Crusade for Christ, had accumulated significant debt in hosting the EXPLO 2000 conference, so I asked if I could teach on financial intercession and call forth those who were anointed specifically to pray for God's provision to cover the event's costs. Out of the 120 people present, only ten people identified themselves as financial intercessors. I instructed them to pray and ask God how much He wanted to provide; then I turned to the rest of the crowd (those who were not anointed for this) and asked them to pray that the ten would hear an exact amount from God. With everyone participating, and with each of the intercessors receiving an amount, I then told them to set their faith to believe for that amount.

The next job for the entire group of 120 was to pray regarding how much they personally were to give. We took an offering and counted it during the break. I then called up each of the ten intercessors and went down the line asking how much they were believing for. As the first person said $1,000, a few members of the audience gasped. Another intercessor said $7,000, which drew an even bigger response of shock—after all, there were only 120 people there. I continued down the line, and each one seemed to top the previous—first $10,000, then $15,000, then $30,000. (For a moment, it felt as if I was an auctioneer.) Finally, I asked the last person, and the crowd was almost hysterical by now. His response: "God said take the highest number and double it."

The offering that day was more than $70,000! Even I was amazed. Although this man did not know what the highest number was, he had set his faith to believe, as had each of those intercessors. Yet the way God orchestrated everything that day proved to us all the value in financial intercessors not sharing with others what they are believing for. Can you imagine how much lower the last man's level of faith would have been if he had asked someone who was not anointed in praying for finances the amount they were believing for? The offering brought in that day was nothing short of impossible, and yet God worked through the faith of ten average people training in financial intercession to astound us all.

7. *Mercy Intercessors.* Jeremiah is often referred to as the weeping prophet (see Jeremiah 9:1), though he did not weep for himself but for the state of his people. He was moved to tears by the Spirit as he interceded for his nation. If you are a mercy intercessor, your tears are your prayers, and you have undoubtedly experienced similar prayer times. Mercy intercessors have an emotional sensitivity to the cries of the Holy Spirit like few other prayer giftings. They feel God's heart, particularly for people.

Unfortunately, mercy intercessors are also the most dishonored of all the intercessory types. Part of this is because we do not know how to handle tears in many cultures. We teach our males from an early age that boys don't cry. Even women grow up believing that tears are a sign of weakness, and we often hold back from crying for fear of being ashamed.

Mercy intercessors, however, cannot hold back the tears when the Spirit moves upon them as they pray. That is not only a good thing, it is a necessary thing. Every time Jesus was moved with compassion, a miracle followed. The truth is, tears soften hardened ground. And if we hope to soften the rock-solid hearts of many key players on the Seven Mountains, we must start with tear-filled intercession. Despite often being misunderstood, unappreciated, and dishonored, mercy intercessors play the pivotal role of watering the ground for culture-changing, mountain-moving miracles. They are instigators for breakthrough!

Unfortunately, mercy intercessors—particularly immature ones— are also prone to grieving to the extent that they give up their lives in despair rather than laying them down in prayer to plant seeds of hope and change. It is one thing to be moved by the Spirit but another to remain in the flesh. Many times the enemy will use identificational tears birthed in intercession as seeds of depression. Mercy intercessors must be mature enough in their faith to know the boundaries where God has not commissioned them to go past, if only mentally or emotionally. They don't own the burden; they bear the burden and give it to the Lord. The danger comes when mercy intercessors hold on to the burden and won't release it to the Lord. This can result in depression.

8. *Warfare Intercessors.* The Bible presents many examples of warfare intercession, but perhaps none is as mature in its expression as the prayer lifted up to God by Jehoshaphat in 2 Chronicles 20. Facing "a great multitude" (v. 2) of enemies bent on going to war, the king of Judah offered a prototypical prayer for entering into battle by stating the truth. Though Jehoshaphat addressed God, in essence he was declaring to the entire spiritual realm, particularly those spiritual enemies who desired to see Judah demolished: "O LORD, the God of our fathers, are You not God in the heavens? And are You not ruler over all the kingdoms of the nations? Power and might are in Your hand so that no one can stand against You. Did You not, O our God, drive out the inhabitants of this land before Your people Israel and give it to the descendants of Abraham Your friend forever?" (vv. 6–7).

Jehoshaphat's rhetorical questions reminded the darkness that his God was the powerful, overwhelming Light. The king partnered with truth, just as any wise warfare intercessor does. He declared truths from lies, light from darkness, and (ultimately) victory from defeat.

I am a warfare intercessor. If I were reading this chapter aloud to you, you would be able to hear the passion in my voice. It is part of the reason this book contains many warfare and military themes. I get excited about warring in the spiritual realm and reminding the demonic forces of God's all-defining truth. But I have also received enough battle scars that prove the pitfalls of being a warfare intercessor. One of the major ones for us is a tendency to go from battle to battle without taking time to rest—both in the spirit and in the natural. When my husband served in the Vietnam War, the Air Force sent him home to rest after a season of serving. Today, when I travel, I routinely encounter soldiers returning from the line of duty for a time of rest.

Warfare intercessors must understand how vital rest and healing is to our unique calling. It does us—and the entire body of Christ—no good if we are perpetually wounded when we go out to fight. We must first be healed, rested, and refreshed before we think about further ministry. Just as we would never send out a wounded troop of soldiers into battle, intercessors must be strong before engaging the forces of darkness.

9. *Worship Intercessors.* Although David and Asaph wrote some of the Bible's most renowned intercessory psalms, Hannah stands as a prime example of a worship intercessor. (See 1 Samuel 1–2.) Her prayer of thanksgiving (2:1–10) came in the form of a song, yet it also found her standing in the gap with declarations of eternal truth and reminders of who God is. As many worship intercessors are, Hannah was also misunderstood. The high priest Eli misread her heartsong intercession as drunkenness or foolish talk. Today, church leaders often mistake many worship intercessors as merely being creative or artistic in their expression, when in fact they are standing in the gap with praise, worship, and intimacy with the Lord. Worship intercessors' songs *are* their prayers.

Keep in mind, however, that such worship intercession does not always have to be a musical expression. We are often guilty of qualifying musical ability with worship, yet Jesus defined true worshipers as those who worship "in spirit and truth" (John 4:23). You do not have to have a great singing voice to be a worship intercessor, nor do you have to play five different instruments. The Lord is seeking those who—whether using song or not—will open up the heavens over each of the Seven Mountains with worship that not only moves His heart, but also changes the atmosphere.

Worship is a weapon of warfare. It opens the heavens. The war in the heavens has always been over *who* will be worshiped.

The first time I experienced worship intercession was more than seven years after I had become a Christian. A well-known minister was visiting a friend's house, and based on all the wonderful things I had heard about him, I was excited to finally hear him in person. Instead of speaking, however, he picked up his guitar and began to sing a phrase from Psalm 124:7: "My soul escaped, like a bird out of the snare of the fowler / The snare is broken and we have escaped / Our help is in the name of the Lord."

He sang it over and over again, to the point that I began counting. By the time he reached twenty, I was a little agitated. Upon reaching thirty and forty, I grew mad; I was tired of hearing someone sing about his soul escaping like a bird. I got up, went to the kitchen where no one could see me, and began talking to God: "Lord, this is ridiculous. You know I have better things to do than listen to this!" Sixty, seventy, eighty—when was he ever going to stop singing this silly song? In my mind, I was screaming and fuming.

Then something broke. I was not looking for it, was certainly not in the right "spirit," and yet suddenly my soul "escaped like a bird." I felt a swelling inside me and couldn't help but jump up and down. I danced around the kitchen, feeling like a free bird soaring in the heavens, and at that moment, he stopped singing! Years later, I finally grasped that the man was interceding for me through worship—powerful, spirit-altering worship.

I have experienced this countless times since, yet I will never forget the impact it had during a trip to Allahabad, India. A city steeped in Hindu tradition, Allahabad is believed to be where all the gods of India converge—yes, all 350 million gods! I had been training intercessors, preparing them for this "god invasion" for several years prior. While on this trip, we put our training to practice and took twelve intercessors to a cathedral in the heart of Allahabad, where during the British rule, thousands of people would come to worship the one true God. At that time, however, the numbers had dwindled to a mere thirty or forty people gathering, which showed just how powerful the Hindu influence had become.

As we stood in this "old well" of a church, we began to sing a variation of the song "Come, Now Is the Time to Worship" by my friend Brian Doerksen. The Lord instructed us to sing it not as an invitation but as a command, and so we did: "Come, Allahabad! *Now* is the time to worship. Come, Allahabad! *Now* is the time to give your heart.... One day, Allahabad, every tongue will confess Him as God; one day, Allahabad, every knee will bow." For almost half an hour we sang these lyrics to the north, south, east, and west parts of the city. We were commanding the people to come; we were not inviting them.

Within days, still during the festival for the converging gods, the city experienced a rainstorm strong enough that only a few people showed up—meaning only a few gods showed up too! And today, instead of a mere thirty or forty people worshiping at the cathedral, almost thirty thousand come to lift the name of Jesus. Now *that* is powerful worship intercession!

10. *Government Intercessors.* A perfect example of a government intercessor, Daniel actually shifted the ruling government of his land. Though his intercession—more specifically, through identificational repentance, in which he identified with the sins of past generations—Daniel stood in the gap for an entire people group. He did not say "they sinned," but instead took it upon himself to say "*we* sinned." As a result, he stood as a mediator for God's people amid a secular government.

Government intercessors not only pray for the government, they actually embrace apostolic intercession. They know when to shift from pastoral prayers of petition to making proclamations, declarations, and decrees as they convene the courts of heaven.

Government intercessors typically are up to date on current events, are knowledgeable about the movers and the shakers, and quickly recognize how judicial decisions affect certain areas or populations. This is not only true for those who intercede for a national government, but also those who are anointed to pray for church government, local authorities, regional representatives, and all other types of government. Yet with a passion to know the who, what, when, why, and how of all things government-related, often these intercessors can fall prey to an intolerance for those who do not share a similar passion, prayer calling, or even understanding. Not coincidentally, they can succumb to the same spirits of pride and power that rule the political arena.

With these two forces often comes a spirit of people-pleasing. Politicians are notorious people-pleasers, saying whatever it takes to win over others and secure a vote. Unfortunately, that same spirit can entrap even the strongest intercessors who become more concerned about being accepted among the political elite than about following the instructions of the Holy Spirit. In an effort to get the "inside scoop" from the ruling parties, these well-meaning prayer warriors compromise their integrity and beliefs. Their unholy sense of awe over governmental positions causes them to fear people more than God.

When seeking someone whom God has anointed to pray for government, make sure their primary focus isn't warring for or against a specific candidate, party, or even legislation but instead calling forth the righteousness of God's kingdom across the land. The most effective government intercessors fear God more than man, and out of this holy fear comes a kingdom perspective that understands the necessity of declaring God's righteous rule and judgment over both geographical land and, more importantly, the people who dwell there.

11. *People Group Intercessors.* Like the Samaritan woman whom Jesus met at the well (John 4:5–42), these intercessors stand in the gap for a specific ethnic group. If you have ever heard someone speak of having "a heart for Norway" or China, for Palestinians or the Sudanese "lost boys," then you have likely encountered a people group intercessor. God endows these prayer warriors with a powerful love for a specific group of people, and standing in the gap for that country, region, or ethnic tribe becomes a personal calling of sorts. People group intercessors are not afraid to cross generational, cultural, gender, ethnic, or status boundaries.

Often God places a burden to pray for a specific people group for a season. When I went to Rwanda immediately following the genocide, God had me interceding for the Hutu and Tutsi people for a year or two after I left—and then the season ended. I have also been praying for Koreans since 1981—and that prayer calling remains strong!

Despite the love God gives people group intercessors for their specific prayer target, sadly many of these prayer warriors develop a sense of resentment for those who do not share a similar burden. This is frequently seen among the most predominant sector of people group intercessors—those who pray for Israel. As they "pray for the peace of Jerusalem" (Ps. 122:6), they develop a sense of pride (are you noticing a pattern of pride?) that questions all those who dare not pray for the Holy Land, much less God's chosen people. These intercessors can further this bitterness by taking on offense on behalf of the Jewish people.

Satan often uses this intercessory gift against these prayer warriors, turning a seed of offense into genuine judgment and even hatred for those who come against Israel. It is impossible to intercede effectively from a place of offense; be wary of those who try—whether they carry that offense for Jews, Iranians, Indians, or Samoans. Intercession seeded in an offensive spirit undoubtedly leads to rotten fruit.

12. *Prophetic Intercessors.* As we clarified in chapter 6, being prophetic is simply saying what God says, while intercession is standing in the gap for people, situations, and lands. Prophetic intercession, then, is saying what God says over people, situations, and lands—it's that easy!

Like Moses or John the Baptist, prophetic intercessors prepare the way for God's will to be done upon the earth. At times that requires proclamations; other times it calls for declarations; and still at other times making decrees is necessary (see chapter 8). Yet all three require the prophetic act of following or repeating what God says. Though this is not a definitive theological definition, a prophetic act is doing something in the natural that appears to have no power in the natural, yet when combined with God's word and a measure of faith, actually wields great power.

For example, sacraments such as baptism or communion are prophetic acts. By itself, being sprinkled with or dipped in water has no power in the natural. If it did, then everyone who takes a bath or shower would have a life-changing encounter with the Most High God. Yet when combined with the word of God and a person's faith, baptism takes on a great power. Likewise with communion: drinking grape juice or wine and eating bread has zero power in the natural realm. Otherwise, can you imagine what a bar scene would look like during happy hour as God manifests Himself with every bite and sip? When combined with faith and the power of God's word, however, communion takes on an entirely new—and very real—power.

Under the same power given by the Holy Spirit, prophetic intercessors enact the will of God on this earth through their prophetic prayers, which include both words and actions. Their intercessory cries often unlock the heavens to break longstanding curses, thwart the enemy's purposes, and dispel the forces of darkness.

Whenever I lead an intercessory team on a trip overseas, I always ask God for a strategy as we prepare to enter into foreign "mountains." Just as Jehoshaphat had to seek God for a unique strategy for each battle, I spend time waiting upon the Lord for His divine direction for each trip. On one journey to Romania, I waited and waited and continued to ask God for a strategy, yet never received one. About a week before our trip, I walked into a church service during worship and heard the worship team singing the words, "Songs that bring Your hope, songs that bring Your joy / Dancers who dance upon injustice." I did not know any other part of the song "Did You Feel the Mountains Tremble?" by the band Delirious at the time, but I immediately knew the Lord was telling me that this was my strategy: we were to dance upon injustice!

The irony was that no one on the team was a dancer. Despite each of us having two left feet, we tried to dance upon the injustices committed against the Romanian children at every orphanage we visited. On the last day, we crossed a bridge on an empty road and decided this was the place we needed to cut loose. As goofy as we might have looked, we danced our hearts out, skipping around and declaring through our fumbled steps the Lord's victory and redemption over every atrocity and injustice that had been committed against generations of children.

We left and made our way into a small town. There in the center of town was a mound where a statue of a former leader once stood. The sculpture represented years of oppression, of abandoned children, of neglect, cruelty, and abuse upon the younger generations, yet it was now a mere mound of dirt. As we prayed over this area, my friend, who normally has no singing voice, stood up, pointed her finger to the sky, and began to sing an incredible song of the Lord. As the rest of us recovered from our initial surprise, children from all over began to crowd around us. I grabbed their hands, formed a circle with them, and we started dancing around the mound. The children didn't know they were doing spiritual warfare—they were simply having fun with us. Yet our simple prophetic intercession created a heavenly breakthrough as God used a group of children to dance upon the injustices committed against previous generations of children in their nation. Only He could have orchestrated such a beautiful scene, yet by receiving His divine strategy—and enacting it through prophetic intercession—we were able to see His victory.

Such dramatic scenes are not irregular for prophetic intercessors. Yet because of this, one of the pitfalls for these prayer warriors is trying to outdo the previous prophetic prayer, word, or deed. I have known a few prophetic intercessors who became so wrapped up in their prophetic acts that their prayer times became outlandish displays of "Can you top this?" Indeed, prophetic prayer warriors can fall prey to finding their identity in the prophetic rather than in the God who gives it. As a result, they may refuse to allow their prophetic word or act to undergo scrutiny from authority—an overt sign of pride. Likewise, these prayer warriors may feel compelled to add to what God has said in an effort to appear super-spiritual. This can even include adding personal opinion or impressions into a "prophetic word" that brings judgment over a person, people group, or land.

HOW TO PICK A WINNING TEAM

With so many different types of prayer anointings, it can seem overwhelming for the average leader deciding which types of intercessors he needs to surround him as part of his prayer shield. Yet the process can actually be as simple as Jesus' instructions in Luke 11:9:

"So I say to you, ask, and it will be given to you; seek, and you will find; knock, and it will be opened to you."

1. *Ask*. Leaders can ask God for who He wants to undergird them. Jesus already stands in a place of intercession on their behalf, and He also knows who is already doing the same for them in prayer. Whether these leaders know it, often there are prayer warriors already interceding for them; the real task is for leaders to hear from God regarding who these people are. That begins with simply asking.

2. *Seek*. As leaders seek to hear from God, He will respond—often by bringing to mind names of those prayer warriors who would be a perfect fit and who have the right gift mixes to comprise an effective prayer shield. Leaders should respond by listing these names and continuing to pray over them.

3. *Knock*. After pinpointing specific names to recruit as intercessors, leaders can then make contact with these people and ask them if they would commit to the task. Most leaders are surprised to discover how eager many intercessors are to use their spiritual gifts for the cause of advancing cultural mountain climbers.

On the flip side, there are a few ways leaders can help those who make up their intercessory prayer shields become more effective in their task. Too often intercessors report a lack of information, input, feedback, openness, and even trust from the leaders they pray for. As a result, they feel limited and restricted in using their gifts to undergird and support.

To avoid this, leaders must first communicate with their intercessors on a regular basis—depending upon the level of prayer shield, of course. It is not necessary for a leader to communicate every week with those within his I-3 shield, for example. It is, however, crucial that the lines of communication remain open and consistent for I-1 intercessors.

Second, leaders should encourage their intercessors. This does not have to be a lengthy letter or call. But as any intercessor can attest, a brief message that confirms that their specific prayers are on target (e.g., divine revelations about the leader given to the intercessor during prayer) can go a long way in encouraging a deeper level of intercession.

Third, leaders must remember that those who make up their prayer shield are not their prayer partners. *Webster's Talking Dictionary* defines the word *partner* as "a person who shares or is associated with another *on the same level* in some action or endeavor" (emphasis added). Suzanne and I have been prayer partners since 1978. We pray for each other, for our families, and for our callings. We war for each other and rejoice with each other. This relationship is mutual and reciprocal. But a prayer partner is different from being a member of your prayer shield. My prayer shield wars for me. They are the ones who fight for me. I am not warring for them, though I do pray for them, specifically that they hear from God; I pray prayers of blessings. Members of my prayer shield commit to pray for me. Intercessors need intercessors! However, a leader is not expected to be a prayer partner for his intercessors; rather, it is the intercessors' privilege to serve the leader in prayer.

A leader's prayer shield is similar to a NASCAR race team. In NASCAR, there is only one driver of one car, yet each member of the team is vitally important to the race. The pit crew has certain responsibilities to keep the gas tank full, the tires changed, and the fluids topped off. The coach has a computer read-out of exactly what is going on with the car, the driver, and the race. He communicates directly with the driver and gives specific instructions. The driver can't win the race without a team who stays focused on their specific assignments and works together with the rest of the crew. And for each member, the end goal is to give the driver the best chance possible to win the race. So it is with those who make up a leader's prayer shield.

Finally, leaders should encourage intercessors to discover their own anointing. I encourage my prospective intercessors to read *Intercessors: Discover Your Prayer Power* and tell me what their gift mix is so I can place them in the right shield. Sometimes this means realizing a certain intercessor is not the best fit and that he would be more effective praying for a different leader who needs more of the unique gifting he brings to the table. Or sometimes I realize that an intercessor needs to be moved to a different shield or circle. Leaders should keep in mind that this is a process; they don't have to get everything right on the first try. God gives abundant grace, and so should they.

CHAPTER 12 NOTES

1. Barbara Denman, "40,000 Haitians Profess Faith in Christ Since Jan. 12 Quake," Baptist Press, February 25, 2010, http://www.bpnews.net/bpnews. asp?id=32370 (accessed July 31, 2011).

2. Sermon Index, "Revival in Haiti: A Call to Fasting and Prayer," video clip, http://www.youtube.com/watch?v=v5vEntWb7AI (accessed July 31, 2011).

Chapter 13

THE WAR CHEST

IF NOTHING ELSE, sixteen years in exile taught Chinese revolutionary Sun Yat-sen one thing: you cannot win a war without money. From 1895–1911, the "father of modern China," as he is called today, plotted multiple uprisings against the corrupt Qing government, despite his being relegated to planning from foreign soil. Each rebellion failed primarily because of a lack of finances, forcing Sun to travel throughout Europe, the United States, and Japan on a fundraising mission.[1]

His message to potential financial supporters was simple: *No matter how passionate those fighting on our behalf, no matter how well-constructed our strategy for battle, to conquer land we need money.* His failed coups and rebellions were proof that often wars are lost purely because of finances. Those whose war chests are deepest gain the higher ground for battle.

Wars are expensive. Not twenty-four-carat diamond ring expensive or Lamborghini expensive. No, wars are so expensive they keep countries in business and maintain a global economy unto themselves. Large-scale warfare takes such serious money that, after a while, the numbers become almost incomprehensible.

The United States' so-called "war on terror," for example, started in 2001 immediately following the terrorist attacks of September 11. What was supposed to be a swift, successful military retaliation in the rugged terrain of Afghanistan has turned into a decade-long struggle with a current tab of $300 billion. The Iraq War, meanwhile, began in March 2003 and, as of this writing, continues to drain American taxpayers to the tune of a staggering $747.3 billion. Combined, these two present-day wars—both with no end in sight—amount to a mind-blowing *$1 trillion-plus.*

What could you do with $1 trillion? You could provide sufficient healthcare to 294,734,961 adults or 440,762,472 children for the next year. You could supply 1,035,282,468 homes with renewable electricity for 365 days. With $1 trillion, you could award the maximum amount for the Pell Grant ($5,500) to every one of the 19 million college and university students in the US—*for the next nine years!* And if you are still wondering just how massive $1 trillion is, consider this: even if you earned $1 million each year, it would still take you another *million years* to become a trillionaire.[2]

Wars cost. They cost money, and they cost lives. The Vietnam War cost the United States more than 58,000 fatalities, while more than 1.3 million Vietnamese (North and South) lost their lives.[3, 4] By comparison, World War I accounted for more than 16 million deaths on and off the battlefield, while World War II cost an astounding 60 million-plus people—soldiers and civilians—their lives.[5, 6]

Ask a veteran of these or any other war who has watched fellow soldiers lose their lives in the line of fire, and he will attest to the immeasurable price of war. There is no dollar amount for lives lost, and it is foolish to even attempt to place such a price tag on the human casualty cost of any war.

If wars in the natural are this costly, why do we think it would be any different when combining the natural and spiritual realms as Christians seek to scale the Seven Mountains of culture and confront the controlling enemy forces? Regardless of where we are positioned on each of the mountains, we must understand that as the level of fighting escalates, so does the cost involved. Although I could spend many pages explaining and proving the toll this war takes in terms of human lives, for this chapter I want to focus on the element on which the church has so egregiously erred: finances.

POOR US

When it comes to the messages we have relayed in church regarding money, we have not just fumbled the ball—to use a football analogy—we have willingly handed it over to the opponent in our own end zone! For hundreds of years, generation after generation of believers has taught that it is more righteous to be poor. Instead of believing "the *love* of money is a root of all sorts of evil" (1 Tim. 6:10, emphasis added), we have convinced ourselves that *money* is the root of all evil, an earthly tool of the devil that inevitably corrupts the soul. Therefore, we think that the less we have, the more spiritual we are.

In more modern countries and times, believers have consistently struggled with the concept of wealth, particularly among affluent nations. Today, we find yet another surge of leaders in the United States promoting the idea that truly following Jesus means taking a vow of poverty—selling all we have in accordance with His "instructions" to the rich young man in Matthew 19:21.

This is all part of a poverty mind-set, which is driven by the religious spirit. Peter Wagner calls the spirit of poverty "a demonic agent of Satan, intent on preventing people from enjoying God-given prosperity" and adds, "One of the most effective tactics of the evil spirit of poverty has been to persuade Christian leaders that poverty is somehow noble."[7] Prophet Chuck Pierce says a poverty mind-set "keeps us from entering our full potential. Those bound by expectations of poverty never look beyond the narrow scope of the immediate lack in order to find God's rich promises for the future." Pierce also argues that at its core, poverty says, "God is not capable!"[8] The poverty mentality is not only linked with our possessions, but with every issue of supply in our lives, including such things as relationships with God and with one another.

Poverty is characterized throughout the Bible as a curse—and rightly so. The Lord pronounced a potential curse upon the Israelites in Deuteronomy 28:48 should they disobey God: "Therefore you shall serve your enemies whom the LORD will send against you, in hunger, in thirst, in nakedness, and in the lack of all things." Proverbs 13:18 says, "He who ignores discipline comes to poverty and shame, but whoever heeds correction is honored" (NIV). In fact, Paul specifically points out how Jesus took poverty upon Himself for our sake: "For you know the grace of our Lord Jesus Christ, that though He was rich, yet for your sake He became poor, so that you through His poverty might become rich" (2 Cor. 8:9).

The word *rich* used there does not necessarily mean we will have Bill Gates' bank account. This is where the majority of the church today either misunderstands this concept or completely abuses it. Jesus took upon Himself the poverty of this world so we could be free from its curse. That does not mean everyone who follows Him is entitled to or should expect Bentley cars and million-dollar houses, but it does mean we will live without lack. The key, then, is ridding ourselves of a poverty mind-set that keeps us ensnared in the lack that so easily holds us back—just as the enemy of our souls would want. Deuteronomy 28:11 says, "And the LORD will make you abound in prosperity, in the offspring of your body and in the offspring of your beast and in the produce of your ground, in the land which the LORD swore to your fathers to give you." It is important to note the sequence of Deuteronomy 28. Before God mentions the potential curse of poverty that comes with disobedience to His will (as cited in verse 48 above), He clearly establishes His original intent of blessing. He desires to bless us and to prosper us! And as was the case with the Israelites, those who obey God will receive His best, which is the essence of prosperity. This is the path He intends for all who follow Him. As John wrote, "Beloved, I pray that in all respects you may prosper and be in good health, just as your soul prospers" (3 John 2).

If God's natural pathway, His highest way of life, is one of prosperity, it doesn't take a genius to figure out what Satan—the great counterfeiter—would use as the way toward destruction. The opposite of prosperity is poverty. Satan wants nothing less than to keep those ascending the cultural mountains encumbered and ensnared by a poverty mindset that believes God is incapable of providing and therefore His followers must live in a continual state of lack.

The truth is, our enemy has succeeded for almost two thousand years. The church has erroneously bought into the lie that piety is directly proportional to poverty. This notion began when Constantine divided the church in A.D. 313, separating clergy from laity. His unnatural division in turn planted the seeds of a mind-set that believed certain people were holier and more righteous than others simply because of their role as church leaders—a belief that was further watered and tended three hundred years later when the Benedictine monks began taking vows of obedience and chastity to prove their commitment through celibacy. By the twelfth century, clergy had solidified themselves as the religious elite—a select class widely accepted as more spiritual, holy, and righteous than the common person. Within this environment, already ripe with the religious spirit, Francis of Assisi imposed another vow: poverty. Now, in a twisted sense of "high" religion, the poorest among the poor became the holiest as clergy swore to a life of complete lack.

Today, the church in general has rejected all vows but one—that of poverty. For reasons that suit our enemy just fine, the body of Christ continues to cover itself with a spirit of poverty, all in the name of being holy.

POVERTY AND WORKPLACE LEADERS

How does this affect the war waged on the cultural mountains? More specifically, what does all this talk of poverty have to do with intercessors praying for workplace leaders, who are the largest targets and therefore encounter the greatest warfare upon those mountains? In a word: *everything*.

The poverty mind-set limits intercessors in how effective their prayers can be upon the spiritual battlefield. If deep inside they believe God cannot provide adequately, that when all is said and done He is not strong enough to overcome every obstacle and enemy, then how will these prayer warriors' doubt-filled prayers be taken seriously by the forces of darkness? That is like listening to a sales pitch for the latest exercise machine from a four-hundred-pound, out-of-shape salesman. Not only are the words not convincing, they are powerless, given the person who is offering them.

On the flip side, workplace leaders with a poverty mind-set have an effect on those praying for them. As long as these leaders cling to a mind-set of defeat and lack, they restrict and hinder the intercessors trying to undergird them in the spirit. God, of course, can break through this flawed pattern of belief. But as His foot soldiers, we give the enemy ground as long as we uphold mind-sets standing in direct opposition to God's kingdom values. These faulty mind-sets include the notions that:

❖ The world of commerce and finances is inherently evil; therefore, those working in the business world are in constant need of cleansing. (Because of this, why would anyone want to undergird in supportive prayer those who are involved in evil on a daily basis?)

❖ Those who are more righteous—the clergy—are doing God a favor by being poor.

❖ Pastors should be poor, and it is the role of a congregation to make sure the pastor is kept "in need of God's provision." (I have traveled to countless churches in wealthy nations— not third-world ones, mind you—that have this mentality.)

❖ Business people should give free service to clergy. Sadly, many ministers around the world have adopted the notion that, because of their role as "mediators" between God and the congregation, they should receive freebies whenever, wherever, from whomever—lawyers, doctors, restaurant owners, mechanics, etc.

❖ Jesus was materially poor. (Food for thought: If Jesus was so poor, and if His ministry involved nothing more than

living off of everyone else's graces, then why did He need
a treasurer?)

The more believers buy into these and other lies, the more they
establish a spiritual framework for a poverty mind-set to move in and
take up residence. They begin to hear the voice of poverty echoing
through the chambers of their spirits: *God is not able. God will not provide.
God will not come through.* Yielding to the lies of these whispers, they
start to believe that the Lord will never launch them into the destiny He
has for them, but that instead He has abandoned them.

Adopting a mind-set of poverty restricts, hinders, and binds. That is
true whether you are a workplace leader or an intercessor for a leader,
whether you are a millionaire or a beggar. It makes no difference how
much money you have or how depleted your bank account is; the spirit
of poverty has the same effect on the rich as it does on the poor.

In addition, we can never forget that poverty itself is not just a mind-
set. It is an evil spirit, a demon assigned by Satan to prevent people
from prospering by keeping them in a constant state of lack and insuf-
ficiency. Poverty is a curse. It does not make us holy; it only makes us
poor!

MAMMON'S ALL-STAR TEAM

In a war, it is always important for soldiers fighting on the ground
to understand both their immediate surroundings and the bigger
picture. In World War II, for example, American soldiers fighting in the
Philippines knew they were there to help the massive cluster of islands
defend itself from Japanese forces. Yet for a multitude of reasons—from
morale to strategy—it was crucial that each soldier understood he was
not just fighting for Philippine territory or to hold off Japan from further
expansion throughout the Asia-Pacific region; his battle was part of the
larger war against the Axis forces bent on world domination.

Poverty, as powerful as it can be, is merely a spirit and is not to be
confused with the larger principality called Mammon, of which poverty is a part. Jesus identified this principality in Matthew 6:24 when He
stated, "No one can serve two masters; for either he will hate the one
and love the other, or else he will be loyal to the one and despise the
other. You cannot serve God and mammon" (NKJV). Out of all the things
Jesus could have identified in addressing such an important topic, why
did He mention Mammon? Because He was not about to waste time

dealing with piddly spirits and demonic weaklings; Jesus honed in on the bigger issue. This is important for intercessors to understand and essential for prayer warriors who are standing in the gap for workplace leaders currently bound by poverty. By better understanding the principality of Mammon and what it is comprised of, intercessors can identify the deeper issues at hand when praying for those on the seven cultural mountains.

Whenever the principality of Mammon is at work, you will find a team of spirits involved. In the same way an All-Star team is made up of the best individual players, Mammon's "team," or roster, is filled with some of the best the forces of darkness have to offer. First, there is the spirit of greed. Avarice, as this spirit is also known, is not just a simple desire for more things. It is, as *Webster's Dictionary* defines it, *"too great a desire to have wealth"* (emphasis added).[9] Avarice is all-consuming and insatiable in its quest for more material possessions. It is excess to the nth degree. When the average person is content owning one car, someone under the influence of avarice (the spirit) desires twenty cars. While everyone else is fine with a nice cell phone, avarice drives a person to "need" every new cell phone that is released with all the latest bells and whistles.

I quoted the first part of 1 Timothy 6:10 earlier, but notice the words that follow: "For the love of money is a root of all sorts of evil, and some *by longing for it* have wandered away from the faith and pierced themselves with many griefs" (emphasis added). Though not as powerful as Mammon, avarice is the source of this unrelenting longing and love for more, more, and yet more.

The second demonic spirit we find on Mammon's team is the spirit of covetousness. This is the same spirit that stirs up envy to the point that people act out—often rashly and uncharacteristically—in their desire to have what cannot be had. To covet is to want something that is someone else's, something that is forbidden. Covetousness inherently leads to idolatry, which keeps us from prospering. For this reason, Paul tells us in Colossians 3:5, "Therefore put to death your members which are on the earth: fornication, uncleanness, passion, evil desire, and covetousness, which is idolatry" (NKJV).

The third member of Mammon's All-Star team is the spirit of parsimony. That is not a word we hear often these days; today, we are more likely to use the word *stinginess*. When you hear of the spirit of parsimony, think of a clenched fist with a crumpled dollar bill in it. A hand that is clenched tight and holding on to material wealth is incapable of giving. That is exactly the posture in which the spirit of parsimony intends to keep people. This even applies to those who are rich and have enough possessions to share with their entire neighborhood. A miserly person is not just someone who is a penny-pincher; he is unwilling to let go of his money and holds it so close to him that it suffocates any potential life left in him.

Finally, Mammon's team is rounded up by the spirit of self-reliance. A cousin of pride, self-reliance presumes to displace God as the source of every good thing. Those who are self-reliant have often worked hard enough and persevered long enough that they eventually discovered success. And that success, particularly when repeated over time, reinforced the belief in them that they can do anything on their own. *I've built my own empire. I've made it big-time on my own and have everything I could ever want—what else do I need? I certainly don't need God!* When we are convinced that we do not need God, we are walking in self-reliance.

Using the spirits of greed, covetousness, parsimony, and self-reliance, Mammon has remained a powerful principality throughout the world since the fall of mankind. Its four-pronged offense has infiltrated the church for years and left entire communities of believers in desolation and defeat. It does not help that too often Christians focus only on the most common fruit of Mammon—poverty—instead of realizing there is a larger, more powerful principality at work.

THE DIVINE EXCHANGE

Just as the opposite of a clenched fist is an open one, the opposite of greed is giving. You cannot give away something with a closed fist, and you cannot be greedy if you walk through life with an open hand. No matter how much money you earn, God never intended you to hoard what He has blessed you with. He is a giving God, and He desires His children to mirror this through a giving lifestyle.

How can you give away if you do not have anything? That is exactly where the poverty mind-set returns to try to dissuade people from entering into a life of freedom through giving. Satan would love to hold captive every person in a place that believes God will not give him anything. As long as Christians are bound by that poverty mind-set, they will never prosper—because the opposite of poverty is prosperity. As John P. Kelly, CEO of International Christian Wealthbuilders

Foundation, says: "We have to hate poverty to defeat it. And we have to love prosperity, and desire for success, in order to achieve it."

When you are released from the demonic spirit of poverty, you can naturally embrace the reality that God is a giving God who wants you to prosper. Does He want to prosper you so you can keep all your money and possessions to yourself, holding them with a clenched fist? Of course not! His desire is to bless you so that you, in turn, will be a blessing to others.

This is the heart of God. In fact, it is at the core of God's purpose for establishing His presence among people. He birthed the nation of Israel upon this divine premise and established a covenant with Abraham that was passed along to generation after generation: "I will make you a great nation, and I will bless you, and make your name great; and so you shall be a blessing; and I will bless those who bless you, and the one who curses you I will curse; and in you all the families of the earth will be blessed" (Gen. 12:2–3).

Approximately two millennia later, despite Israel's defiance, God continued to make a way for His people to be blessed. Jesus Christ was the greatest gift ever given, the ultimate blessing sent down to us so that we too could reciprocate that blessing by living as Christians. As if that was not enough, Jesus accomplished something through His life that no one else but Him could have done: He took our poverty so that we could in turn have His riches. Jesus recognized the power of poverty and understood how detrimental it was to God's eternal plan of blessing all people. And so Christ came with a heavenly transfer in mind, just as the apostle Paul describes in 2 Corinthians 8:9: "For you know the grace of our Lord Jesus Christ, that though He was rich, yet for your sake He became poor, that you through His poverty might become rich."

What a divine exchange! After centuries of pursuing His people to bless them so that they would in turn bless all the nations of the world, God established a permanent means—His only Son—to accomplish the task. Jesus' poverty forever opened the doors for our eternal riches. Now that's good news!

Those riches are not limited to earthly goods, nor are they meant for mere earthly purposes. These are the spoils of heaven—God's war chest opened wide, if you will. The Bible, therefore, lets us in on a secret when it presents at least two general uses for riches. First, we see God's stewardship plan initiated whenever we receive riches. This is His divine principle of blessing, by which, if we walk in righteousness,

God will multiply what He has given. Jesus' parable of the talents in Matthew 25:14–30 clearly depicts the Father's intent and higher purpose for bestowing riches upon His servants. To each slave who doubled his portion—as meager as it was—the master said, "Well done, good and faithful slave. You were faithful with a few things, I will put you in charge of many things; enter into the joy of your master" (vv. 21, 23). Yet the master was enraged with the slave who did nothing with what he was given. He threw him out and labeled him a "worthless slave." Through this parable, Jesus makes obvious the kingdom principle of stewardship: "For to everyone who has, more shall be given, and he will have an abundance; but from the one who does not have, even what he does have shall be taken away" (v. 29).

THE BUSINESS OF BLESSING

There is another biblical purpose involved when God pours out His riches on someone. It is the underlying reason why we must never forget the lopsided trade Jesus made of exchanging our poverty for His riches. His higher purpose was to establish a wealth of "supplies"—in the form of blood-bought souls—who would enact Holy Spirit–inspired strategies for the sake of God's good-news plan. What good news? That God desires to bless and prosper all those who were purchased by His Son. Stated another way, He wants us to spread the wealth of His Son's salvation—using His abundant riches!

Too often Christians can succumb to the same mentality as the world regarding finances. We can easily adopt the spirit of fear by which Satan establishes his foothold, and from there we develop a poverty mind-set that believes—in fear—that God will not provide and therefore we must cling to the little we have. This spirit of poverty will turn even the most abundantly blessed Christian into a money-clenching miser, causing God's purpose of blessing to once again be derailed. Jesus took our poverty once and for all so that we could continuously reflect the Father's heart to bless those around us unconditionally. Christ was set on establishing God's kingdom business on earth through this exchange.

We must have that exact same mind-set, which says that all financial blessing (which comes from God in the first place) is meant for kingdom purposes first. That means businesses are not simply vehicles to prosper individually and gain more money so their owners can pile up riches upon riches. Businesses are intended to advance the kingdom of God.

Their divine purpose is to bless the nations of the earth. Every business in this world is meant to reflect the heart of God!

Consider Deuteronomy 8:18: "But you shall remember the LORD your God, for it is He who is giving you *power to make wealth*, that He may confirm His covenant which He swore to your fathers, as it is this day" (emphasis added). The word *wealth* used in that verse is not limited to money. The original Hebrew word, *chayil* (khah'-yil), also connotes strength, might, ability, virtue, efficiency, and valor. *Chayil* is a word picture of an army, and the original King James Version actually translates it on a few occasions as "a band of men (soldiers), a company, or (great) forces."[10] Obviously, God's intent in giving us "power to make wealth" involves the heavenly battle for prosperity. He desires His army on earth to be equipped in strength and finances.

Because that is God's ultimate kingdom purpose, He intends for the gifts of His Holy Spirit to be used fully in the workplace. It should be commonplace for Christian business owners to walk under the power of the Holy Spirit in divine wisdom, knowledge, faith, healing, miracles, prophecy, spiritual discernment, and tongues—and even the interpretation of those tongues (see 1 Cor. 12:8–13). If the workplace leader you are praying for does not operate in these gifts, intercede on his behalf that the windows of heaven will pour out such divine riches. Remember, this is not about accumulating wealth for pure pleasure and excess; it is about being in and doing God's kingdom business of blessing.

Chapter 13 Notes

1. CNN.com, "The Father of Modern China: Sun Yat-sen (1866–1925), *Visions of China*, http://www.cnn.com/SPECIALS/1999/china.50/inside.china/profiles/sun.yatsen/ (accessed July 31, 2011).

2. Urbana-Champaign Independent Media Center, "Crossing the $1 Trillion Cost of War Line," http://www.ucimc.org/content/crossing-1-trillion-cost-war-line (accessed July 31, 2011).

3. National Archives Military Records, "Statistical Information About Casualties of Vietnam War," http://www.archives.gov/research/military/vietnam-war/casualty-statistics.html (accessed July 31, 2011).

4. Associated Press, "Vietnam Says 1.1 Million Died Fighting for North," *The Ledger-Star*, April 4, 1995, http://web.archive.org/web/20071222122211/http://scholar.lib.vt.edu/VA-news/VA-Pilot/issues/1995/vp950404/04040331.htm (accessed July 31, 2011).

5. Wikipedia.org, "World War I Casualties," http://en.wikipedia.org/wiki/World_War_I_casualties (accessed July 31, 2011).

6. Wikipedia.org, "World War II Casualties," http://en.wikipedia.org/wiki/World_War_II_casualties (accessed July 31, 2011).

7. C. Peter Wagner, *Dominion* (Grand Rapids, MI: Chosen Books, 2008), 185.

8. Chuck D. Pierce, "40 Days to Revamp: Day 22—Sept. 15, 2009," Glory of Zion International Ministries, http://media.gloryofzion.org/devotion/archivedisplay.php?did=78 (accessed July 31, 2011).

9. *Webster's New World College Dictionary*, 4th ed., s.v. "avarice."

10. *Biblesoft's New Exhaustive Strong's Numbers and Concordance with Expanded Greek-Hebrew Dictionary* (Biblesoft and International Bible Translators, Inc., 1994).

Chapter 14

MARCHING ORDERS

OST AMERICANS WHO hear the phrase *I have a dream* understand the power behind Martin Luther King's famous 1963 speech from the steps of the Lincoln Memorial. Likewise, few patriots can listen to the words *Fourscore and seven years ago* without recognizing the inspiration packed into Abraham Lincoln's renowned Gettysburg Address. Our nation will forever remember these monumental speeches.

Yet for those on the frontlines—the soldiers tasked with putting their lives at risk with every second of warfare—possibly the most unforgettable words heard are those given before a potentially culminating battle. For these warriors, a commander's speech before the fight goes beyond tactical instruction and last-minute strategy; it is a source of inspiration and motivation. It is, in the most literal and figurative sense, a true charge.

At the tail end of World War II, as the Allied forces sensed momentum shifting their way in a long, costly war against Adolf Hitler's empire, US Lieutenant General George S. Patton Jr. delivered such a charge. His legend had already preceded him, with word buzzing among the troops as they waited that May day in 1944 in England: Patton's here—*the* General Patton is here! By the time he arrived in a long, black car and stepped out, impeccably dressed with a holstered Colt .45 Peacemaker on his right side, the anticipation among the crowd was almost tangible.

"America's fightingest general" lived up to the hype, using his words, presence, and raw charisma to command the attention of every soldier within earshot. In typical Patton style, his speech was littered with profanity and vulgar references. Yet history records the powerful effect the moment had upon these young soldiers as they listened to such a legendary figure offer them a powerful charge:

> You are not all going to die. Only two percent of you right here today would die in a major battle. Death must not be feared. Death, in time, comes to all men. Yes, every man is scared in his

first battle. If he says he's not, he's a liar. Some men are cowards, but they fight the same as the brave men or they get the hell slammed out of them watching men fight who are just as scared as they are.

The real hero is the man who fights even though he is scared. Some men get over their fright in a minute under fire. For some, it takes an hour. For some, it takes days. But a real man will never let his fear of death overpower his honor, his sense of duty to his country, and his innate manhood.

Battle is the most magnificent competition in which a human being can indulge. It brings out all that is best and it removes all that is base....Remember that the enemy is just as frightened as you are, and probably more so. They are not supermen.[1]

Throughout this book we have identified the forces that lie behind enemy lines. We have exposed the fear-filled tactics of Satan and his demonic realm, and we've recognized that the enemy's effectiveness in ruling the Seven Mountains with darkness hinges upon weapons such as miscommunication, deception, pride, and the spirits of religion and poverty. Satan currently uses these, among others, to maintain a position atop each of the cultural mountains.

Yet just as Patton said of his enemy, Satan and those who fight on his behalf are not supermen. As one who exists in a state of constant fear, the devil is infinitely more frightened than we are—and not just because he knows his impending doom when Christ returns. I believe Satan is now beginning to shake in fear as he sees a church rising in power and truth, a church that understands and is gradually exposing his tactics and, even more, relies upon what God has declared as its foundational battle plan.

Our weapons, as we have discussed in this book, are spiritual, not carnal. Yes, they have been dulled, neglected, and even forgotten for generations. But the church is awaking! As the assault of darkness upon this earth increases, Jesus' glory—represented in His body, the church—is simultaneously increasing and, by its very nature, casting out all darkness with the pure light of God's kingdom.

A Model for War

One of the key ways we establish this radiating glory in every corner of the earth is through prayer. Obviously, this book has been all about using intercession to invade the seven cultural mountains and ultimately take them as earthly territories within which God's kingdom is free to reign. Yet too often Christians can read a book such as this—one with revelatory truths that, if correctly applied, can help to establish that kingdom—and walk away no more empowered than when they first picked it up.

How is that possible? Because they read solely with their carnal minds, without letting God's revelatory truths into their spirits. Knowledge and education are wonderful and necessary when approaching a war. But infinitely more important is the spirit that carries you into the battlefield.

I hope this book has fed your spirit and that you have allowed your spirit to take in what I believe are keys to establishing God's kingdom via intercession. But I also know many times the greatest way to "soak up" truth, revelation, or anointing is to see those elements enacted. We all need models from which we can learn. When you learn to drive, for instance, you don't study from a book and then one day hop in a car to drive through downtown traffic. You first watch someone model how to drive, *then* you gradually put into practice what you saw (preferably in a parking lot or a back road, for starters!).

In 2008, I created a network to put into action the model God placed in my spirit years ago. The framework came from principles God has taught me over my thirty-plus years of leading prayer teams. During that time, I have consistently been involved with changing the atmosphere of so-called "secular" environments into places that welcome God's presence and power. Most of these were, in fact, workplace settings—small businesses, mega-corporations, public schools, private universities, government halls, and the like. I would meet with the leaders of these settings and, almost without fail, receive an open invitation to pray for them, their families, their companies, their employees, and anything else they mentioned. As God opened door after door for intimate yet powerful times of prayer with these leaders, it became obvious that the Lord was giving me (and other prayer warriors) not just a new role, but also a new job description. We were to be apostolic intercessors for these workplace leaders, hired by them specifically to declare into the heavenly realm what God had already promised.

Therein lies the heart of the Apostolic Intercessors Network (AIN), which has since connected hundreds of businesses and individuals with powerful, uniquely appointed apostolic intercessors. As I travel the world, I encounter countless workplace leaders and CEOs desperately wanting God's presence in every facet of their businesses. Most have also seen, at some point, how invaluable intercession is to the success of their companies. They recognize that when God's people pray, the heavens move—and therefore create opportunities otherwise impossible on earth. Many of these leaders initially connect with me on a personal basis, asking only for me to undergird them as individuals in intercession. Yet some soon realize their entire companies need the same attention given in prayer, and that a support structure such as AIN is the perfect solution.

Most business leaders struggle to find intercessors they can trust not only with sensitive information but also with the task of faithfully praying for however long it takes. As we covered in chapters 11 and 12, creating the right gift mix of prayer anointings (both for personal and corporate purposes) and the right intercessors can be a difficult task. AIN rises to that challenge by coming alongside leaders to identify and develop intercessory prayer teams, which are custom-designed for their businesses. It also serves a twofold purpose of connecting workplace leaders with apostolic intercessors *and* connecting apostolic intercessors with leaders, thereby enhancing the relationship between the two groups.

I am often asked why business leaders can't just pray for their companies on their own. Why do they need "hired guns" to undergird the business? The answer is similar to why professional basketball teams hire shooting coaches for their players. You wouldn't think men earning millions of dollars, who have grown up spending days and nights shooting innumerable shots—and who are already coached by the best of the best in the world—would need anyone else to come alongside them and coach them on how to shoot better. And yet every NBA team in the league has a shooting coach, if not several. Some teams even hire coaches for a single player! The reason behind this is pure investment: by paying these expert coaches, teams understand they will reap the rewards in more shots made, which most likely will result in more victories, which can mean more championships. (And in sheer business terms, this translates into more money.)

Apostolic intercessors have a unique gifting. Just as shooting coaches excel in the techniques and finer points of shooting a basketball, apostolic intercessors have been called out by God specifically to rend the heavens. Some believers may be great in evangelizing, and others may have an incredible heart and talent for worship; apostolic intercessors have been gifted to excel in the realm of prayer. Because of this gift, it is worth a business leader's time, effort, and, yes, money to invest in someone who can stand and war in the heavenly realm on a company's behalf.

These prayer warriors can often see things from a new perspective, one the business owner may not have considered. Granted, apostolic intercessors are not coaches—let me reiterate that point. The intercessors who are part of AIN are not paid or called in to offer their opinion on business deals, management, or any other similar area. They are to hear God's directives for a specific company or leader and not taint that word with their own preference or thoughts.

THE MODEL IN ACTION

How, then, does this work on a practical level? First, a business leader meets with an AIN consultant and team director from my overarching ministry, GateKeepers International, to go over the current business situation. After listening to the business leader, the consultant and team director will assess the workplace needs for intercession and strategize with the leader on how to meet those needs quickly and effectively. The intercessors will then assist the business leader in developing and implementing apostolic strategies for the workplace.

One of the most significant differences such business leaders see in hiring AIN for support is the position of prayer taken by apostolic intercessors. These prayer warriors shift from petitioning God to standing with the business leader, inviting Jesus Christ into the workplace, and officially announcing, declaring, and decreeing what God has promised He will do for those in the workplace. As we discussed in chapter 8, this type of prayer takes the offensive position rather than defensively reacting to the enemy's plans to destroy a business. Apostolic intercessors release commanding actions with great faith, knowing that what is spoken will be manifested on earth. Such systematic, powerful, anointed intercession opens the doors of heaven for those in the workplace to experience the fullness of what God has for them.

There is more to the picture, however, than just saying a confident blessing over a company. AIN's representatives also assist workplace leaders in learning how to hear from God for themselves—and, more specifically, how to seek Him for divine strategy for their businesses. AIN's trained consultants will, in turn, train business leaders to operate in the gifts of the Spirit within their workplace environments and to apply the fivefold ministry model to their businesses. Consultants will coach business leaders on identifying and recruiting additional intercessors (both personal and corporate), on networking with other business leaders who desire to do business God's way, on deploying an intercessory prayer shield, and on applying the prophetic words spoken specifically for that workplace. Truly, AIN uses an equipping and empowering model for getting these businesses and their leaders to operate on a higher level.

The immediate goal is to remove, through prayer, every obstacle that hinders advancement in a business. Yet the ultimate goal is for workplace leaders to receive the revelation of Christ's purposes, plans, and strategies for their companies. God strategically positions these leaders "for such a time as this" (Esther 4:14); once they can operate without being encumbered by the enemy's tactics to "steal, kill, and destroy" (John 10:10), they will be empowered to fulfill their destiny, resulting in the reclamation of the Seven Mountains and the overall transformation of society.

Proof is in the Pudding (and the Results of Prayer)

Despite the potential for such turnaround, many people balk at the notion of paying intercessors to pray for a business. Most believe prayer is a spiritual tool given to us as a gift from God, and therefore it should not be sold. I have even had major leaders of the church's intercessory prayer, prophetic, and apostolic movements approach me with concerns over AIN's "pray for pay" structure. In every case, I have posed the same question: if paying someone to pray is wrong, why, then, is it acceptable to pay senior pastors, worship leaders, executive pastors, evangelists, prophetic ministers, or anyone else who is compensated in the church setting for using their spiritual gift? (For the record, almost everyone who has heard it stated this way recognizes that compensating intercessors is not "unholy," evil, or wrong.)

The word *volunteer* is in the language of the Religion Mountain. It does not exist on the cultural mountain of business. The business realm deals with workers, staff members, clients, consultants, and more. There are *no volunteers!* If you work, you get paid—it's as simple as that. Yet somehow, we in the church have adopted a "work for free" mentality when it comes to anything remotely associated with prayer. We will pay someone to sing songs and entertain us under the guise of worship. We will pay guest speakers to use their gift in eloquently preaching God's Word. And we will even pay some itinerate ministers more than what many in our congregations earn in an entire year just so they will come and deliver a prophetic message that tickles our ears. Yet somehow we expect intercessors to go to war for us in the battlefields of the spirit, using a gift that is just as essential to the body of Christ as preaching, teaching, or singing, and receive nothing in return.

Often all it takes to change someone's mind regarding compensating intercessors is evidence of the fruit they bring. Business people have no problem paying someone, especially when that person produces. In the church, we often hesitate to compensate someone, mainly because we have grown accustomed to a poverty mind-set that expects to receive everything for free. Yet for both groups, I can count on one hand the number of AIN clients who have been disappointed with their "investment." The results speak for themselves.

One of our recent clients, for example, says that within the first four weeks of partnering with AIN, his business encountered more unsolicited multimillion-dollar initiatives than in the previous four years combined. Another small-business owner was owed three thousand dollars from a client at the time he hired AIN. In a matter of days, the client not only paid up but also gave a bonus for a total of more than fourteen thousand dollars!

Rather than relay secondhand some of the ways AIN has affected workplace leaders and their environments, let me offer a couple of accounts personally written by those who have hired us. The first is from a woman who is currently working in sales at a business while trying to accumulate enough capital to launch her own company:

> The monthly target [where I work] is $200,000 before I'm eligible for commission. This is a real obstacle because the $200,000 target is actually unrealistic and, for the most part, unachievable. I, nor my colleagues, nor previous staff have ever achieved more than $200,000 in sales per month.

We took this client's prayer request to the AIN team, and within seventeen days, the client wrote us back:

> Oh, how wondrous are Your works, O Lord. His provision of your wonderful, gifted saints is so very much appreciated. My sales are $859,586! Praise God, He really vindicated me.

Another personal account comes from a business owner who listed several positive results from AIN standing with him:

> First, we are on track to have our best year ever, as our first-quarter earnings were 20 percent ahead of last year. Second, the problems with the previous management team have been completely resolved, and the office is running the best it ever has. Third, we have been receiving much favor from the franchise corporate offices and are being asked to help bring our expertise to other franchises that have the opportunity to bid on some very large contracts. Finally, my family is doing very well in health, school, and spiritually.

Not every case deals with monetary or business-related success. Recently, AIN members interceded on behalf of Al and Kacey Hauck's daughter Jess, who had just survived a horrific snowmobile accident. After a season of AIN's apostolic intercessors standing in the gap for Jess in intense prayer, we received a letter describing multiple miracles. Although nurses at one of Jess' hospitals told her she would never be able to walk normally again, she defied the odds and, months ahead of schedule, walked so smoothly that, without seeing her back brace, it was difficult to detect she had ever been injured. In addition, her physical healing was accelerated in almost every area, with one orthopedic surgeon describing her rate and quality of healing as "phenomenal." To this day, Jess still has no recollection of the day of her accident, yet she miraculously relearned the entire previous semester of her graduate school classes and resumed her academic schedule, despite being told that she would likely have to miss up to a year of schooling. To top it off, Kacey informed us that our specific prayers for financial provision had been answered; all of Jess' medical bills and additional needs had been covered. And a recent update from her father informed us that their daughter just received her pilot's license, and she will be receiving her doctorate degree next May!

Finally, another testimony from a client shows the unique role AIN serves in providing workplace leaders with prophetic insight. The client was involved in negotiations over a large project and needed an investor. During the process of searching for this investor, an AIN team member dreamed of a vulture dressed in a business suit and sitting at one end of a long conference table, with our client at the other end. Beyond the negative undertones in the dream, we also interpreted it to mean that there would be a takeover of the client's company.

When our client had secured a final investor and was at the closing meeting, sure enough, the investor sat at one end of a long conference table and our client sat at the other. Our client couldn't help but recall the dream about the vulture and felt a sudden caution in his spirit. When the investor placed the contract on the table, our client particularly remembered the prophetic warning involving the word *takeover*. He re-read the document and discovered the investor had changed his own share of ownership to 51 percent. Without having been given the dream and interpretation, our client would not have thought to re-read the contract before signing, and the company would have been handed over because of sheer oversight!

To War!

If you are a workplace leader, you may not be in a position where you can afford the services of AIN. One of the purposes of AIN is to provide affordable intercession for those in the workplace. We have three levels of pricing, one for "seed" companies, one for startups, and one for established businesses. The monthly prayer fee is based on the number of intercessors on the team and the level of the company. Although I believe every business owner or leader should invest in establishing a prayer-support structure that will undergird your company, there may be some exceptional cases that make this a virtual impossibility. If so, I still challenge you to find prayer warriors around you who will commit to supporting you and your business in the spirit. As we have discussed in the latter chapters of this book, every leader hoping to scale a cultural mountain needs the support of those equipped to engage in war on those mountains.

If you are an intercessor, I challenge you to use the gift God has given you to its fullest. Go beyond being just a one-dimensional closet prayer soldier; become a warrior on the battlefield by serving in an army. Find fellow intercessors with whom you can stand for a united purpose. Join a network such as AIN that can strategically apply your gift to the perfectly matched situation.

The underlying point, whatever your gift or role, is to recognize that we are at war. Our enemy, Satan, currently occupies the Seven Mountains of society. He has done and will continue to do whatever is necessary to take out those who attempt to scale higher on the mountains. He is devoted to distracting and isolating warriors, confusing strategists, creating fear among the troops, and keeping the generals and leaders in defeatist mind-sets. So far, he has done a good job.

Yet the church is rising from its slumber, and this awakening is beginning with those on the frontlines of the spiritual battlefield—the apostolic intercessors who see things beyond what they are now and instead call them into being. We will not be content with an ever-deteriorating culture that is content to be ruled by the kingdom of darkness. We want God's kingdom to reign throughout every inch of this world, including each of the Seven Mountains. We are after no less than the transformation of this world!

Only weeks after Patton offered his speech to the American troops stationed in England, then-Supreme Commander Dwight Eisenhower delivered a starkly different, albeit equally rousing message to the United States' military forces. For months, Eisenhower had prepared and directed Allied leaders with his plan of liberating Europe from Nazi occupation by first invading Normandy, France. On the morning of June 6, 1944—known ever since as D-Day—Eisenhower activated his strategy in a calm yet assured radio broadcast to troops giving the order of the day:

> Soldiers, sailors, and airmen of the Allied Expeditionary Force: You are about to embark upon the Great Crusade, toward which we have striven these many months. The eyes of the world are upon you. The hopes and prayers of liberty-loving people everywhere march with you. In company with our brave Allies and brothers-in-arms on other fronts, you will bring about the destruction of the German war machine, the elimination of Nazi tyranny over the oppressed peoples of Europe, and security for ourselves in a free world.
>
> Your task will not be an easy one. Your enemy is well trained, well equipped, and battle-hardened. He will fight savagely.

But this is the year 1944. Much has happened since the Nazi triumphs of 1940–41. The United Nations have inflicted upon the Germans great defeats in open battle, man to man. Our air offensive has seriously reduced their strength in the air and their capacity to wage war on the ground. Our home fronts have given us an overwhelming superiority in weapons and munitions of war and placed at our disposal great reserves of trained fighting men.

The tide has turned.

The free men of the world are marching together to victory. I have full confidence in your courage, devotion to duty, and skill in battle. We will accept nothing less than full victory.

Good luck, and let us all beseech the blessing of Almighty God upon this great and noble undertaking.[2]

Indeed, the tide has turned for the church. It turned more than two thousand years ago when Jesus conquered Satan, claimed victory over the grave, and established a kingdom of everlasting life for those who would follow Him. Today we have the honor of enacting that victory—of reclaiming territory stolen by the enemy and restoring the kingdom rule throughout the world.

Yes, the task will not be an easy one. Yes, our enemy is well prepared. And yes, he will fight savagely. Yet notice what even Eisenhower pointed out as one of the greatest keys to victory in war: an air offensive. In the case of World War II, winning the war of the air resulted in opening up the path to victory below. This has been a universal truth for every war since: whoever wins the war above wins the war below.

We have seen this to be true on the seven cultural mountains, where the enemy has retained the higher ground. Our key to victory, then, must be to win the war *above* the mountains—the battle over the airways. We must defeat the enemy in the spirit realm.

In the case of the greatest world war ever engaged, winning the battle of the spirit through intercession will establish a dominant kingdom below. Jesus prayed to the Father, "Your Kingdom come, Your will be done, on earth as it is in heaven" (Matt. 6:10). We, the church, can now pray the same prayer to establish an "air offensive," the likes of which the kingdom of darkness has never seen. Satan may currently be the "ruler of the kingdom of the air" (Eph. 2:2, NIV), but this only remains because the church has yet to launch its full offensive in the spirit. Our intercession can turn the tide even further. The wars we win above—in the realm of intercession—will open up clear passageways for those fighting on each of the Seven Mountains. Our assault, both in the air and on the mountains, will ultimately end in victory, but we must first understand the power we wield. If we hope to see society transformed through the regeneration of each of its Seven Mountains, we must truly understand the power of this great weapon God has equipped us with, and we must follow His strategy for war.

We have spent an entire book discussing how to do this; now let's invade the Seven Mountains with intercession and reclaim stolen territories!

Chapter 14 Notes

1. Charles M. Province, "The Famous Patton Speech," http://www.pattonhq.com/speech.html (accessed July 31, 2011).

2. KansasHeritage.org, "General Dwight D. Eisenhower (Ike) D-Day Message," http://www.kansasheritage.org/abilene/ikespeech.html (accessed July 31, 2011).

Appendix A

PRAYING GOD'S WORD OVER THE SEVEN MOUNTAINS

RELIGION MOUNTAIN:

❖ Then he said to Him, "If Your presence does not go with us, do not lead us up from here. For how then can it be known that I have found favor in Your sight, I and Your people? Is it not by Your going with us, so that we, I and Your people, may be distinguished from all the other people who are upon the face of the earth?"

—EXODUS 33:15–16

❖ Now it will come about that in the last days the mountain of the house of the LORD will be established as the chief of the mountains, and will be raised above the hills; and all the nations will stream to it. And many peoples will come and say, "Come, let us go up to the mountain of the LORD, to the house of the God of Jacob; that He may teach us concerning His ways and that we may walk in His paths." For the law will go forth from Zion and the word of the LORD from Jerusalem.

—ISAIAH 2:2

❖ Thus says the LORD, "Let not a wise man boast of his wisdom, and let not the mighty man boast of his might, let not a rich man boast of his riches; but let him who boasts boast of this, that he understands and knows Me, that I am the LORD who exercises lovingkindness, justice and righteousness on earth; for I delight in these things," declares the LORD.

—JEREMIAH 9:23–24

❖ Then Jesus said to His disciples, "If anyone wishes to come after Me, he must deny himself, and take up his cross and follow Me."

—MATTHEW 16:24

❖ For God so loved the world, that He gave His only begotten Son, that whoever believes in Him shall not perish, but have eternal life. For God did not send the Son into the world to judge the world, but that the world might be saved through Him.

—John 3:16–17

❖ I urge you therefore, brethren, by the mercies of God, to present your bodies a living and holy sacrifice, acceptable to God, which is your spiritual service of worship. And do not be conformed to this world, but be transformed by the renewing of your mind, that you may prove what the will of God is, that which is good and acceptable and perfect.

—Romans 12:1–2

❖ Finally, brothers, whatever is true, whatever is noble, whatever is right, whatever is pure, whatever is lovely, whatever is admirable—if anything is excellent or praiseworthy—think about such things. Whatever you have learned or received or heard from me, or seen in me—put it into practice. And the God of peace will be with you.

—Philippians 4:8–9, NIV

❖ For this reason, I bow my knees before the Father, from whom every family in heaven and on earth derives its name, that He would grant you, according to the riches of His glory, to be strengthened with power through His Spirit in the inner man; so that Christ may dwell in your hearts through faith; and that you, being rooted and grounded in love, may be able to comprehend with all the saints what is the breadth and length and height and depth, and to know the love of Christ which surpasses knowledge, that you may be filled up to all the fulness of God.

—Ephesians 3:14–19

❖ "For I know the plans that I have for you," declares the Lord, "plans for welfare and not for calamity to give you a future and a hope. Then you will call upon Me and come and pray to Me, and I will listen to you. You will seek Me and find Me when you search for Me with all your heart. I will be found by you," declares the Lord.

—Jeremiah 29:11–14

❖ Our Father which art in heaven, Hallowed be thy name. Thy kingdom come, Thy will be done in earth, as it is in heaven. Give us this day our daily bread. And forgive us our debts, as we forgive our debtors. And lead us not into temptation, but deliver us from evil: For thine is the kingdom, and the power, and the glory, for ever. Amen.

—MATTHEW 6:9–13, KJV

FAMILY MOUNTAIN:

❖ A father of the fatherless, a defender of widows, is God in His holy habitation. God sets the solitary in families; He brings out those who are bound into prosperity; but the rebellious dwell in a dry land.

—PSALM 68:5–6, NKJV

❖ Behold, I am going to send you Elijah the prophet before the coming of the great and terrible day of the LORD. He will restore the hearts of the fathers to their children and the hearts of the children to their fathers, so that I will not come and smite the land with a curse.

—MALACHI 4:5–6

❖ Wives, be subject to your own husbands, as to the Lord.... Husbands, love your wives, just as Christ also loved the church and gave Himself up for her....Children, obey your parents in the Lord, for this is right. Honor your father and mother (which is the first commandment with a promise), so that it may be well with you, and that you may live long on the earth.

—EPHESIANS 5:22, 25; 6:2–3

❖ "As for me, this is my covenant with them," says the LORD. "My Spirit, who is on you, and my words that I have put in your mouth will not depart from your mouth, or from the mouths of your children, or from the mouths of their descendants from this time on and forever," says the LORD."

—ISAIAH 59:21, NIV

❖ I will utter hidden things, things from of old—what we have heard and known, what our fathers have told us. We will not hide them from their children; we will tell the next generation the praiseworthy deeds of the LORD, his power, and the wonders he has done. He decreed statutes for Jacob and established the law in Israel, which he commanded our forefathers to teach their children, so the next generation would know them, even the children yet to be born, and they in turn would tell their children. Then they would put their trust in God and would not forget his deeds but would keep his commands.

—PSALM 78:3–7, NIV

❖ The righteous man will flourish like the palm tree, He will grow like a cedar in Lebanon. Planted in the house of the LORD, they will flourish in the courts of our God. They will still yield fruit in old age; they shall be full of sap and very green, to declare that the LORD is upright; He is my rock, and there is no unrighteousness in Him."

—PSALM 92:12–15

EDUCATION MOUNTAIN:

❖ And I have filled him with the Spirit of God, in wisdom, in understanding, in knowledge, and in all manner of workmanship, to design artistic works, to work in gold, in silver, in bronze, in cutting jewels for setting, in carving wood, and to work in all manner of workmanship.

—EXODUS 31:3–5, NKJV

❖ Teach me good discernment and knowledge, for I believe in Your commandments.

—PSALM 119:66

❖ Say to wisdom, "You are my sister," and call understanding your intimate friend.

—PROVERBS 7:4

❖ But the goal of our instruction is love from a pure heart and a good conscience and a sincere faith.

—1 TIMOTHY 1:5

❖ Train up a child in the way he should go, even when he is old he will not depart from it.

—PROVERBS 22:6

❖ "Learn to be wise," he said, "and develop good judgment and common sense! I cannot overemphasize this point. Cling to wisdom—she will protect you. Love her—she will guard you. Getting wisdom is the most important thing you can do! And with your wisdom, develop common sense and good judgment. If you exalt wisdom, she will exalt you."

—PROVERBS 4:5–8, TLB

❖ And do not be conformed to this world, but be transformed by the renewing of your mind, that you may prove what the will of God is, that which is good and acceptable and perfect.

—ROMANS 12:2

GOVERNMENT MOUNTAIN:

❖ When the godly are in authority, the people rejoice. But when the wicked are in power, they groan.

—PROVERBS 29:2, NLT

❖ For a child will be born to us, a son will be given to us; and the government will rest on His shoulders; and His name will be called Wonderful Counselor, Mighty God, Eternal Father, Prince of Peace. There will be no end to the increase of His government or of peace, on the throne of David and over his kingdom, to establish it and to uphold it with justice and righteousness from then on and forevermore. The zeal of the LORD of hosts will accomplish this.

—ISAIAH 9:6–7

❖ Let every soul be subject to the governing authorities. For there is no authority except from God, and the authorities that exist are appointed by God. Therefore whoever resists the authority resists the ordinance of God, and those who resist will bring judgment on themselves. For rulers are not a terror to good works, but to evil. Do you want to be unafraid of the authority? Do what is good, and you will have praise from the same. For he is God's minister to you for good. But if you do evil, be afraid; for he does not bear the sword in vain; for he is God's minister, an avenger to execute wrath on him who practices evil.

—ROMANS 13:1–4, NKJV

❖ Therefore I exhort first of all that supplications, prayers, intercessions, and giving of thanks be made for all men, for kings and all who are in authority, that we may lead a quiet and peaceable life in all godliness and reverence. For this is good and acceptable in the sight of God our Savior, who desires all men to be saved and to come to the knowledge of the truth.

—1 TIMOTHY 2:1–4, NKJV

❖ Choose wise and discerning and experienced men from your tribes, and I will appoint them as your heads...So I took the heads of your tribes, wise and experienced men, and appointed them heads over you, leaders of thousands and of hundreds, of fifties and of tens, and officers for your tribes. Then I charged your judges at that time, saying, "Hear the cases between your fellow countrymen, and judge righteously between a man and his fellow countryman, or the alien who is with him. You shall not show partiality in judgment; you shall hear the small and the great alike. You shall not fear man, for the judgment is God's."

—DEUTERONOMY 1:13, 15–17

MEDIA MOUNTAIN:

❖ Like cold water to a weary soul, so is good news from a distant land.

—PROVERBS 25:25

❖ Get yourself up on a high mountain, O Zion, bearer of good news, lift up your voice mightily, O Jerusalem, bearer of good news; lift it up, do not fear. Say to the cities of Judah, "Here is your God!"

—ISAIAH 40:9

❖ How lovely on the mountains are the feet of him who brings good news, who announces peace and brings good news of happiness, who announces salvation, and says to Zion, "Your God reigns!"

—ISAIAH 52:7

❖ The Spirit of the Lord GOD is upon me, because the LORD has anointed me to bring good news to the afflicted; He has sent me to bind up the brokenhearted, to proclaim liberty to captives and freedom to prisoners; to proclaim the favorable year of the LORD and the day of vengeance of our God.

—ISAIAH 61:1

❖ These are the things which you should do: speak the truth to one another; judge with truth and judgment for peace in your gates. Also let none of you devise evil in your heart against another, and do not love perjury; for all these are what I hate," declares the LORD.

—ZECHARIAH 8:16–17

ARTS AND ENTERTAINMENT MOUNTAIN:

❖ David, together with the commanders of the army, set apart some of the sons of Asaph, Heman and Jeduthun for the ministry of prophesying, accompanied by harps, lyres and cymbals.

—1 CHRONICLES 25:1, NIV

❖ And it came to pass when the priests came out of the Most Holy Place (for all the priests who were present had sanctified themselves, without keeping to their divisions), and the Levites who were the singers, all those of Asaph and Heman and Jeduthun, with their sons and their brethren, stood at the east end of the altar, clothed in white linen, having cymbals, stringed instruments and harps, and with them one hundred and twenty priests sounding with trumpets—indeed it came to pass, when the trumpeters and singers were as one, to make one sound to be heard in praising and thanking the LORD, and when they lifted up their voice with the trumpets and cymbals and instruments of music, and praised the LORD, saying: "For He is good, for His mercy endures forever," that the house, the house of the LORD, was filled with a cloud, so that the priests could not continue ministering because of the cloud; for the glory of the LORD filled the house of God.

—2 CHRONICLES 5:11–14, NKJV

❖ There is nothing better for a man than to eat and drink and tell himself that his labor is good. This also I have seen that it is from the hand of God. For who can eat and who can have enjoyment without Him?

—ECCLESIASTES 2:24

❖ It is good to praise the LORD and make music to your name, O Most High, to proclaim your love in the morning and your faithfulness at night, to the music of the ten-stringed lyre and the melody of the harp. For you make me glad by your deeds, O LORD; I sing for joy at the works of your hands.

—PSALM 92:1, NIV

BUSINESS MOUNTAIN:

❖ But you shall remember the LORD your God, for it is He who is giving you power to make wealth, that He may confirm His covenant which He swore to your fathers, as it is this day.

—DEUTERONOMY 8:18

❖ Let the favor of the Lord our God be upon us; and confirm for us the work of our hands; yes, confirm the work of our hands.

—PSALM 90:17

❖ For thus says the LORD of hosts, "Once more in a little while, I am going to shake the heavens and the earth, the sea also and the dry land. I will shake all the nations; and they will come with the wealth of all nations, and I will fill this house with glory," says the LORD of hosts. "The silver is Mine and the gold is Mine," declares the LORD of hosts. "The latter glory of this house will be greater than the former," says the LORD of hosts, "and in this place I will give peace," declares the LORD of hosts.

—HAGGAI 2:6–9

❖ No servant can serve two masters; for either he will hate the one and love the other, or else he will be loyal to the one and despise the other. You cannot serve God and mammon.

—LUKE 16:13, NKJV

❖ Whatever you do, do your work heartily, as for the Lord rather than for men, knowing that from the Lord you will receive the reward of the inheritance. It is the Lord Christ whom you serve. For he who does wrong will receive the consequences of the wrong which he has done, and that without partiality.

—COLOSSIANS 3:23–25

❖ For the love of money is a root of all sorts of evil, and some by longing for it have wandered away from the faith and pierced themselves with many griefs.

—1 TIMOTHY 6:10

❖ "Oh, that You would bless me indeed, and enlarge my territory, that Your hand would be with me, and that You would keep me from evil, that I may not cause pain!" So God granted him what he requested.

—1 CHRONICLES 4:10, NKJV

❖ And they spoke to him, saying, "If you will be a servant to these people today, and serve them, and answer them, and speak good words to them, then they will be your servants forever."

—1 KINGS 12:7, NKJV

❖ You shall not have in your bag two kinds of weights, a large and a small. You shall not have in your house two kinds of measures, a large and a small. A full and just weight you shall have, a full and just measure you shall have; that your days may be prolonged in the land which the LORD your God gives you.

—DEUTERONOMY 25:13–15, RSV

❖ Instruct those who are rich in this present world not to be conceited or to fix their hope on the uncertainty of riches, but on God, who richly supplies us with all things to enjoy. Instruct them to do good, to be rich in good works, to be generous and ready to share, storing up for themselves the treasure of a good foundation for the future, so that they may take hold of that which is life indeed.

—1 TIMOTHY 6:17–19

Appendix B

OCCUPATIONS AND ROLES ON THE SEVEN MOUNTAINS

Religion Mountain:

- ❖ Administrative assistant
- ❖ Administrator
- ❖ Bishop
- ❖ Clergy
- ❖ Intercessor
- ❖ Itinerate minister
- ❖ Missionary
- ❖ Nonprofit ministry director
- ❖ Parochial teacher
- ❖ Pastor (senior, executive, worship, children's, women's, youth, etc.)
- ❖ Priest
- ❖ Religious director
- ❖ Sunday school leader
- ❖ Worship leader

Family Mountain:

- ❖ Aunt
- ❖ Brother
- ❖ Cousin
- ❖ Father
- ❖ Godparent
- ❖ Grandparent
- ❖ Guardian

❖ Homemaker

❖ Housekeeper

❖ Mother

❖ Nanny

❖ Nephew

❖ Niece

❖ Sibling

❖ Sister

❖ Stepchild

❖ Stepparent

❖ Stepsibling

❖ Uncle

Education Mountain:

❖ Administrator

❖ Curator

❖ Dean

❖ Lecturer

❖ Librarian

❖ Library technician

❖ President

❖ Principal

❖ Professor

❖ Researcher

❖ Student

❖ Teacher

❖ Teaching assistant

❖ Trainer

❖ Tutor

Government Mountain:

❖ Administrative judge

❖ Arbitrator or mediator

❖ Congressman/woman

❖ Court reporter

❖ Fire chief

❖ Firefighter

❖ Judge or magistrate

❖ Law clerk

❖ Lawyer

❖ Legal secretary

❖ Legal support worker

❖ Mayor

❖ Military

❖ Paralegal and legal assistant

❖ Police chief

❖ Police officer

❖ President

❖ Senator/state representative

❖ Town/city clerk

❖ Vice president

Media Mountain:

❖ Advertising executive

❖ Announcer

❖ Audio engineer

❖ Blogger Broadcast technician

- ❖ Camera operator
- ❖ Copywriter
- ❖ Critic
- ❖ Designer (Web, graphic, etc.)
- ❖ Director
- ❖ Disc jockey
- ❖ Editor
- ❖ Film and video editor
- ❖ Journalist
- ❖ Manager
- ❖ Marketing executive
- ❖ News analyst
- ❖ Photographer
- ❖ Printer
- ❖ Press operator
- ❖ Producer
- ❖ Production artist
- ❖ Production assistant
- ❖ Proofreader
- ❖ Publicist
- ❖ Publisher
- ❖ Reporter or correspondent
- ❖ Researcher
- ❖ Scriptwriter
- ❖ Sound technician
- ❖ Technical director
- ❖ Technical writer

❖ Translator

❖ Writer

Arts and Entertainment Mountain:

❖ Actor

❖ Animator

❖ Art director

❖ Artist (fine arts, multimedia, etc.)

❖ Athlete

❖ Audio and video technician

❖ Broadcast technician

❖ Camera operator

❖ Choreographer

❖ Coach

❖ Critic

❖ Dancer

❖ Editor

❖ Entertainer

❖ Film and video editor

❖ Music director or composer

❖ Musician or singer

❖ Photographer

❖ Poet

❖ Producer or director

❖ Public relations specialist

❖ Radio or television announcer

❖ Screenwriter

❖ Sound technician

- ❖ Trainer
- ❖ Translator
- ❖ Writer

Business Mountain:

- ❖ Accountant or auditor
- ❖ Bookkeeping or accounting clerk
- ❖ Budget analyst
- ❖ Buyer
- ❖ Chief executive officer
- ❖ Chief financial officer
- ❖ Chief operating officer
- ❖ Compensation and benefits manager
- ❖ Compensation and benefits specialist
- ❖ Credit analyst
- ❖ Economist
- ❖ Emergency management specialist
- ❖ Employment specialist
- ❖ Financial analyst
- ❖ Financial examiner
- ❖ Financial manager
- ❖ Financial specialist
- ❖ Health services manager
- ❖ Human resources manager
- ❖ Human resources specialist
- ❖ Loan counselor
- ❖ Loan officer
- ❖ Logistician

❖ Management analyst

❖ Manager

❖ Market research analyst

❖ Owner

❖ Personal financial advisor

❖ Purchasing agent

❖ Tax examiner or revenue agent

❖ Tax preparer

❖ Training and development manager

❖ Training specialist

Appendix C

WEALTH AND PROSPERITY PROCLAMATIONS, DECLARATIONS, AND DECREES

I declare wealth and honor comes from the Lord. God is the ruler of all things. In His hands are strength and power to exalt and give strength to _____. (1 Chronicles 29:12)

I proclaim _____ is blessed because he fears the Lord and he finds great delight in God's commands. _____'s children will be mighty in the land. Wealth and riches are in _____'s house. _____'s righteousness endures forever. Even when darkness tries to overtake _____, light will come bursting in. I declare _____ is kind and merciful and all goes well for him because he is a generous man who conducts his business fairly. I decree _____ will not be overcome by evil circumstances. God's constant care of him will make a deep impression on all who see it. I declare _____ does not fear bad news or live in dread of what may happen. _____ is settled in his mind that Jehovah will take care of him, and that is why _____ is not afraid and can calmly face his foes. _____ gives generously to those in need. His deeds will never be forgotten. He shall have influence and honor. I proclaim evil-minded men will be infuriated when they see all this; they will gnash their teeth in anger and slink away, their hopes thwarted. (Psalm 112:1–10, TLB)

I proclaim it is the Lord God who gives _____ the power to become rich. God does this to fulfill His promise to _____'s ancestors. (Deuteronomy 8:18)

I decree the power of the wicked will be broken. I declare the Lord upholds _____ because he is righteous. Day by day the Lord observes the good deeds done by _____ and gives him eternal rewards. I proclaim God cares for _____ when times are hard; even in famine, _____ will have enough. (Psalm 37:17–18, TLB)

I declare _____ is filled with happiness and joy because he does not follow evil men's advice. _____ does not hang around with sinners scoffing at the things of God. _____ delights in doing everything God wants him to do. Day and night _____ mediates on God's laws and thinks about ways to follow God more closely. I proclaim _____ is like a tree along a riverbank bearing luscious fruit each season without fail. His leaves shall never wither and all he does shall prosper. (Psalm 1:1–3, TLB)

I declare Jehovah God is _____'s Light and Protector. He gives _____ grace and glory. No good thing will the Lord withhold from _____ because he walks along God's paths. (Psalm 84:11, TLB)

I decree _____ will be made rich in every way so that he can be generous on every occasion. _____'s generosity will result in others giving thanksgiving to God. (2 Corinthians 9:11, NIV)

I proclaim that _____, who is uncompromisingly righteous, shall flourish like the palm tree. He will be long-lived, stately, upright, useful, and fruitful. _____ shall grow like a cedar in Lebanon that is majestic, stable, durable, and incorruptible. I declare _____ is planted in the house of the Lord. He shall flourish in the courts of our God. As _____ grows in grace, he shall still bring forth fruit in old age. I proclaim _____ shall be full of sap, of spiritual vitality, and rich in the verdure of trust, love, and contentment. _____ is a living memorial to show that the Lord is upright and faithful to His promises. I decree the Lord is _____'s Rock, and there is no unrighteousness in Him. (Psalm 92:12–15, AMP)

I declare that _____ is a generous man who will prosper. As he refreshes others, he will be refreshed. (Proverbs 11:25, NIV)

ABOUT THE AUTHOR

TOMMI FEMRITE, FOUNDING apostle of GateKeepers International and Apostolic Intercessors Network, is an ordained minister with a doctorate of practical ministry from Wagner Leadership Institute. A highly respected teacher with more than 30 years of ministry experience around the world, she is recognized as a spiritual strategist who is able to assess the enemy's grip, receive God's strategic battle plans, and communicate this wisdom with humor and prophetic accuracy. Tommi is an active participant in the International Coalition of Apostles and the Eagles' Vision Apostolic Team. She authored *Praying with Passion: Life Changing Prayers for Those Who Walk in Darkness, Conquering the Religious Spirit*, and co-authored *Intercessors: Discover Your Prayer Power.* Tommi and her husband Ralph, a former Air Force fighter pilot, live in Colorado Springs, Colorado.

CONTACT THE AUTHOR

Tommi Femrite, Founding Apostle
Dianne Emmons, AIN Administrator
Apostolic Intercessors Network
A Division of GateKeepers International
P.O. Box 1026
Wallis, TX 77485
AIN Tel: 979-533-4767
AIN Fax: 979-478-6586
Email: info@AIN-GKI.org
www.AIN-GKI.org

Tommi Femrite, President
Kelli Drury, GKI Administrator
GateKeepers International
7670 Kaleb Grove #913
Colorado Springs, CO 80920
GKI Tel: 719-488-8148
Email: Info@GateKeepersIntl.org
www.GateKeepersIntl.org